Encounter at Shimoda:
Search for a New Pacific Partnership

Other Titles in This Series

Westview Special Studies on China and East Asia

Encounter at Shimoda:
Search for a New Pacific Partnership
edited by Herbert Passin and
Akira Iriye

The United States and Japan are the two largest democracies in today's world. The United States is still a superpower economically, militarily, and intellectually, but its traditional independence has changed to a position that requires cooperation and mutual understanding with its major allies and especially with Japan. Japan, also an economic superpower, enormously rich in human, economic, and intellectual resources, but very weak in natural resources, has an equal need for cooperation, military support, and teamwork on all levels. Both nations accept an obligation to contribute their resources fully toward the solution to the world's problems. Consequently, new forms of dialogues and new instruments of cooperation must be devised based on a sophisticated, mutually agreed upon data base. These discussions from the Fourth Shimoda Conference (September 1-4, 1977) explore some of those new directions.

Herbert Passin is professor of sociology at Columbia University. Akira Iriye is professor of history at the University of Chicago. He was recently elected president of the Society for Historians of American Foreign Relations.

Published in cooperation with
The Japan Center for International Exchange
and
The Japan Society

Japan Center for International Exchange

In response to a growing concern about Japan's role in the international community, a number of Japanese business and intellectual leaders founded the Japan Center for International Exchange in 1971. It is a private, nonprofit, nonpartisan organization devoted to the improvement of Japanese communication with the rest of the world and to the encouragement of more positive Japanese participation in international activities. JCIE is working to achieve these goals through conferences, exchange programs, research projects, publications, and other forms of involvement with organizations in Japan and abroad.

Japan Society, Inc.

The Japan Society, founded in 1907, is an association of individuals and corporations actively engaged in bringing the peoples of Japan and the United States closer together in understanding, appreciation, and cooperation. It is a private, nonprofit, nonpolitical organization, devoted to cultural, educational, and public affairs, and to discussions, exchanges, and studies in areas of vital interest to both peoples. Its aim is to provide a medium through which both nations may learn from the experiences and accomplishments of the other.

Encounter at Shimoda:
Search for a New Pacific Partnership

edited by Herbert Passin
and Akira Iriye

Westview Press / Boulder, Colorado

Westview Special Studies on China and East Asia

Copyright © 1979 by Westview Press, Inc.

Published in 1979 in the United States of America by
 Westview Press, Inc.
 5500 Central Avenue
 Boulder, Colorado 80301
 Frederick A. Praeger, Publisher

Library of Congress Cataloging in Publication Data
Main entry under title:
Encounter at Shimoda.
 (Westview special studies on China and East Asia)
 Papers presented at the 4th Shimoda Conference held in Sept. 1977 in Shimoda, Japan.
 1. United States—Relations (general) with Japan—Congresses. 2. Japan—Relations (general) with the United States—Congresses. 3. United States—Relations (general) with East Asia—Congresses. 4. East Asia—Relations (general) with the United States—Congresses. 5. United States—Foreign relations—1945- —Congresses. I. Passin, Herbert. II. Iriye, Akira.
 E183.8.J3E5   301.29'73'052   79-4238
 ISBN 0-89158-467-6

Printed and bound in the United States of America

Contents

Part 3
Political and Economic Development in Southeast Asia

Part 4
Japan and International Politics

Part 5
Japan, the United States, and the World Economy

Appendixes

Tables and Figures

Figures

Abbreviations

ASC	Asian Socialist Conference
ASEAN	Association of Southeast Asian Nations
APSO	Asia and Pacific Socialist Organization
CIA	U.S. Central Intelligence Agency
CIEC	Council on International Economic Cooperation
DSP	Democratic Socialist Party of Japan
EC	European Community
EEC	European Economic Community
EURATOM	European Atomic Energy Community
GATT	General Agreement on Tariffs and Trade
GNP	Gross National Product
IAEA	International Atomic Energy Agency
IDA	International Development Association
IEA	International Energy Authority
IMF	International Monetary Fund
INFCEP	International Nuclear Fuel Cycle Evaluation Program
JCP	Japan Communist Party
JSP	Japan Socialist Party

LDC	Less developed country
LDP	Liberal Democratic Party of Japan
MNC	Multinational corporation
NATO	North Atlantic Treaty Organization
NGO	Nongovernmental organization
NHK	Japan Broadcasting Corporation
NLC	New Liberal Club
NPT	Nuclear Nonproliferation Treaty
ODA	Official development assistance
OECD	Organization for Economic Cooperation and Development
OPEC	Organization of Petroleum Exporting Countries
UNCTAD	United Nations Conference on Trade and Development
WAES	Workshop on Alternative Energy Strategies

Foreword

The Fourth Shimoda Conference was held in September 1977 when the Carter administration was in its ninth month. Issues such as trade, nuclear fuel reprocessing, and the proposed withdrawal of U.S. ground troops from Korea were much in mind.

Although official contact between Japan and the United States has reached an unprecedented level, as the issues before the Fourth Shimoda Conference demonstrate, there is need for informed and private consultations. We feel that this conference, coming at the time it did and including an extraordinary group from each country, was particularly valuable.

The bilateral Japanese–U.S. relationship has not been the primary focus for American foreign policy, but in recent years the liaison has become one of the two or three most important for the United States. For Japan the relationship was primary, and even though the importance of other ties is increasing rapidly, the relationship with the United States is still central. Thus, there has been a convergence of interest for these two great Pacific democracies. Each has broad involvement in world affairs, each has other important bilateral ties. Yet each depends on the relationship with the other for the success of its foreign policy. Sustained, informal, unofficial contacts such as those fostered by the Shimoda conference are vital to this relationship.

The Japan Center for International Exchange (JCIE) and the Japan Society cooperated in the preparation of the Fourth Shimoda Conference. As the host institution, more of the burden fell on the JCIE. This Shimoda conference vividly demonstrates the commitment of both organizations to increasing the joint analysis of common policy issues. Both the JCIE and the Japan Society are deeply grateful to several other organizations that provided grants for the 1977 meetings at Shimoda. The Ford Foundation supported the earlier Shimoda conferences and was generous in its support for the fourth. In addition, the Japan Foundation and the Rockefeller Brothers Fund provided substantial grants. It should be noted, however, that the views presented at the conference and in the current papers are the authors' own and do not necessarily reflect the positions of the funding agencies.

Tadashi Yamamoto
Director
Japan Center for International Exchange

David MacEachron
Executive Director
Japan Society, Inc.

Introduction

Shimoda has been associated with Japanese–U.S. relations from the beginning. It was near Shimoda that Commodore Perry first anchored to negotiate for the U.S.–Japan Amity Treaty, and it was here that Townsend Harris established the first U.S consulate in 1857. Shimoda was therefore particularly appropriate for a series of Japan–U.S. conferences.

The First Shimoda Conference was held in 1967, the year of the Meiji Centennial, with the assistance of Columbia University's U.S. Assembly and the Japan Center for International Exchange; in the following decade three more were held. During that decade domestic conditions changed considerably in both countries, but even more drastic were developments in the international situation. These changes contributed to a new emphasis on multilateral communication and coordination, most notably among the United States, Europe, and Japan. Close policy consultation among these three advanced areas became a matter of vital necessity for the creation of a new international political and economic order.

With the second largest Gross National Product in the world, following the United States, Japan is now an economic superpower by any standard. While Japan is still in the process of identifying and defining its appropriate international role, it has become increasingly clear that it must go beyond the narrow confines of Japanese–U.S. alliance to reach out and establish solid lines of communication and exchange with other countries. As a superpower without military force, Japan is extremely sensitive to international criticism, and as a trading nation without its own natural resources, it is highly vulnerable to external pressures. (See

Chapter 1 for a discussion of the dramatic changes that occurred in the 1967-77 period.)

The Shimoda conferences are the result of private initiative on each side, and this is highly significant. Privately sponsored meetings to discuss public policy issues serve a special function. As compared to official conferences, they offer the possibility of greater candor in the discussion of sensitive issues, a variety of viewpoints from each national group, more continuity among the respective delegations, and constructive informality. The most recent Shimoda conference provided examples of each of these attributes.

The most vivid example of the greater candor that private conferences can tolerate was the discussion of U.S. troop withdrawal from Korea. Both Japan and the United States differed considerably in viewpoint over this issue. Official conferees could have alluded to such differences, but at the recent Shimoda conference Americans debated vigorously with each other over the merits of this policy, and the Japanese did likewise. Americans divided sharply along the lines of support or objection to U.S. troop withdrawal. The Japanese views ranged from those expressing worry about a declining commitment in Asia to those urging a different approach in Northeast Asia, including the opening of U.S. contacts with North Korea.

The delegations to the recent Shimoda conference achieved considerable diversity. Seven Japanese delegates from the Diet attended, representing all parties but the Communist. Seven government officials, including Mr. Kiichi Miyazawa, former foreign minister, also were present. In addition, business leaders, one labor leader, academicians, and journalists attended. Among the Americans were five congressmen, including Senator John Glenn, chairman of the Subcommittee on East Asian and Pacific Affairs of the Senate Foreign Relations Committee. Ambassador Mike Mansfield attended throughout. The White House, the State Department, and the Defense Department all were represented by senior officials. The diversity of the nonofficial delegation matched that of the Japanese. More non-Japan specialists were included on the U.S. side to broaden the spectrum; also, more younger leaders and government officials in private capacity were able to interact.

The continuity that these private meetings can achieve is striking in contrast to official meetings between democratic governments. Among the forty-five Japanese and thirty-four Americans who participated in the Fourth Shimoda Conference, twelve Japanese and three Americans had participated in one or more previous conferences. Continuity for its own sake is, of course, meaningless if the result diminishes the flow of new ideas or lowers responsiveness to changing circumstances. The record of the four Shimoda conferences is available, and those who are interested may judge for themselves.

We believe, however, that continuity helps to create personal acquaintances—a situation that makes forthright, even critical, comment not only acceptable but desirable. Furthermore, it leads to a more profound discussion because there is less need to establish positions, reiterate basics, or review the history of the relations. As a result, within a given time period a great deal of useful exchange can take place to affect significantly the thinking of the participants.

The informality of the unofficial conference is a subtle matter of degree. Even the most formal official meetings can provide informal contacts, but the atmosphere of a private gathering is conducive to more intellectual experimentation. Trial balloons can be lofted to succeed or be shot down in an environment that does not involve national prestige. Early warnings of emerging problems can be conveyed in ways that do not carry the ominous overtones of official warnings.

The problems confronting the two governments cannot be effectively solved until a better mutual understanding on a people-to-people basis has been established. Failure to attain such understanding and consensus can weaken the foundation of Japanese–U.S. relations, causing, perhaps, a more direct and damaging result than heretofore. National understanding and popular support for its foreign policy and commitments abroad are essential for the Carter administration. Popular support is particularly needed in a political milieu marked by serious domestic economic difficulties and the experiences of the Vietnam War and Watergate.

The political scene in Japan is likewise fluid now that the margin between the ruling Liberal Democratic Party and the opposition is paper-thin in both houses of the Diet. Japanese foreign policy, centered as it has been on cooperation with the United States, is no longer a matter under exclusive control of the conservative party. As many observers predict, bipartisan consensus and cooperation, based on broad popular support, will be necessary for Japan's diplomacy to remain functional.

Problems requiring Japanese–U.S. consultation are becoming increasingly complex and harder to solve. Specifically, the problems include the security of Northeast Asia, especially in the Korean peninsula, and the stability and development of Southeast Asia in the aftermath of the Indochina war. As the only industrial country in Asia, Japan now is under increased pressure from the United States and other nations to create its own alternatives and articulate its role in solving these problems. This means that Japan's dialogue and consultation with the United States must be conducted on a new and higher plane than the past pattern of binational communication.

Demonstrating convincingly the tangible results of such a gathering is rarely possible. The quicksilver of ideas is elusive. *Post hoc, ergo propter hoc* is all too easy a fallacy.

We do believe that the forthright discussion at the Fourth Shimoda Conference concerning security in Northeast Asia was healthy and may have contributed to the modification of U.S. policies. Likewise, it was useful for the Japanese to be reminded again of the degree of economic distress that Japanese exports were causing in some areas of the United States. Possibly of longest term importance, however, was the suggestion of more collaboration on fusion research, which was discussed with Prime Minister Fukuda when he attended the final session of the conference. His subsequent specific proposal may introduce an important new era in cooperation between the two largest economies in the democratic world.

Within democracies, active groups that help to inform, shape, and articulate public opinion are essential. As Japan and the United States deal with each other on an ever more intimate basis on issues of greater complexity, contacts of the sort provided by the Shimoda conference grow in importance.

The format and content of private meetings will, of course, change continually, but the process is a vital element in forging the truly mutual cooperation that is so important to the welfare of both nations.

Robert S. Ingersoll
Cochairman

Nobuhiko Ushiba
Cochairman

About the Contributors

Barber B. Conable, Jr., a Republican congressman from western New York, is the ranking minority leader of the Committee on Ways and Means and is a member of the Budget Committee and the Joint Committee on Internal Revenue Taxation.

John H. Glenn, Jr., the first American to orbit the earth as a NASA astronaut, is a U.S. senator from Ohio and chairman of the Subcommittee on East Asian and Pacific Affairs, the Committee on Foreign Relations, and the Subcommittee on Energy, Nuclear Proliferation and Federal Services, Committee on Governmental Affairs.

Takashi Hosomi, advisor to the Industrial Bank of Japan, Ltd., and chairman of IBJ International, Ltd., formerly served as director-general of Japan's Tax Bureau, vice-minister of Finance for International Affairs, and special advisor to the minister of Finance.

Akira Iriye, professor of history at the University of Chicago and a Far Eastern specialist, is president of the Society of Historians of American Foreign Relations and the author of *After Imperialism: The Search for a New Order in the Far East, 1921-1931* and *Across the Pacific: An Inner History of American-East Asian Relations.*

Koichi Kato, a Sinologist and formerly an officer in Japan's Ministry of Foreign Affairs, is a representative (Liberal Democratic Party) in the Japanese Diet and a member of the Agriculture and Fishery Committee as well as the Special Committee on Prices.

Tamio Kawakami, a representative (Japanese Socialist Party) in the Japanese Diet, member of the Committee on

Foreign Affairs, and a professor of politics and history in Tokai University's Department of Political Science and Economics, has participated in official delegations to the PRC and the United States and is the author of *Requirements for Contemporary Politicians.*

Tokusaburo Kosaka, a representative (Liberal Democratic Party), formerly president of Shin-Etsu Chemical Industries, Ltd., is the chairman of the Public Relations Committee of the Liberal Democratic Party and serves as a member of the Committee on Social and Labour Affairs.

Herbert Passin has lived and done research in various capacities in Japan since the occupation and has authored numerous publications in English and Japanese; he is professor of sociology at Columbia University.

Gustav Ranis, whose numerous publications include *Development of the Labor Surplus Economy: Theory and Policy,* is professor of economics at Yale University and has served as consultant to the Pearson Commission, the CED Subcommittee on Japan, the Ford Foundation, and other agencies.

John C. Sawhill, president of New York University, has served as associate director for Natural Resources, Energy, and Science in the U.S. Office of Budget and Management, as federal energy administrator in 1974, and is a member of the Trilateral Commission, serving as principal rapporteur of its energy task force.

Stephen J. Solarz, congressman from Brooklyn, serves on the House International Relations Committee (Subcommittee on Asian and Pacific Affairs) and the Post Office and Civil Service Committee.

Ro Watanabe, whose publications include books on nationalism and socialism, participated in the formation of Japan's Democratic Socialist Party, has been actively involved in party affairs as deputy director of the International Bureau, and is a member of the House of Representatives, where he serves on the Foreign Affairs Committee.

Toru Yano is associate professor of political science at Kyoto University's Center for Southeast Asian Studies, a member of various governmental advisory committees, and the author of numerous publications, among which is *Japan's Southeast Asian Commitment in Historical Perspective.*

Encounter at Shimoda:
Search for a New Pacific Partnership

Part 1
The New Era of
Japanese-U.S. Relations

1
Shimoda—The View from 1967

Herbert Passin

The first of the Shimoda conferences took place in 1967, the fourth in 1977.[1] During those ten years, Japanese–U.S. relations changed dramatically. To put it very simply, Japan grew larger, the United States smaller.

The Change

In the mid-1960s I used the analogy of two countries looking at each other through the opposite ends of a telescope. To the Japanese, the United States was an enormous presence filling almost all of the lens space; to the Americans, Japan was a very small spot on the lens of U.S. global responsibilities. And this was quite natural. The U.S. economy was about five times the size of that of the Japanese, and its per capita gross national product (GNP) was 2.5 times larger. By 1977, however, Japan had come within hailing distance of the United States, her GNP about 40 percent of that of the American, and her per capita GNP about 80 percent. The views from the opposite ends of the telescope were no longer so different as far as size was concerned. For both sides the adjustment was hard: many Japanese still preferred to act small, and many Americans preferred to act big.

The changed view is the result of change not only in relative economic weight but also in the world environment at large. With the recovery of the belligerents from World War II, the upward surge in the Third World, the increased weight of the

Soviet bloc, and the emergence of the OPEC nations, it was inevitable that the relative position of the United States, despite its not inconsiderable growth, would decline. The United States remained the most powerful single country in the world, no matter what indicator one wished to use, but it was no longer as overwhelmingly dominant as it had been. After a decade of Vietnam, the Black revolution, the student explosions, the environmental backlash, and the oil shock, the position of the United States could never be the same.

The View from 1967

In light of these changes, it is instructive to look at the structure of the Japanese–U.S. relationship as it appeared in 1967 and then compare it to the structure of the relationship in 1977.

In 1967, as already noted, the United States was large and Japan was small. The United States was still the dominant power in the world, even though the beginnings of the shift already were becoming apparent. By contrast, despite its rapid rise to the position of third-ranking economic power in the Free World, Japan could still continue to think of itself as small. In the sloganizing of the period, the issue was *taikoku Nippon*—big Japanism—versus *shokoku Nihon*—little Japanism, and the debate raged throughout the mass media.

In the Shimoda conference that year, the aura of World War II winner and loser still clung to the relationship. Japan, still thinking of herself as a defeated country—*haisen Nihon*, as the phrase goes—was highly dependent on the United States not only for trade relations but also for defense, for sponsorship in a still less-than-friendly world, and for support. This dependence, in turn, generated resentments and the beginning of a nationalistic reaction that manifested itself in a growing clamor for "independence," for "autonomy" in foreign affairs, and for less "subservience" to the United States.

Japan's economy and growth were heavily dependent upon the United States. If not for the stimulus of the Korean War, U.S. military procurement, U.S. technology export, and later even the Vietnam War—although not to the same extent—the Japanese economy would not have grown so dramatically. And the Japanese–U.S. trade balance, although just beginning to show portents of change, remained "typically," as economist William Lockwood noted at the time, in the U.S. favor.[2]

On virtually all major issues the United States was the active element and Japan the passive. The power of decision lay with the United States, and all that Japan could do was respond— sometimes happily, sometimes grudgingly—or, if possible, resist.

The View from 1977

By 1977 this basic relationship was unrecognizable. No longer was it a question of a weak, dependent Japan facing the overwhelming, giant United States. Japan was still a very vulnerable country and to some degree was still dependent upon the United States, but now it no longer came to the game totally without assets.

The changes were reflected in the Shimoda conferences. Most dramatic was the change in tone over the ten-year period. In 1967 the Americans talked a lot and the Japanese listened. The Japanese appeared hesitant, fearful of debate, and were often silent, generally exemplifying a low-posture style that corresponded to Japan's low-posture diplomacy.

In 1977 the U.S. participants were surprised—sometimes agreeably, sometimes disagreeably—to find all this changed. Many Japanese spoke in English in order to communicate their views directly to the Americans, but whether in English or in Japanese, they spoke with great openness, force, and cogency. Again, while in 1967 the Japanese participants hesitated to expose differences among themselves, by 1977 there was not the slightest hesitation about expressing disagreement in public. To the Americans in 1967, all the Japanese, whether on the government or the opposition side, sounded alike. Consequently, when Americans spoke to "the Japanese side," it was as if the differences among the parties were not important. In 1977 the Americans were fully aware of the differences.

On many issues the divisions of opinion were not along national lines so much as along policy lines. U.S. doves found themselves closer to Japanese doves on such issues as security, troop withdrawal from Korea, and relations with the Indochinese countries, than to the hawks on their own side. And on the burning trade issues, Japanese participants who represented constituencies other than the agricultural often found themselves closer to U.S. free traders than to their own agricultural bloc. The problem for the free traders on both sides was their own protectionist fellow nationals rather than the other side. For example, the business, manufacturing, and urban interests were quite willing to see beef and citrus fruits come in freely and wanted to drop virtually all of the remaining tariff and nontariff barriers on manufactured goods. However, it was the small and medium business interests that resisted. For Americans firmly convinced that "Japan, Inc." was a united monolith, the discovery that this was not so was important.

A Different Discussion

Equally significant was the change in the content of the debates. Many of the issues that had been important in 1967 no longer seemed important in 1977. In some cases this was because the problem had been solved (e.g., the number one issue of 1967—Okinawa reversion). In other cases it was because the problems seemed to have been outdated or bypassed by events.

The textile problem—so tense that it was often described as a "war"—dominated the Second Shimoda Conference in 1969 and still reverberated in the third in 1974. In 1977 it was as if the problem had never existed. While the textile industry remains a sore spot with both countries, it is no longer a purely bilateral Japanese–U.S. issue. Now that the competitive advantage in textiles has shifted to the more ambitious developing countries with their remaining reserves of cheap labor, the industry is obsolete in both Japan and the United States. Japanese talking today about textile imports from Korea or Taiwan sound just like Americans talking about Japanese textile imports in 1969.

Okinawa

In 1967 Okinawa virtually dominated the Shimoda discussions—it was the most explosive issue in the relationship, a potential "second Trieste," as one of the Japanese participants characterized it.[3] In 1969, even though the reversion had already been agreed upon in principle in the Nixon-Sato communiqué, debates continued to rage about the exact character of the reversion. Should the U.S. bases remain, should they be allowed to store nuclear weapons, or should they be placed on the same basis as the main-island bases? Should U.S. soldiers be subject to the Okinawan courts for off-base offenses? Should the base land returned by the United States go to civilian use or be taken over by the Japanese Self-Defense Forces? The conference was punctuated by meetings with Okinawan delegations, reporters, and experts, and the issue was on everybody's mind. No one seems to have noted, however, that the Bonin Islands, which had also been in contention, already had been quietly returned in 1968.

In 1977 hardly a word was spoken about Okinawa. This is not to say that no problems remained in 1977, because they did. For one thing, the Okinawan "progressives" still objected strongly to the continuing U.S. presence on the islands as well as to the presence of the Japanese Self-Defense Forces, and their complaints about the bases sounded to many like an echo from the past. Even the opposition politicians from the main islands, who had to support the Okinawan position in public, seemed uncomfortable with it, as if their hearts were no longer in it.

A more serious latent issue was the question of the use of the bases in the event of necessity. The reversion settlement left some ambiguity about the use of the bases for operations not directly related to the defense of Japan. Instead of the free use of the prereversion days, now prior consultation with the Japanese government was required. This raised two questions: First, did prior consultation mean that the United States must secure the *agreement* of the Japanese government or only that it must *inform* it? Second, if agreement were required, would the Japanese government give it? The issue surfaced in 1977 because of the American troop withdrawal from Korea. If the United States were to come to the military aid of Korea, would or would not the Americans be able to use Okinawan bases? Some Japanese were afraid that the United States might; some Americans were afraid that it might not.

Korea

In 1967 the Korean question scarcely stirred a ripple in the flow of the discussion. The heated debates were over other problems. Korea and Japan had signed a treaty of normalization in 1965 in spite of the strenuous domestic opposition within both countries, and while their relations remained uneasy, the Japanese–U.S. relationship was not involved. Nor was it an important issue in 1969, in spite of the fact that the United States had just withdrawn 40,000 troops—while the Vietnam War was still raging—in conformity with the then newly announced Guam Doctrine.

By the 1977 Shimoda meeting, however, Korea was one of the two most hotly debated issues (the other was trade). But this time there was an ironic reversal: it was the Japanese who were most disturbed by the prospects of U.S. withdrawal. Such an action would destabilize the delicate balance on the Korean peninsula and in Northeast Asia generally, they argued; South Korea's independence and security were vital for Japan's security.

The withdrawal was supported by some of the Americans and some of the Japanese, particularly on the antigovernment side (although not by all). While the U.S. prowithdrawal position hewed fairly close to the Carter line, the Japanese prowithdrawal position was more diverse, ranging from acquiescence and reluctant agreement that withdrawal was not necessarily harmful to Japan's security all the way to strong support for establishing relations with North Korea. Opinions divided more along the hawk-dove axis than along national lines. The hawks on both sides expressed anxiety over the consequences of the withdrawal, the unbalancing of the finely drawn equilibrium in Northeast Asia, the increasing power of the Soviet Union, and the general reduction of the U.S. commitment to Asia. The doves on both sides emphasized the undemocratic character of the Park regime, the desirability of an opening to the North, the Koreagate scandals and the growing rumors about "collusion" between Korean and Japanese politicians, and the importance of North–South unification.

In spite of the fact that most of the Japanese regarded South

Korea as vital to Japan's security, they were not prepared to accept the proposition that Japan should itself do anything about it. This position, which was characterized by one distinguished Japanese participant as "self-serving"—and was certainly regarded as such by the Americans—appeared contradictory. To the Americans, the Japanese seemed to be saying, "Korea is vital to our security." But when asked, "If Korea is so vital to your security, what will Japan do about it?" the answer was, "Nothing." "In that case, what do you propose?" the Americans asked, to which the answer was, "You Americans should do it." If the Japanese were not prepared to do anything about Korea, the Americans found it hard to believe that it was as vitally important to Japan's security as had been argued, a conclusion that only reinforced the views of those who felt that withdrawal did not entail any serious risks.

The Korean question tied back into the base problem because it was quite obvious that an effective U.S. defense of South Korea would require backup support from bases in Japan, and particularly Okinawa. Would the Japanese government allow the use of the bases for the defense of South Korea? Here, however, the Japanese response was ambiguous, not to say evasive: it depended upon circumstances; if a left coalition came to power, certainly not; even if the LDP (Liberal Democratic Party) government were willing it might have too slim a majority to do so; and so on. To many Americans, the hesitation to assure base use for what the Japanese presumably wanted the United States to do appeared disingenuous at best.

The United States in Asia

But Korea raised a larger question than the fate of the Korean peninsula: that of the U.S. commitment in Asia. In 1967 there had been a general chorus of lament about the U.S. "overpresence" accompanied by much shaking of forefingers and sad nodding of heads. The United States was heavily involved in Indochina, Thailand had just become the newest addition to the United States's string of bases in Asia, and many Japanese were worried about the use of Japanese bases for conducting the Indochinese war.

Overpresence remained a problem even in the Second Shimoda Conference in 1969, despite the Guam Doctrine and the 40,000 troop cutback in Korea. The worldwide student revolution was still in full force in Japan, although it had by then crested in most countries, and the Vietnam War was still lurching agonizingly towards its conclusion.

By the third conference (in 1972), however, the issue looked different. The Nixon-Kissinger Doctrine, which was based upon a recognition of the new multipolar balance of power, was no longer in doubt. In Asia the doctrine clearly seemed to imply a reduced U.S. military presence. But the focus of the issue had now shifted. To the Americans, the reduction of their military presence meant that their allies, including Japan, had the obligation of taking up a larger share of the security burden and of filling in the gaps created by the U.S. withdrawal. There was a vacuum, and something had to fill it. This concept of burden sharing did not commend itself to most Japanese, and the Shimoda discussions revealed deep differences in the perception of the problem on the two sides.

In 1977, however, the only overpresence discussed was that of Japan in Southeast Asia. The problem was the American "underpresence," the growing signs of isolationism. Many of the Americans participating pointed out that withdrawal was as much necessitated by the current mood of the Americans as by deliberate policy considerations. Since Vietnam, the U.S. public simply would not support a high-risk, high-cost military policy; it no longer wanted to be the "policeman of the world." This came as no surprise to the Japanese, but it was disturbing: another confirmation of their fears.

By and large, the Japanese participants were the ones opposing U.S. withdrawal from Asia, and the Americans were defending it or, if not defending it unreservedly, were arguing that it was not really as much of a withdrawal as it seemed. This was an ironic twist on Yukichi Fukuzawa's *datsua-ron*, which argued in the early Meiji period that Japan should withdraw from Asia. "Is the United States abandoning its commitments?" as one Japanese participant put it. "Is the United States shifting its interest to Europe, the Middle East, and Africa?" asked another. "Is the United States no longer concerned about the military balance with the Soviet Union?" The U.S. side was far from united on these issues, and the evidence of disunity added another dimension to the anxiety of some Japanese.

The Security Treaty

In 1967 the United States–Japan Security Treaty was a major issue. The common view was that the United States had "imposed" the treaty on a reluctant Japan for U.S. interests. The Japanese public was divided over the issue, and the political parties were sharply polarized. While the LDP government regarded the treaty as central to its foreign policy, its position did not command universal support, even among its own members. Many people simply acquiesced in the treaty; others reluctantly supported it for want of a realistic alternative. But very few were happy about it. Not only was the physical presence of large numbers of U.S. troops on Japanese soil more than twenty years after the war an irritant, but many people were fearful of Japan's involvement in U.S. actions as, for example, in Vietnam, or even of becoming a target for foes of the United States. The Japan Communist Party (JCP) and the Japan Socialist Party (JSP) called for immediate abrogation of the treaty and a neutralist position between the two great power blocs; the Komeito called for abrogation of the treaty but in stages;[4] and the Democratic Socialist Party (DSP) called for withdrawal coupled with the right of emergency use. The traumatic events of 1960 were still on everybody's mind, and the Japanese chapter of the worldwide student revolt was moving towards its climactic year.

In Shimoda that year the debates were very tense, and the drafters of the final report were barely able to reach a compromise on a delicately phrased statement that had to be read carefully between the lines: "After considering the possibilities for mutual security arrangements available under present circumstances, it is difficult to find a generally agreed-upon alternative to a Mutual Security Treaty between our two countries at this time."[5]

The Second Shimoda Conference took place in 1969, just one-half year before the treaty was scheduled for review. With

the student revolt still not over and the Vietnam War at a new
climax, the treaty issue remained as troublesome as before.
There was a strong sense of countdown about the discussion.

In the third conference, in 1972, countdown to disaster was
replaced by a feeling of transition, and the Mutual Security
Treaty had receded far from the center of attention. This was
now occupied by the Nixon shocks, the rapprochement with
China, and the trade and balance-of-payments problem. There
was, as Professor Henry Rosovsky wrote, "the very general
assumption that U.S.-Japanese relations are no longer in a
state of equilibrium but rather that we find ourselves in a
transition toward a new and as yet unclear equilibrium."[6]
Nevertheless, with regard to the Mutual Security Treaty,
"There was agreement that the U.S. military presence should
be reduced but no clear consensus on possible future revisions
of the treaty."[7]

By 1977 the treaty issue was curiously muted. Since the
recession of the last antitreaty wave of 1970, the Japanese
public—except for the Okinawans—has seemed not to find it
interesting. It is also striking that the Chinese and the Soviets,
each for their own reasons, no longer opposed the treaty as they
did in the past. Therefore, the external pressure on the Japanese
left to oppose the treaty had disappeared. Recent public
opinion polls have shown, if anything, a substantial increase
in popular support for the treaty.

Because of this development, or perhaps because coming to
power has become a more realistic possibility, the opposition
parties, except for the JCP, have all become more "responsible"
and have tempered their views on the Mutual Security Treaty.
Although the JSP still formally holds to the "immediate
abrogation" slogan of the past, it now interprets this to mean
the negotiation of abrogation and the replacement of the
existing treaty by a treaty of friendship. The Komeito, which
for a while, in the interest of a coalition with the JCP, had
accepted the formula of immediate abrogation, has now returned to its original "step-by-step termination" slogan and in
practice is in no haste about it. The DSP has made the biggest
flip-flop: not only has it abandoned the emergency–use
formula, but it now favors the treaty, if anything, even more

strongly than does the LDP.

Thus, the dialectic of events has now brought about a curious reversal. Today it is the Japanese who are anxious to preserve the treaty and the Americans who are increasingly doubtful about it. Many question its value, particularly in view of the ambiguities about base use. Given the end of the Vietnam War and the reduction of the U.S. commitment in Asia—including Korea—many Americans are coming to feel that the cost is too high. And since Japan will not increase its defense expenditures or carry a significant part of the base cost in Japan, the old issue of the "free ride" continues to plague the discussions.

China

Another recurrent theme in all the Shimoda conferences has been the relationship with the People's Republic of China (PRC). One would have had to conclude from the discussions at the first conferences that Japan and the United States were so far apart in their views of the PRC that there was little likelihood of their ever seeing eye-to-eye. While Japan still continued to recognize Taiwan rather than the mainland, it was clear that most of the Japanese participants would have preferred to move toward normalization with Peking, but felt that they were being prevented from doing so by the United States. While it is realized that "we have to learn to live with her (China)," wrote one of the participants, "here lies a fundamental difference from the American conception."[8] The hope of many Japanese was that Japan would recognize Peking before the United States did, but that hope was being dashed by the reality of the Vietnam War. Since agreement could not be reached, the conference concluded that "we see no objections, but perhaps even some advantages in the two countries approaching these objectives independently and with different timing."[9]

The atmosphere of the second conference had already changed sufficiently, as Tamio Kawakami noted,[10] its final statement called for the reinstatement of the PRC "as a member of international society."

However, by the third conference, in 1972, Kissinger had

already been to Peking, and the process of Sino-American rapprochement had begun. The failure of the U.S. government to inform Japan of its intentions in advance constituted one of the famous Nixon shocks. In the words of one distinguished participant, "I used to have a recurrent nightmare that I would wake up one morning and find that the United States had recognized China before we did. And then the nightmare came true." Although the U.S. action was not precisely "recognition," Prime Minister Tanaka, elected one month after the Shimoda conference, set out to repair the situation by going to Peking at the earliest possible time—September 1972—to establish diplomatic relations.

The main issue at Shimoda was no longer whether the PRC should be recognized or not, but rather whether Kissinger's PRC shock was the proper way for "partners" to treat each other. "We agree that the American initiative toward establishing relations with the People's Republic of China was in the interest of both Japan and the United States," the final report stated, "but we also believe that the U.S. government was maladroit in the way in which these initiatives were communicated to Japan."[11]

By 1977 this was no longer an issue. Japan and the PRC were exchanging ambassadors and had moved very far toward normalization. However, they still were not able to sign a peace treaty. The principal obstacle was the PRC's insistence on the hegemony clause, which the Japanese resisted for fear of offending the Soviet Union. Even though Japan had severed relations with Taiwan (but was nevertheless managing to intensify economic relations at the same time), a number of the Japanese participants urged the United States to go slow in doing so.

In 1967 the debate was over whether there should be any relations with the PRC at all. Ten years later it was possible for one of the participants to propose, and have seriously discussed, the idea of some kind of "loose alliance" among Japan, the United States, and the PRC. This tilt toward the PRC was by no means universally favored, primarily because of the danger of antagonizing the Soviet Union. And some Japanese were even worried that perhaps the United States was now drawing closer to the PRC and away from Japan.

The Soviet Union

The principal reason for the tilt-toward-China concept was the growing tension in the relations between Japan and the Soviet Union. In 1967 the Soviet Union was considered to be primarily a problem for U.S. global policy; all Japan had to do was be studiously correct and friendly. But the Soviet Union increasingly has become a regional as well as a global power, and its tough line toward Japan has raised tensions. The much-vaunted joint development of eastern Siberia has never come off the ground. Ever since the end of World War II, the disputed four islands off the coast of Hokkaido have been a sore point, and the Soviet Union is still not prepared to discuss the issue. Every time a Japanese fishing boat wanders across the Soviet line it is arrested. At times, hundreds of Japanese fishing boats will be impounded by the Soviet coast guard and their crews arrested and fined. When the Soviet Union wants to make a kind gesture to Japan, it releases some of the fishermen or eases up on the seizures.

In 1977 the Soviet Union (as well as the United States) jumped the gun on the United Nations Conference on the Law of the Sea and announced the establishment of a 200-mile exclusive fishery zone. The two impacted areas account for the majority of Japan's fish catch. While the U.S. Congress immediately ratified a temporary fishery agreement with Japan, allowing virtually the same catch as before, negotiations with the Soviet Union were painful and protracted. A comprehensive agreement foundered over the northern islands question, the Soviets rejecting any implication that the matter could still be discussed. After three months of hard bargaining—referred to in one Japanese newspaper as the "100 days"—temporary agreements were reached. As a result, the Japanese quota was reduced to something on the order of one-half the normal catch; in addition, fishermen lost two full months of the North Pacific high fishing season while waiting for the agreement to be concluded.

By the time of the 1977 Shimoda conference, the level of awareness of the Soviet Union was at a high point. Ever since the incident of the defecting MIG, public and media attention had fastened themselves on the movements of Soviet military air and naval craft in Japanese waters. Overflights, formerly unreported, now were reported regularly and sometimes shown to home viewers on the television screen. Security experts began to sound the alarm about the Soviet naval growth in the North Pacific. The appeal of a tilt toward the PRC, in spite of Japan's professed stance of equidistance between the two communist powers, was understandable.

"Is the United States really unconcerned about the effect on the world power balance of the Soviet Union's overtaking her militarily?" one of the Japanese asked the U.S. participants. Detenté, too, came in for some serious questioning but on the whole held up reasonably well. It was clear, however, that a world of Soviet military parity with the United States, or even superiority, was very different from the world of 1967.

Conclusion

Changes in the Japanese–U.S. relationship have to follow. But to bring them about, both sides have to learn much more about the other: first, about their relative weight and position in the world. Each side has to understand not only the other's position but its own as well. Whatever vestiges of the Occupation mentality still linger on have to be abandoned, and a new realism has to enter the relationship. Americans must stop seeing Japan as a minor nation that can be disregarded easily, without running to the other extreme of seeing Japanese as ten feet tall. The Japanese, for their part, have to give up seeing themselves as the "eternal victims," poor, frail, and vulnerable, without giving in to the temptations of chauvinism to which the new situation might so easily lead.

Second, they have to learn more about how the other side works: the relations of executive and legislative, the *modus operandi* among elites, the weight of the press, and the role of public opinion. The old slogans of "Japan, Inc." or of the "U.S. colossus" are no longer useful. The United States and Japan are the two largest democratic industrial societies in the world, and public opinion is important in both of them. For all the much-discussed "crisis of democracy," this public opinion is reflected, for good or for ill, in the decision-making process.[12]

U.S. congressmen and senators have to realize that Japanese Diet members are as constrained by their cattle raisers as they are themselves. And the Japanese have to learn that the U.S. steel industry, both management and union, is as powerful a constraint on the trade policy of the U.S. side as is the farm bloc in Japan.

Change, however necessary, is painful. To borrow an image from a book written several years ago by Eto Jun,[13] growing up brings gains but it brings losses as well. To become more realistic means to lose innocence. Nevertheless, change, however painful, is necessary. What changes might come, no one was fully prepared to say. But clearly this is the agenda for the next period.

Notes

1. The second took place in September 1969 and the third in June 1972.

2. William W. Lockwood, "Political Economy," in *The United States and Japan,* ed. Herbert Passin (Englewod Cliffs, N.J.: Prentice Hall, 1966), p. 118.

3. Kinhide Mushakoji, "The View From Japan," in *The United States and Japan,* ed. Herbert Passin (Englewood Cliffs, N.J.: Prentice Hall, 1966), p. 132.

4. "The United States–Japan Security Treaty is a risky military alliance that can involve us in wars not directly related to us," said a Komeito declaration. "Needless to say," it continues, "we must by all means avoid unnecessary tensions or confrontation between Japan and the United States as a result of the discontinuation of the United States–Japan Security Treaty. The discontinuation of the treaty should be based on mutual agreement reached by diplomatic negotiations between the two countries" (*15th National Convention, January 11-13, 1978, Komeito.* No publishing date, in English, p. 72).

5. Final Report, in Kinhide Mushakoji and Herbert Passin, eds., *Nichibei Kankei no Tenbo.* (Tokyo: Simul Press, 1967), p. 209.

6. Henry Rosovsky, ed., *Discord in the Pacific,* The American Assembly, Columbia Book, 1972, p. 4.

7. Ibid., p. 238.

8. Mushakoji, "View from Japan," p. 137.

9. Final Report, *Nichibei Kankei no Tenbo*, p. 208.

10. *See* Kawakamo Tamio, "Groping for Korean Unification," in this volume.

11. Final Report, *Discord in the Pacific*, p. 238.

12. *See*, for example, Michel Crozier, Samuel Huntington, and Joji Watanuki, *The Crisis of Democracy: Report on the Governability of Democracies to the Trilateral Commission* (New York: University Press, 1975).

13. Eto Jun, *Seijuku to Sonshitsu* (Tokyo: Kawade Shobo, 1975).

2
Japan, the United States, and the International Order

Akira Iriye

For some time uncertainty and instability have characterized Japanese–U.S. relations. Gone are the days—if they ever existed—when statesmen on both sides could take for granted the durability of their alliance or when businessmen could engage in their bilateral dealings in a fairly stable framework of international economic transactions. Instead of stability and durability one hears more often of "critical turning points," "vast transformations," and "unknown futures." While there have been other periods of crisis and uncertainty, it seems that the relationship between the two countries, whether military, political, economic, or cultural, is in desperate need of redefinition if it is to be consolidated and survive temporary clashes of interest and occasional gaps in mutual respect and understanding.

In order to consider the matter with some care, it is best to start by recognizing the obvious fact that Japanese–U.S. relations, like those among any group of countries, have two essential aspects: domestic and international. Japanese–U.S. relations are based on the prior existence of Japan and the United States as independent entities and will reflect changing orientations within the two societies. Each country has its own dynamics, organizational mechanisms, and cultural patterns that function (or malfunction) as a whole. Secular as well as abrupt changes in these factors can be generated from within; they need not be the result of some input from abroad. At the same time, Japan and the United States are part of the international order, and their behavior is necessarily conditioned by developments in this larger framework. Wars, economic dislocations, and food shortages on a global scale have an obvious impact upon domestic affairs. But even without such dramatic events, political and economic forces in the world arena constantly impinge upon individual countries' developments. Moreover, certain cultural outlooks and ideological trends—such as the human rights movement—create an environment and a vocabulary through which governments and peoples engage in discourse.

In short, national societies are both independent and interdependent, so that Japanese–U.S. relations must be viewed in terms of the changes taking place at the domestic and the external levels. Domestic and international developments interact with one another in an intricate fashion, and ultimately this interrelationship between domestic order and international order is the key to understanding world affairs. Questions of peace, stability, and interdependence in the world are closely linked to those of political order, economic development, and social structure at home. This linkage is an extremely complex phenomenon, but some understanding of it is essential for a clear perception of the current issues and future outlook in Japanese–U.S. relations.

To a considerable extent harmony existed between these relations and the domestic developments in the two countries for over two decades after the end of the war. The United States, the victor and the definer of postwar Japanese order, detemined that the world was to reject the regionalism and protectionism of the 1930s and return to the pre-1929 system of economic interdependence, equal opportunity, and liberal political development. It was assumed by U.S. leaders that only such a world—the Wilsonian world order—would ensure lasting peace and increasing welfare among nations. Japan was to be rid of its militarism and be reintegrated into a restored international order where economic rather than military objectives would be the norm, and where interdependence would lead to cooperation, and cooperation to harmony. Japanese society would be reorganized to remove supporters of aggression and pan-Asianism and to encourage the growth of those forces oriented toward peaceful external relations—above all, peaceful economic enterprises. This meant the reordering of a society in which businessmen, bureaucrats, and intellectuals would have a stake in economic development as well as a political environment congenial to it. The new political order in Japan would be oriented toward economic modernization and political liberalism. Naturally, such a system would give power and influence to modernizers and liberals—those who rejected the path of militaristic enterprises at home and abroad and whose interests lay in the U.S.-defined postwar world order.

It was no accident that the Japanese political scene for over twenty years after 1945 was characterized by the return to power of those who had been influential during the 1920s, the decade of Japanese–U.S. economic and political cooperation. They did not reject the path of industrialization and urbanization that the more militaristic leaders pursued in the succeeding decade, but they were intent upon reorganizing society to give prominence to organized business. There was harmony not only between Japanese business and government, but also between them and U.S. policy objectives.

In the United States, too, the end of the war brought general acceptance of a world of economic development and interdependence. It was assumed that the nation would continue to expand its trade and investment activities overseas, to extend loans and aid to war-devastated countries so that they could reintegrate themselves into the international economic system, and to raise the U.S. standard of living in an attempt to nurture a more efficient labor force and to support an expanding domestic market. U.S. society, of course, was not without serious political turmoil, as witnessed during the McCarthy era. It reflected dissatisfaction with the Democratic administration's handling of foreign and domestic policies; however, on the whole both government and its critics accepted the essential objectives of U.S. society such as economic growth, prosperity, and general well-being.

To the extent that the structure of international relations depended on domestic order, developments within the United States parallel expanding world trade and international economic activities. The international economic order, based on the Bretton Woods agreements of 1944, enabled business and labor to thrive on continued industrialization. In this sense, both in the United States and in Japan, domestic interests and orientations were compatible with a commitment to the maintenance of world order.

Of course, this was not the only world order that emerged after the war. There were also the realities of U.S.-Soviet confrontation and of Third World anticolonialism. Japan was much less involved in them than the United States, and for that reason Japan's sense of identification with the postwar international economic system was stronger. The U.S.-Soviet confrontation meant that Japanese trade and investment opportunities in the Soviet Union and in the Soviet-bloc countries could not be maximized, but they would have been small in any event when compared with Japan's economic ties with the Free World. Even so, the Japanese were eager to establish economic connections with the Soviet Union, the PRC, and their allies within bounds dictated by considerations of the U.S. security pact. The Japanese–U.S. alliance, with Japanese security entrusted to the U.S. "nuclear umbrella," provided a simple and plausible framework for Japan's behavior in the context of the cold war. Such a posture required a minimum of armament and freed national manpower, energy, and capital for industrialization and overseas trade. As for Third World nationalism, Japan dealt with it primarily by renouncing its prewar and wartime colonialism and paying reparations to various Asian countries. Japan then proceeded to turn to these countries as markets and as suppliers of natural resources—an integral part of its postwar program of economic development. Thus, Japanese social organization on the whole did not have to suffer from strains generated by the cold war or by Third World anti-imperialism. The interests that benefited from postwar Japan's economic orientation could cope with these external phenomena without having to redefine their objectives or rearrange their priorities.

The United States, on the other hand, had to maintain a balance of power on a global scale, necessitating huge expenditures of money and calling into being the "military-industrial complex." These generated corresponding domestic vested interests, making it progressively more difficult to extricate the country from its cold war orientation. There is little question that the world order defined in terms of the cold war conflicted with the goal of economic interdependence. U.S. resources became split between the two types of objectives, although on occasion it was possible to argue that by strengthening the Free World against communism the United States was making it possible for the advanced industrial countries to promote their prosperity.

The United States also had to confront the emergence of the PRC as a spokesman for Third World countries. Instead of the traditional conception of the two countries having the complementary relationship of an advanced economy supplying capital and technology to a backward economy, which, in turn, provided a huge market for the former, the two came to see each other as hostile. The Chinese denounced the United States as the archenemy of all aspiring countries, while the United States saw the PRC as the major threat to stability in the non-Western parts of the globe, carrying out subversive activities to create trouble for anticommunist nations. The almost complete stoppage of trade between the two countries symbolized the failure of the conception of an interdependent world order to provide a framework of cooperation between the under-developed and developing nations. Despite all these, however, U.S. society on the whole maintained stable features; strains that did exist reflected the tensions in the world arena. In that sense a symbiotic relationship existed between the world and domestic orders.

There was essential stability in Japanese–U.S. relations because of that symbiotic relationship. Events within the two countries could be comprehended within a broader framework; they reflected trends in the world. The dominant orientations of each society derived their inspiration from a given definition of international order, and the two countries tended to behave in ways calculated to perpetuate such an order, be it that of capitalist interdependence, cold war confrontation, or the conflict between developed and developing nations. Japanese–U.S. relations were thus fairly predictable because those who controlled the political and economic systems in each country had a stake in a stable international environment and because international affairs encouraged them to remain in positions of power.

Even those who rebelled against such dominance tended to define the terms of their rebellion in the context of international affairs. For instance, the anti-American riots in Japan during the summer of 1960 were comprehensible in the same framework of international politics that justified the security arrangements between the two countries. Both supporters and opponents of the treaty were governed by the same codes. In the end, the Mutual Security Treaty survived, but the Kishi cabinet that had pushed it did not. This was probably because Kishi had come to stand not only for a U.S. alliance but also for militarism and pre-1945 politics. The security pact was accepted by the Japanese when it was seen as one, but not the only, definition of the nation's foreign policy. When coupled with the Ikeda cabinet's pursuit of economic objectives, it could symbolize Japan's identification with a stable postwar international order.

Against such a background, the recent passing of a familiar phase of Japanese–U.S. relations becomes more intelligible. A greater disjunction now seems to exist between developments within each society and in the world as a whole. In the United States, the 1960s saw the first serious challenge to postwar social order. It expressed itself most spectacularly in the protest against the war in Vietnam. Actually, however, the antiwar movement reflected a major challenge to established authority and accepted orthodoxies in postwar America. It was propelled by the youth, women, and minority groups who not only were opposed to military involvement in Asia but also questioned the values that had so long been taken for granted. Some of them challenged the two-party system, middle-class mannerisms, patriotism, or the family structure, while others revolted against restrictions of various kinds. The primary targets of their assault were domestic taboos and ways of life, but for that very reason their emergence as a potent social and political force made it difficult for the United States to accommodate its international roles to domestic concerns.

Unlike the preceding decades, after the 1960s U.S. domestic

developments and foreign policy seemed on different courses. For instance, the United States pursued a policy of détente with the Soviet Union, but the U.S.–Soviet rapprochement evoked little answering support within U.S. society. Few constituencies or vested interest groups had a stake in the détente. Nevertheless, the succeeding administrations in Washington considered it a cardinal goal of U.S. foreign policy to avoid a nuclear holocaust and reach an arms limitation agreement with the Soviet Union. The U.S. government continued to emphasize policy toward the Soviet Union as its overriding concern, even while developments within the country at large could no longer be considered in relation to that question. In short, one could not assume a stable relationship between domestic and international order.

At the same time, in the international arena many issues not directly related to the U.S.–Soviet cold war or détente were emerging. One was the rapid development of Germany, Japan, and other Western countries as industrial giants, eclipsing the United States's position as the leading economic power. The United States remained the largest trading nation in the world as well as the largest exporter of capital. But others were fast catching up with it in terms of volumes of trade and investments, national income, and productivity. This was a development that the postwar policy of encouraging economic multilateralism had envisaged but one that the United States had not pursued uncompromisingly because of the onset of the cold war. While the United States had had to divert its resources to the cold war, its allies and partners had prospered and gained economic strength. By the late 1960s the United States was beginning to suffer from annual balance-of-trade deficits, but initially there was no concerted movement within the United States to cope with the problem. Labor unions, industrialists, farmers, and other interest groups dealt piecemeal with some trade questions—the Japanese textile issue, for instance—but selective protectionism had always existed, and it did not cause a reorientation of official policy on economic questions.

Even more significant was the rising importance of the world outside both the U.S.–Soviet bipolarity and the industrial nations. The relations between the United States and the Soviet

Union and those among advanced industrial countries came to
account for less of the global realities, as demonstrated
poignantly during the Vietnam War and following the quadrupling of oil prices in 1973. All of a sudden, the Third World
revealed itself in stark reality. In fact, it was not a monolithic
group but was divided into those rich in natural resources and
those without them as well as those intent upon industrial
development and those who remained primarily nonindus-
trial. Some of these countries became instant holders of surplus
foreign exchange and wielders of bargaining power in world
politics. These countries represented the bulk of the world's
population with no sense of involvement in the U.S.–Soviet
cold war or commitment to the preservation of a world order
defined by Western capitalist countries. This, too, was a
development little related to existing orientations and patterns
of social relations in the United States. Because the transformation of U.S. society in the 1960s and the 1970s was
internally generated, it was not responsive to the rapid rise in
importance of the resource-rich Third World countries.
Americans of all classes and interest suffered from a rise in the
price of gasoline, for instance, but this did not affect their styles
of living or their modes of political expression.

In Japan there was a greater sensitivity to external trends,
but a gap existed between the sensitivity and Japan's overall
foreign relations. By the late 1960s, 40 percent of the population consisted of those born after the war, and their concerns
and attitudes tended to confirm the postwar stress on peace,
prosperity, and cosmopolitanism. They generally supported
the new constitution. They worked hard and contributed to
economic growth. They opted for stability in politics, never
giving enough support to the leftist parties to challenge the
domination of the Liberal Democratic Party.

Unlike the United States, however, no profound transformation took place in Japanese social order during the 1960s. Thus,
in a different sense from the United States, a disjunction
between Japan's domestic social order and the international
order became noticeable. It took the oil shocks of 1973-1974 for
the Japanese to start questioning the basic premise of the high-
growth economy. All of a sudden, they became aware of the

risks involved in their country's heavy dependence on the overseas supply of natural resources. They also began to consider
environmental issues, not merely as a separate question but as
part of the entire national outlook on growth. Despite all this
concern, however, Japanese foreign relations did not significantly deviate from the patterns established by the 1960s, where
the primary objective had been economic rather than political
power and where Japan relied on the United States for security
and protection. No movement arose calling for a different
orientation in foreign policy or defense strategy. In this sense,
the country was not responding automatically to a changing
international environment.

In this situation, Japanese–U.S. relations experienced new
strains. Their significance in the world arena altered, while
consciousness of that transformation lagged. The two societies
coped differently with external affairs, and in the end uncertainties prevailed. For instance, the United States withdrew
from Vietnam and made plans to reduce its ground forces in
Korea. These steps could be linked to the general decline of
U.S. power throughout the world relative to the Soviet Union.
The United States's overwhelming military superiority was
passing as was the policy of deterring a radical alteration of the
global status quo. This did not mean, however, that the United
States was no longer interested in a stable international order.
On the contrary, the Ford and Carter administrations both
asserted the nation's overriding commitment to stability.
Stability, however, was to be built not on the basis of the United
States's unilateral military superiority but on arms limitation
agreements, negotiations, and political understandings with
the Soviet Union and other countries. Less clear were the
implications of these policies for Japanese–U.S. relations. For
example, did the United States intend to reduce its commitments to the status quo in the Korean peninsula? Was it not
concerned with the growing Soviet power in the Indian Ocean?
What was it going to do in Southeast Asia, where Vietnam was
emerging as a major factor but where other countries (the
Association of Southeast Asian Nations) were uneasily poised
between the United States and Vietnam? What role did the
United States expect Japan to play? Should Japan undertake

to reorient its policy so as to be less dependent on the United States's nuclear umbrella? If so, should Japan expand its armed forces, or should it seek a political understanding with the Soviet Union? Should it, instead, work for an agreement among the major powers for the neutralization of the Asia-Pacific region?

Neither the U.S. nor the Japanese public was prepared to cope with these and many other urgent issues that resulted from the declining power of the United States. In the United States there was little debate on foreign policy questions after the termination of the Vietnam conflict, and it was not clear how the search for new stability in the international arena was linked to developments at home. The 1970s saw the continued growth of the political influence of minorities as their members registered to vote in massive numbers. Movements for women's and other types of liberation gained momentum, absorbing the energies of the government and the public. In the meantime, rising inflation and unemployment claimed attention. There were fewer assassinations and radical movements compared with the 1960s, but this seeming return to law and order was not related to the search for stability in the world arena. It was far from clear how the building of a new society would affect the nation's myriad foreign policy problems. There was obviously an inward-looking, isolationist trend in U.S. society, but it remained to be seen how such isolationism would fit in with an international order requiring a U.S. military presence.

Similarly, in Japan there was no new movement to redefine the country's military posture (or lack of military posture) abroad. Given the decline in U.S. power, it would have been logical to consider altering Japan's role through increased armament or a more equal contribution to joint defense efforts with the United States. But these choices were hardly, if at all, discussed, reflecting general satisfaction with what Americans could consider "a free ride" on security matters. This also meant that Japanese society managed to assign its internal conflicts and contradictions to predictable categories such as student radicalism and pro-Peking or pro-Taipei lobbies without giving rise to new privileged classes that were wedded to a program of expanding defense spending. There were strong stakes in continuity, and continuity meant keeping within the framework of the Mutual Security Treaty with a minimum of Japanese military contribution.

Likewise, the 1970s saw an erosion of U.S. economic competitiveness in the world, but here again no strong movement emerged within the United States to reorder domestic priorities. Certain interests reacted in a traditional way: by demanding high tariff walls and retaliatory trade policies to cut back foreign imports. But other interests expanded their overseas operations, causing a growth of multinational corporations. Agriculture, computer technology, aviation industry, and other export-oriented interests remained internationalist in outlook. The importation of oil, on the other hand, never abated, contributing to huge trade deficits that in turn weakened the dollar. Traditional mechanisms such as recession, declining consumer demand, unemployment, and an aggressive export drive did not automatically work in coping with these issues in the aftermath of the collapse of the Bretton Woods framework following the oil shocks. The United States's concern was with domestic problems—inflation, layoffs, urban decay, the cost of social welfare, and increasing taxes. The concern was expressed in organized movements of one kind or another, but such movements were only tangentially related to foreign economic policy. There was some movement toward a more nationalistic posture, as seen in the decision to declare a 200-mile coastal fishery zone, in line with similar decisions by other countries. But the decision was not a result of an emerging domestic consensus, and it was not clear how such a nationalistic stance was tied in with other aspects of economic foreign policy and what interests it was trying to accommodate. In short, here, too, no new forms of power and interest appeared corresponding to the vast changes in the international arena.

Japanese society responded more systematically to these changes. Efforts were generated to shift domestic priorities away from rapid economic growth and to stress social welfare, the quality of life, and "civil minima." On the whole, this shift was accomplished without great political turmoil, although the long, drawn-out recession created social tensions as more firms began giving up the policy of lifelong employment. The relative political stability, however, may have made it more difficult to reassess Japanese–U.S. economic relations.

Despite—indeed, because of—the global economic dislocations, the Japanese economy became more than ever export-oriented, and in 1977 its trade surplus reached 17 billion dollars. Much of this surplus could be accounted for by massive Japanese exports to the United States at a time when Japanese purchases from the latter were not showing a significant gain. Inevitably, such a development called forth a serious protectionist sentiment in the United States for which the Japanese were little prepared. They had not reckoned with the fact that this time U.S. protectionism was not an isolated phenomenon but rather was part of the process of domestic reorganization in which new power centers and interest groups were making themselves known. The administration in Washington would not be as effective as in the past to cope with the demands of labor and some industries for protection because the government's power was built on a loose alliance of divergent interest groups whose loyalties were, at best, halfhearted. In such a situation, Japanese–U.S. economic ties could not be taken for granted as a provider of stability in Japan. One could no longer count on a seeming correspondence between Japanese social order and U.S. social order.

As the 1970s approach their end, a need clearly exists to discuss ways in which tensions in the world and in each country can be channeled into a new patterning of national and international affairs. The countries of the world are being called upon to reformulate their goals and create new stakes in some framework of stability, but the reordering of domestic priorities could generate nationalistic forces and severely strain relations among nations. If so, there can be no stable world order. The question is whether the world as a whole can accommodate domestic changes and whether national societies can be organized in a way compatible with the new realities— moral and existential—of international society.

The problems facing Japanese–U.S. relations, then, are no

longer simply bilateral issues but involve fundamental chal-
lenges of global proportions. The two countries will need to
clarify their objectives at home and in so doing redefine social
relations among divergent interests and orientations. To be
more specific, each society will have to determine whether the
exisiting economic mechanisms, the processes of decision
making, and the modes of transmitting cultural norms from
one generation to the next are adequate given the growing
scarcity of resources and energy and given the increasing
seriousness of the problems of the aged, the handicapped, the
impoverished, and the alienated. At the same time, both the
United States and Japan will have to operate in an international environment in which more countries come to possess
destructive nuclear weapons and claim segments of the oceans
and the skies. Few of them are committed to preserving an
international system whose stability depends on a U.S.–Soviet
balance of terror or on the domination of the world economy
by a handful of advanced industrial countries. Most of the
developing countries reject fiercely any attempt at interference
by another nation, but at the same time some groups within
their societies derive their power and influence from political
and economic connections with foreigners.

This is a chaotic picture, and it is far from certain how the
world is going to restabilize itself when conditions in most
countries are so unstable. But at least it seems probable that
Japanese–U.S. relations will come to depend far more on
factors exterior to the two countries than on purely bilateral
questions. For this very reason, paradoxically enough, there
will be much that they can do together to cope effectively
with, if not anticipate and influence, developments elsewhere.
Most fundamental will be the question of human survival. As
two of the most advanced and democratic economic powers,
they are in a position to persuade others to join together for a
common effort. At the same time, however, they must respond
to the charge that they are wasting the earth's resources and
pursuing materialistic, energy-intensive consumption policies
when other peoples are suffering from a lack of food and
shelter. The Third World's clamor for a share of economic

opportunities and its political assertiveness can be ignored only at great risk. But instead of meeting this challenge individually, the advanced industrial democracies must cooperate and coordinate their responses. To do so, they will have to be willing to break away from some of the existing patterns of national politics and social life.

As the papers in this volume indicate, there is enough willingness among leaders of both countries to view Japanese–U.S. relations in the necessary broad framework and to consider ways to cooperate in the world arena. To carry out such cooperation they will need domestic support; there will have to be individuals, groups, and interests with a stake in a stable international system that has not yet emerged. To ensure the emergence of such a system and a corresponding domestic order is a test of leadership and a challenge to the imagination and resourcefulness of the two peoples. The world has never been in greater need of Japanese–U.S. cooperation.

Part 2
Security in Northeast Asia

3

The Role of the United States in East Asia: A Legislative Perspective

John Glenn, Jr.

Although I am a member of the Foreign Relations Committee of the U.S. Senate and in fact am the chairman of its Subcommittee on East Asian and Pacific Affairs, I speak not as a representative of the administration, the Senate, or the Foreign Relations Committee, but as an individual with concerns and hopes for the future regarding our mutual interests.

To put my following remarks in perspective, let me point out an often misunderstood aspect of our U.S. democratic system: the checks and balances between the executive and legislative branches of government. While the president speaks with authority as the leader in foreign policy, that leadership is balanced by the check of congressional, particularly senatorial, approval on major issues.

This can be disconcerting to other countries because these counterbalancing responsibilities and approvals can sometimes give the impression that the voice of U.S. foreign policy leadership is an "uncertain trumpet."

More fundamental than the "uncertain trumpet" is a factor that *will* determine long-term U.S. foreign policy, namely, the views of the American people. And it is very clear that the overwhelming majority of Americans and their representatives in Congress strongly support the continuation of U.S. interests and concerns in East Asia and in Japan in particular.

U.S. policy established at the end of World War II was not to crush, humiliate, or exploit, but rather to start the long process of building political and economic ties that would contribute to peaceful development. Japan stands today as an eloquent testimony to the wisdom of that decision. Coupled with the strength of the Japanese people, that policy has helped make Japan one of the strongest economic powers in the world, an achievement made in the unbelievably short span of the last three decades. To pull back now from that success story is not realistic.

Relationships, however, are not static. They change and develop in response to events. But in spite of the end of the war in Indochina, the dramatic opening of the PRC, and other necessary shifts in U.S. policy toward former adversaries in the region, U.S. determination to maintain close and cordial political and economic ties with Japan has not diminished.

Recent actions of the United States prompted concern and misunderstanding over what many U.S. friends around the Asian periphery saw as signs of a U.S. withdrawal. This is not, of course, the first time in recent years that important U.S. policy moves have appeared to others less than well coordinated and have led to an adverse reaction from Asian friends.

But such interpretations are unnecessarily pessimistic. The primary U.S. objective remains the stability and prosperity of East Asia. Many Asian states have long looked to the United States as a prime supporter of their economic and strategic interests and as a leader in Pacific affairs. Continued U.S. presence is vital, and I am confident that the United States is and will remain an important source of economic and military cooperation; that the United States is and will remain a major market for raw materials and manufactured goods produced by these states and a major source of private capital investment; and that the United States is and will remain committed to balancing other major powers in the area—the Soviet Union and China.

It is no secret that in the recent past the United States has had problems at home. It had Watergate, a recession, an energy crisis, and the 1976 presidential election, all following the collapse of the U.S.-supported governments in Indochina in 1975. U.S. friends in East Asia and Japan became deeply concerned over what they perceived as an increasing loss of interest by the United States in Asian affairs and a shift in the balance of power in the region.

Adding to Asian worries were calls by many U.S. political leaders for reductions in the number and size of U.S. forces in Asia. At the same time, more U.S. leaders were criticizing the growing volume of manufactured imports from the nations of East Asia and were calling for restrictive tariffs and other measures to protect U.S. industries. There was also mounting criticism in the United States regarding the status of human rights in several East Asian countries closely aligned with the United States.

Some Asian concerns are understandable. But if the United States is to take a realistic approach to changing the world situation, other concerns are not justified. For instance, I know of no one in the United States who prefers that U.S. military forces remain spread around the world as a "police force" in perpetuity, even though the United States very properly maintained many of its world military alignments during the post–World War II stabilizing period. The size and disposition of those forces obviously will and should change as nations are able to assume larger responsibilities. As another example, it is realistic to assume that as productive capacity grows and international commerce increases, agreements on trade must be forthcoming.

But there are other, more immediate, East Asian concerns. While it was understandable that a new U.S. president wished to move forcefully and rapidly, new policy initiatives in many instances did not succeed in reassuring the nations of East and Southeast Asia. With the obvious advantage of perfect hindsight, it would undoubtedly have been advisable to establish more positively a broader understanding of U.S. overall commitment and general policy in the region before proceeding with individual initiatives.

A succession of East Asian ambassadors have come to my office in recent months expressing their doubts and uncertainties regarding U.S. actions and policies. I believe that if this conference and other exchanges are less than candid and forthright in addressing these concerns, the good that can accrue from them will be limited.

Let me be more specific and share with you some of their views, comments, and questions:

First: "The United States seems to be far more concerned about improving relations with Hanoi, Peking, and even Pyongyang than in strengthening relations with long-standing friends."

Second: "Would our expressed concerns about human rights seriously alter our relationships with such places as South Korea, the Philippines, or Indonesia?"

Third: "In light of Soviet moves into the Indian Ocean, how can we even consider 'complete demilitarization' of the Indian Ocean?"

Fourth: "Why are we not more concerned about the movement of Soviet fishing fleets into the Southwest Pacific and even about Soviet air base construction in that area?"

Fifth: "Were press reports true, although later denied, that the United States would really consider closing its naval and air bases in the Philippines because of the increased lease-payment demands?"

Sixth: "Did the proposed cutoff of last year's military assistance funds to Indonesia and Thailand, even though it did not pass the Senate, indicate lessening commitment?"

Seventh: "Did the sudden trade sanctions against the import of Japanese television sets indicate a changing trade relationship?"

Eighth: "Will changes in our nuclear policies affect Japan's critical energy needs?"

Ninth: "What will be our relationship with Taiwan in the future? Can that long-standing relationship be changed without reduction of confidence in U.S. commitments? Will we sell arms to Taiwan?"

Tenth: "Does our reduction of troops in Korea, even if it is to take place over a five-year period, indicate reduced commitment to the overall East Asian balance of power? How long will our air and naval forces remain?"

These examples are sufficient to provide the general tenor.

With the Vietnam experience a recent memory, it is easy to understand why serious questions are raised in the minds of East Asian leaders. In addition, not one item on the above list seemed to be singularly critical in the minds of those to whom I talked, but taken together they formed a pattern most disturbing to those in leadership positions. As expressed bluntly by one ambassador, "Can we still rely on the United States? We feel inundated by a tidal wave of change. What does it all mean? We don't know why you are doing what you are doing." While I could reassure him of my confidence in U.S. long-term commitment, specific answers to the many questions are not easy to supply, either singly or as a whole.

However, in recent months U.S. leaders have taken greater pains to reassure Asian allies and have managed to establish a better consultative framework in U.S. Asian policy. Thus, the United States has recently worked hard to underline its continuing defense commitment to South Korea. Most notably, when Defense Secretary Brown met with President Park of Korea on July 25, 1977, he gave the South Korean leader a personal letter from President Carter that reaffirmed the "firm and undiminished" U.S. commitment to support South Korea and advised that "neither North Korea nor any other nation should have any doubt about the continuing strength of this commitment."

The Brown mission subsequently announced that the bulk of U.S. combat troops in Korea would not be withdrawn until 1981-1982 and that the administration had pledged—subject to congressional approval—to provide the South Koreans with an estimated $2 billion in military sales and credits as U.S. troop strength was reduced. He also spelled out in more detail the continuing commitment of U.S. air and naval forces, which would remain indefinitely. These were precisely the positive signals needed for reassurance.

Elsewhere, the administration substantially altered its position on demilitarization of the Indian Ocean. During talks with Australian Prime Minister Frazer in June 1977, President Carter dropped his earlier call for "complete demilitarization" and endorsed the view that the United States should maintain a strategic balance in the area. He also reassured Frazer that the

United States would remain "a major power in Asia and the Pacific and would maintain a strong security position in the region."

Regarding the issue of U.S. security assistance to Asian friends, Congress was not swayed by the arguments that major cuts should be made in the administration's proposals for military aid in the area. Prior to final committee action, military assistance funds for Indonesia and Thailand were restored, and that positive action was sustained by the full Senate.

At the same time, prominent U.S. spokesmen—notably Secretary Vance in a major address on Asian policy on June 29, 1977—expressed a deeper realization of the difficulties of some Asian states to conform to Western standards of human rights. Thus, Vance expressed understanding that some Asian traditions—unlike the traditions of the West—stress the rights and welfare of the group over those of the individual and emphasize the fulfillment of basic human economic needs over political rights.

Finally, the administration and Congress reassured Asian friends regarding U.S. trade policies by working well together to avoid protective tariffs or other harsh measures that would close U.S. markets to Asian goods and seriously disrupt the joint economic welfare. The administration strongly reaffirmed the U.S. commitment to policies of free trade during President Carter's meeting with Japanese Prime Minister Fukuda at the London summit meeting in May. It subsequently negotiated compromise agreements with Japan, Taiwan, and South Korea that established voluntary restrictions on the number of color television sets and shoes entering the United States from East Asia.

This spirit of cooperative friendship will also be evident, I believe, when the Association of Southeast Asian Nations (ASEAN) meets formally, for the first time with the United States, to discuss opportunities as well as problems that the ASEAN nations may have with current U.S. trade policies. The above are but a few examples of other continuing assurances that will go a long way in restoring any erosion of confidence that may have occurred in the recent past.

Apart from those general East Asian views, let us turn to specific Japanese–U.S. relationships. U.S. ties are firmly and properly grounded in the self-interest of both nations and are essential to global stability. The consultative mechanisms between the two countries are extensive but must be even further strengthened if misunderstandings in the future are to be avoided. No government likes surprises. Decisions made abroad with little or no prior consultation and that drastically affect a nation's future naturally evoke a negative reaction as a defense to gain time for adequate analysis of new proposals. The Nixon shocks, for instance, arose in part because of the belief that the Japanese were unwilling to recognize legitimate U.S. grievances. However, these feelings dissipated following the Tanaka visit of August 1973, when the final communiqué expressed a willingness to share on a more equal and reciprocal basis. In 1975 Japan for the first time participated as an equal with the major Western powers in an economic summit. The point is that the U.S. commitment to Asia is permanent but must be based on mutual understanding. Determined diplomatic efforts to resolve problems, as in the case of Okinawa, are necessary.

And what of the Japanese–U.S. military relationship? Critics in the United States habitually talk of the "free ride" or "free umbrella" provided Japan by the United States, and it is no small item. When the United States is running sizeable trade deficits and Japan has a current-account surplus, it is difficult to understand why Japan cannot increase its defense efforts in cooperation with the United States. Certainly the present U.S. administration and a majority in Congress recognize the domestic constraints on a major expansion of Japanese military forces. However, to ensure qualitative sufficiency for Japanese self-defense forces, improvements should be made in such areas as antisubmarine warfare equipment and fighter and patrol aircraft, all of which may require far less strict adherence to the artificially selected 1 percent GNP barrier now used as a limit for defense budgeting. By comparison, NATO countries average over 4.5 percent of GNP in defense expenditures. In time of need, less than an adequate defense force will be a poor bargain, whatever the percentage of GNP.

What of the economic relationship between the two countries? This is an area of both opportunities and problems that Ambassador Mansfield recently addressed in considerable detail and that will be the subject of much of the meeting time at Shimoda. The complications of further negotiations are indicated by the necessity of maintaining an economic system geared to exports that has led to a possible $7 billion current-account surplus in 1977. Without further cooperative efforts to reduce that surplus, domestic politics are bound to hamper the trade relationship. Added to that is the concern over how, and to what degree, direct investment between the two nations will be permitted to dominate particular product lines with their obvious impact on employment. Reciprocity must exist, or protectionism will arise.

There are no easy solutions, particularly when non-agricultural U.S. exports may sometimes suffer less from tariffs or quotas than from nontariff, cultural barriers that are harder to penetrate—a marketing problem, in other words.

Looking beyond the Japanese–U.S. economic relationship alone, however, Japan is in a position to play a major and constructive role in grappling with the problems of a new economic order. Japan has the potential for being a pivotal nation in devising a new creative economic diplomacy emphasizing cooperation and peace. Prime Minister Fukuda's recent meetings with ASEAN leaders and the pledge of substantial aid are highly commendable examples of Japan's ability to contribute strongly to regional stability. As another example, the newly established $20 million "special assistance for the expansion of food production fund" will help others in the region to cope with a pressing problem.

But a word of caution is necessary. Other Asian states are keenly conscious of Japan's economic presence. Many of the other East Asian nations have memories of past Japanese militarism that have not yet disappeared. While they have no military fears today, they express concern about the economic domination that might result from overrapid Japanese expansion in the Asian area, an expansion that could overpower their own economic improvement efforts. In other words, Japanese aid and economic help must not be excessive or dominating.

Since economic development, like self-government, cannot be exported, the infusion of capital and knowledge can best be used to supplement indigenous efforts, assuming there is to be a harmonious relationship. Japanese national interests and an expanded international role do come together in the economic sphere. Increased foreign aid, less tied to export commodities, and private investment for development can help other nations to meet their goals and ensure a more stable international system.

Economic power alone, however, is insufficient. Political muscle must accompany economics for major impact on global developments. For example, an activist Japan that mediates between the socialist and noncommunist states of the region, as the prime minister suggested to ASEAN leaders, would help to stabilize the international environment and also produce a greater sense of national identity. Japan has a historically unique opportunity. Never before has a rich and powerful nation chosen to exert itself in the international system through solely political and economic alignments. Japan now has that opportunity.

The largest and perhaps the most basic problem of all, however, is energy. Last fall I flew over the Strait of Hormuz, the few-hundred-yards-wide outlet from the Persian Gulf, and was told that while 18 percent of the United States's total oil comes through that strait, some 70 percent of Western Europe's oil and an astounding 85 percent of total Japanese oil passes through those narrow waters. For industrial Japan to be so dependent on that small, faraway piece of geography certainly emphasizes the magnitude of the problem and the importance of international relationships in an increasingly interdependent world. Because of Japan's resource dependency—99.7 percent of its oil is imported—its interests in energy security are paramount.

I need not elaborate that point further here, except to say that we are committed to finding a mutually agreeable, practical solution to the nuclear fuel reprocessing issue. Certainly the U.S. atomic weapons nonproliferation objectives are not directed against Japan. I would hope that the unique Japanese experience would encourage Japan to assist the United States in trying to stem the proliferation of nuclear weapons. Like-wise, Japanese–U.S. differences must be resolved so that Japan can become more self-sufficient in the energy field through the proper use of nuclear power. This is a field in which I have been particularly active, and I have authored several pieces of legislation dealing with nuclear matters. I also am firmly convinced that we must have some supplies of nuclear fuel internationally administered, and independent of national politics. I have introduced legislation to establish such an International Nuclear Fuel Authority.

We are entering a new era of Japanese–U.S. relations—a time of more equality, a time of more partnership, but still an era with many unanswered questions. What will be the Japanese role in international politics? Will it center only on trade? Is Japan the Pacific bulwark of a Western economic and strategic system, or is it primarily an Asian power, uniquely nonmilitaristic, that is also the principal economic power in the region? The answer, of course, is both, but then we must ask whether Japanese interest can be secured by passive diplomacy, or must a more active role be forthcoming? What, then, is the yet-to-be-defined role of Japan in Asia and the international system?

In February 1973 the secretary general of the Liberal Democratic Party cited the lack of a permanent seat on the United Nations Security Council as evidence of the lack of a Japanese role commensurate with the country's power. Ambassador Mansfield, while in the Senate, urged such a shift. President Carter reaffirmed that objective when Prime Minister Fukuda met with him earlier this year. The rapid rise, fall, and rebirth of modern Japan attests to the skill and character of the Japanese people, and these talents certainly deserve a wider international forum.

Looking to the future, not only must the above be considered, but a myriad of other issues with continual, close consultation as well. Taking a legislative branch viewpoint from Washington, I see no lessening of the U.S. commitment to work together with Japan and other East Asian nations. The United States is not in retreat—far from it. That Japanese–U.S. cooperative efforts can succeed in the worldwide arena of competing ideologies is a foregone conclusion.

What is the wave of the future? Is it the supersocialistic approach, lesser brands of communism, or free enterprise? Recent history has the answer. At no place or time in history has the rapid advance in the status and welfare of hundreds of millions of people been recorded as that which occurred in those nations whose development followed free enterprise lines after World War II. When the economic development of Japan, Germany, South Korea, and Taiwan is contrasted with what has happened under the deadening influence of the socialist states, the answer emerges with startling clarity. The systems of freedom are certainly far from perfect, and we must work unremittingly to make them better, but they certainly speak directly to age-old hopes for freedom, dignity, fair play, and for the right to determine one's place in a society, a nation, and the world. These are to me the wave of the future.

The challenge is to work together as partners in this framework of freedom toward a better, more stable, and peaceful world. It will require our best efforts.

4

Japan and the United States: Security Issues in the Far East

Stephen J. Solarz

Both the United States and Japan have a significant stake in the preservation of peace throughout the Far East. For Tokyo, the outbreak of war in the Western Pacific would endanger the Japanese economy and threaten the country's tranquility. For Washington, an armed conflict in East Asia would result in economic uncertainty and political turmoil.

The United States is, after all, a Pacific power, and it is likely to remain so for as long as it holds a place of preeminence in the family of nations. Since the end of World War II, the United States has twice shed the blood of the best and the bravest of its younger generation in Asia. The graves of over 100,000 U.S. men provide mute but moving testimony to the intense interest of the United States in the maintenance of a balance of power in East Asia. One of the states lies deep in the Pacific Ocean. One U.S. trust territory is located even further west than Hawaii. Asia accounts for more than one quarter of U.S. foreign trade, and the jobs and livelihood of millions of Americans are dependent on the free flow of goods and services across the vast expanse of the Pacific Ocean. Seven Far Eastern nations—Japan, South Korea, Taiwan, the Philippines, Thailand, Australia, and New Zealand—are the beneficiaries of U.S. contractual defense commitments.

Through history, tradition, economic advantage, and military necessity, the United States is bound, inevitably and inextricably, to the future of its Asian allies. The reformulation of U.S. foreign policy in the post-Vietnam period notwithstanding, a U.S. withdrawal from its Asian associations would be unthinkable. A contraction of U.S. commitments, yes; but a repudiation of U.S. obligations, no.

The Japanese–U.S. relationship is both the touchstone and the cornerstone of the U.S. foreign policy in the Far East. The rise of Japan from the ashes of war to the ranks of the world's great industrial powers is a tribute to the industriousness and ingenuity of the Japanese. With the third largest GNP of any nation in the world, Japan is involved in two-way trade with the United States in excess of $25 billion per year. The United States is Japan's largest trading partner, and Japan, after Canada, is the largest trading partner of the United States.

At the heart of this particularly productive relationship, which has meant so much to the economies of both countries, is the Mutual Security Treaty. First signed in 1951, it has been a major factor in the establishment of a great-power equilibrium in the Far East. By enabling Japan to concentrate its resources on development rather than defense, the treaty has facilitated one of the great economic success stories of our times. By bringing Japan under the defense umbrella of the United States, it has enabled the West to balance the growing industrial and military power of the communist states. By justifying the continuing Japanese determination to remain a lightly armed, nonnuclear power, it has brought a measure of calm and confidence to the populous and politically significant states of Southeast Asia that might otherwise have felt threatened by a resurgence of Japanese militarism. And perhaps most significantly of all, the treaty has provided an example to the world of how to achieve industrial progress without military might.

For all these reasons, the care and maintenance of the Japanese–U.S. relationship must necessarily be one of the cardinal objectives of U.S. foreign policy. If Japan were to lose faith in the credibility of the U.S. commitment, the consequences might be catastrophic, not only for the relationship between the two countries, but for the entire international balance of power as well. It is, of course, possible that in the wake of such a development Japan might opt for a policy of neutrality. Instead of a mutual defense pact with one great power, it may conclude that its interests might be served better by nonaggression pacts with all of the great powers.

But given the economic progress that they have already made and the military potential that their industrial base makes possible, it is doubtful that Japan would be comfortable with such an arrangement. Confronted by countries whose ideological interests and economic aspirations may come in conflict with those of Japan, it seems much more likely that under such circumstances Japan would choose to be in a position to defend itself instead of having to rely on the goodwill and good intentions of its neighbors.

The chances are, therefore, that if Japan lost faith in the value of the Mutual Security Treaty, it would decide to rearm as rapidly as possible. Since the end of World War II and the decision of Japan to rely on the United States for its own security, its annual expenditures on defense have averaged less than 1 percent of its GNP. The United States, by comparison, has spent around 6 percent of its GNP on defense each year, and the Soviet Union, according to the best estimates, has been devoting between 12 and 14 percent of its GNP to defense. Therefore, there is ample room for a substantial increase in defense spending by Japan—if it should decide to forego the advantages of the Mutual Security Treaty. And given the advanced industrial base from which it would begin, it would not take Japan long to become one of the major military powers in the world. If Japan does decide to rearm, the possibility cannot be precluded that it would decide to develop a nuclear capacity as well. Informed sources have estimated that Japan is producing enough plutonium to manufacture about two hundred atom bombs per year. Clearly, the obstacles in the path of a Japanese decision to go nuclear are primarily political rather than technical.

While Japanese rearmament may seem more like a hypothetical horror than a realistic political possibility, it cannot be completely discounted, particularly if Japan were to lose faith in the efficacy of its existing arrangement with the United States. And precisely for this reason it may be worthwhile to examine briefly the likely consequence of such a development.

At the very least, the situation would create consternation on the part of those Southeast Asian and Western Pacific countries whose memories of World War II have left them with a residual fear of Japanese militarism. But it undoubtedly would also be a cause for concern to both the Chinese and the Russians, who would see in Japanese rearmament a potential threat to their own security. The increase in tensions that a massive military buildup by Japan would inevitably produce would have an enormously destabilizing impact on the existing great-power equilibrium in the Western Pacific. Both the People's Republic of China and the Soviet Union would probably feel compelled to increase their own defense spending in order to deal with the military challenge of a rearmed Japan. And this, in turn, would necessarily obligate the United States to spend more on defense as well. Should Japan decide to go nuclear—a possibility that, in the context of rearmament, cannot be precluded—these problems would assume an especially dangerous dimension. Indeed, if Japan ever joins the nuclear club, it would pretty much mean that the United States had lost its last chance, if not to put the nuclear genie back into the atomic bottle, at least to prevent the spread of such weapons in the hands of many states that do not now possess them.

Since no one can predict with certainty the internal impact on Japan of a decision to rearm, one cannot exclude the possibility that it would facilitate a fundamental change in the political orientation of the Japanese. In these terms, it is not inconceivable, although it is admittedly unlikely, that Japan might decide at some future date to make common cause with the PRC or the Soviet Union. Needless to say, were the population of the PRC or the military might of the Soviet Union harnessed to the industrial power of Japan, it would have the most profound consequences for the international balance of power.

This is not to suggest that any, let alone all, of these possibilities are likely to take place. But stranger things, after all, have happened in the checkered history of mankind. Who, for instance, would have predicted twenty-eight years ago that the two great communist powers, joined as they were in revolutionary solidarity, would one day be each other's most bitter enemy? Yet this illustrates the potentially destabilizing developments that could take place if Japan were to conclude that it could no longer rely on the U.S. defense commitment.

It is in these terms that the continuing debate over burden sharing must be evaluated. From time to time complaints have been heard in the United States about the alleged failure of Japan to assume its fair share of the cost for its own defense. The enormous growth of the Japanese economy, these critics contend, has made it possible for Japan to spend substantially more on its military establishment without in any way endangering its economic viability. Considerations of equity, as well as a backlog of unmet social and economic needs in the United States, also have been cited as arguments in favor of greater military spending by Japan. After all, not a single developed country in the world today, and few developing ones, spend a smaller percentage of their GNP on defense than Japan. And if there is a will to do more for their own defense, the Japanese surely can find a way to do it.

Such an argument, however fiscally attractive it may be to Americans bent on balancing the budget, must ultimately be considered a classic example of a policy that is economically wise but strategically foolish. Given all of the potential problems that might result from a Japanese decision to become a major military power, it seems clear that mutual interests are far better served by a continued Japanese reliance on the United States for defense. A little rearmament could very easily end up like a little pregnancy: getting larger and larger until it bore little resemblance to what it looked like when it first began. Indeed, from a political point of view, the forces that would have to be mobilized to justify a substantially greater expenditure on defense are primarily the same factions that would be behind a Japanese determination, should that day ever come, to join the ranks of the world's major military powers. Consequently, instead of urging Japan to assume a larger share of the defense burden, the United States should be encouraging a commitment to a defense policy based on the concept of Japan as a lightly armed, nonnuclear power relying on the Mutual Security Treaty with the United States for the protection of its most vital interests. If the Mutual Security Treaty is an essential ingredient in the maintenance of the existing equilibrium in the Western Pacific, then the credibility of the U.S. commitment is the key factor in determining the viability of the current arrangement. For more than twenty-five years, despite an occasionally divisive domestic debate, the majority of the Japanese, and certainly the ruling Liberal Democratic Party, has been willing to rely on the U.S. military umbrella for its defense.

With the collapse of the U.S.-sponsored effort in Indochina, however, new doubts have been raised about the value and viability of the United States's commitment to its Asian allies. And President Carter's announced intention to withdraw gradually all U.S. ground forces from South Korea over the next four to five years has served, among other things, to focus additional attention on the nature and extent of the U.S. role in the Far East. To the extent that Tokyo has traditionally considered the security of South Korea as essential to the security of Japan, such a policy is, quite understandably, a matter of grave concern. North Korea is, after all, one of the most rigid and repressive regimes in the world today. Under the complete control of its president, Kim-Il kung, it remains dedicated in word as well as in deed to the reunification of the Korean peninsula under communist control. Based on his history, his ideology, his personality, and his politics, it seems fair to say that reunification remains Kim's major personal and political priority. He tried once before to achieve his ambition through the force of arms and failed. But few doubt that Kim would be prepared to attempt another attack *if* he thought he could succeed.

The possibility of another war in Korea is not as remote as some might think. From the perspective of Pyongyang there would appear to be few, if any, alternative methods of achieving the much sought-after objective of reunification. Neither the PRC nor the Soviet Union, on whom North Korea would have to depend for logistical assistance and diplomatic support in anything other than a very brief conflict, appear to have much of an interest in seeing another war on the Korean peninsula. From their point of view, such a conflict would be dangerously destabilizing. For the Soviet Union, it would threaten the whole policy of détente, and for the PRC, it would probably halt the process of normalization that began with the Shanghai communiqué. It could even result in a catastrophic conflict with the West. It seems safe to say, therefore, that the Soviet Union and the PRC would undoubtedly try to dissuade Kim from attempting to achieve by war what he could not accomplish through peace.

Yet for all of Kim's dependence on the PRC and the Soviet Union, the fact remains that their revolutionary communist credentials are somewhat dependent on him. The very existence of the Sino-Soviet split, which in some respects has been an unusual element in the maintenance of a balance of power between East and West, has in other respects given communist countries like North Korea a measure of political flexibility that they otherwise would not have had. If war did break out on the Korean peninsula, however much they wished it had not, both the PRC and the Soviet Union undoubtedly would feel compelled, given the ideological and political competition between them, to support North Korea. The fear of losing favor with Pyongyang would probably prevail in the calculations of both Moscow and Peking over their fear of alienating the West. And Kim Il-sung, who is very much aware of these elementary political constraints, is thus more or less free to pursue whatever course of action he thinks is in his own best interests. It is precisely for these reasons that the maintenance of a balance of power in Korea is so important. Let the North develop a decided and demonstrable military superiority over the South, and a reasonably good chance exists that Kim, especially if he thought the United States was not prepared to defend Seoul, would conclude that the time had come to strike again.

The outbreak of another war on the Korean peninsula would in and of itself be a cause of great concern to Japan. It would be a source of divisiveness among the 600,000 Koreans in Japan whose loyalties would be split between the North and the South. Assuming that the United States would seek to utilize its base facilities in Japan to provide South Korea with the air support and logistical assistance it needed to repel an invasion, the Japanese would become politically polarized between those who supported the U.S. commitment and those who opposed it.

Should Pyongyang prevail and Seoul suffer a defeat, the consequences would be even worse, for in the process of permitting the forcible reunification of the Korean peninsula, the United States, from the perspective of Japan, would have facilitated the transformation of a political problem into a military threat. Whether, in fact, a unified Korea under communist control would pose a serious military challenge to Japan, it would certainly be perceived as posing such a threat by the Japanese. Certainly, were the United States to stand by while the North overran the South, or even seized Seoul, despite the Mutual Defense Treaty, it would raise the gravest doubts in Japan about the value of their treaty with the United States. The collapse of resistance in the South, coupled with a failure on the part of the United States to prevent it, would produce a major debate within Japan about the best course of action to follow, probably resulting in a decision to rearm, accompanied by the consequences previously described.

It is, therefore, perfectly understandable that Japan should be skeptical, to put it mildly, about the decision on the part of the Carter administration to begin withdrawing all U.S. ground forces from South Korea. No one can doubt that the presence of the Second Division has contributed to the deterrent value of the U.S. commitment to South Korea. And legitimate questions have been raised about the extent to which the withdrawal of these forces may ultimately lead to the outbreak of the very war that they are there to prevent.

It seems, however, that there are a number of sound and substantial reasons why the plan and process initiated by President Carter, if properly carried out, can contribute to a shoring up of the U.S. commitment to South Korea. Paradoxical as it may seem, by making it appear less likely that U.S. troops will once again become involved in a ground war on the Asian mainland, it is more likely that the United States will be able to muster the broad-based political support back home that will be necessary to defend South Korea should it be attacked.

Under the present circumstances, most military experts agree that the indigenous balance of power on the Korean peninsula favors the North over the South. Table 4.1, taken from the latest edition of the worldwide military balance published by the Institute for Strategic Studies in London, provides the basic data on which such a judgment can be made.

As anyone who has studied the military significance of an order of battle well knows, statistics alone do not tell the whole story. And, to be sure, a number of factors in the equation militate in favor of the South rather than the North. Many of the planes available to Pyongyang, for example, are more or less outdated, and of those that are not, a substantial number are designed for home defense instead of ground support. Assuming that the North went on the offensive, the South would have the benefits of being on the defensive. And since there are only two established invasion routes on the road to Seoul, the South also would enjoy the advantage of preparing in advance for such an attack. Perhaps most importantly, however, the South not only has almost 100,000 more men under arms than the North, but many of its soldiers are battle-hardened veterans of the war in Vietnam, giving them a distinct advantage in combat experience.

On balance, however, it appears that the North does have substantial superiority over the South in the critical categories of air, armor, and artillery. In recent months the estimates of the number of tanks and artillery pieces in the North Korean inventory have been upgraded substantially. And most military analysts would agree that the North has a significant edge over the South in terms of the amount of firepower. The reason for this indigenous imbalance is basically that over the course of the last decade and more the North has devoted a much larger share of its GNP to military expenditures than the South. Between 1963 and 1972, for example, Pyongyang spent approximately 14 percent of its GNP on defense, while Seoul utilized only 4 percent of its resources for such purposes. Since that time, the figures have remained comparably disproportionate, although the absolute amounts have changed somewhat. Supposedly secure under the protection of the U.S. defense umbrella, which made up for the developing disparity in the indigenous balance of power, the government in Seoul obviously chose to concentrate on development rather than defense. Such a policy, to be sure, required South Korea to pay

TABLE 4.1   North and South Korea: The Military Balance

North Korea (Democratic People's Republic)

Army: 430,000

   2 tank divisions
 22 infantry divisions
   3 independent infantry brigades
   6 independent tank regiments
   3 AA artillery brigades
250 T-34, 900 T-54/-55 and T-59 med, 150 PT-76, 50 T-62 lt tks; BTR-40/-60/-152, M-1967 APC; 3,000 guns and how up to 203mm; 700 RL; 2,500 120mm, 160mm mor; 82mm RCL; 57mm ATk guns; 24 *FROG*-5/-7 SSM; 2,500 AA guns, incl 37mm, 57mm, ZSU-57, 85mm, 100mm

Navy: 20,000

   8 submarines (4 ex-Soviet W-class, 4 ex-Chinese R-class)
 21 submarine chasers/escorts (ex-Soviet SO-1 class)
 10 *Komar*- and 8 *Osa*-class FPBG with *Styx* SSM
 50 MGB (20 under 100 tons, 15 *Shanghai*-, 8 *Swatow*-class, 27 inshore)
150 torpedo boats (all under 100 tons, 45 ex-Soviet P-4, 30 P-6 class)

Air Force: 45,000

600 combat aircraft
   2 light bomber squadrons with 70 Il-28
 13 FGA sqns with 30 Su-7 and 300 MiG-15/-17
 10 fighter sqns with 150 MiG-21 and 50 MiG-19
100 transports, incl An-2, Il-14/-18, Tu-154
    Hel incl 20 Mi-4, 20 Mi-8
    Trainers incl Yak-18, MiG-15UTI/-21UTI, Il-28U
   3 SAM brigades with 250 SA-2

Para-Military Forces 40,000 security forces and border guards, and a civilian militia of 1,800,000 with small arms and some AA artillery.

Army: 520,000	18 infantry divisions
	2 armored brigades
	2 infantry brigades
	5 airborne brigades
	2 air defense brigades
	7 tank battalions
	30 artillery battalions
	1 SSM battalion with *Honest John*
	2 SAM battalions with *HAWK* and *Nike Hercules*
	840 M-47/-48 med tks; 500 M-113/-577 APC; 2,000 105mm, 155mm, 175mm and 8-in guns/how; 107mm mor; 57mm, 75mm, 106mm RCL; *Honest John* SSM; 48 *HAWK*, 45 *Nike Hercules* SAM.
	RESERVES: 1,000,000

Navy: 25,000	7 destroyers (*Gearing-, Sumner-, Fletcher-* classes)
	9 destroyer escorts (6 excort transports)
	14 coastal escorts
	44 patrol boats (under 100 tons)
	12 coastal minesweepers
	18 landing ships (8 LST, 10 med)
	70 amphibious craft
	(120 *Harpoon* SSM on order)
	RESERVES: 33,000

Marines: 20,000	1 division
	RESERVES: 60,000

Air Force: 30,000	204 combat aircraft
	10 FB sqns: 4 with 72 F-4D/E; 2 with 50 F-86; 4 with 70 F-5A/E
	1 recce sqn with 12 RF-5A
	44 transports, incl 20 C-46, 12 C-54, 12 C-123 Trainers incl 20 T-28D, 30 T-33A, 20 T-41D, 20 F-5B
	6 UH-19, 5 UH-1D, 2 Bell 212 hel
	(18 F-4E, 60 F-5E/F on order)
	RESERVES: 55,000

Para-Military Forces	A local defense militia and 750,000 Homeland Defense Reserve Force.

a military price. But it also provided a significant economic payoff. Bouncing back from the internal and international recession produced by the fourfold increase in the price of oil in 1973, South Korea experienced a phenomenal 16 percent rate of growth in 1976 and projected a 12 percent growth rate for 1977. Clearly, however great the existing military imbalance may be, South Korea has the industrial potential and financial capacity to make it up.

Time, in these terms, is very much on the side of the South rather than the North. The plain and persuasive fact is that there is no reason in principle why South Korea ultimately should not be able to defend itself. Indeed, President Park acknowledged as much himself when he said in August 1975 that in five years there would no longer be a need for the active assistance of U.S. ground forces. A quick look at the underlying demographic and economic realities of the Korean peninsula should make it clear that the South has a much stronger human and financial foundation than the North. At 34 million, the population of South Korea is more than twice as large as the population of 16 million in North Korea. And the GNP of South Korea, which reached a level of 18.7 billion in 1975, is also slightly more than twice the size of the GNP in North Korea, which was only 9 billion in that same year.

Following the fall of the Thieu regime in Vietnam and the Lon Nol government in Cambodia, South Korea finally decided to utilize its underlying economic power for strengthening its capacity to defend itself. In cooperation with the United States, South Korea embarked on an ambitious force improvement program designed to bring itself up to par militarily with North Korea. The plan should take five years to complete and should cost somewhere in the vicinity of five billion dollars. Approximately half of the necessary funds for this modernization program will come from a 20 percent surcharge levied by Seoul on existing taxes, which is supposed to generate about $500 million in new revenues each year. The remainder is expected to come in the form of foreign military grants and credits from the United States. By the time it is finished, the United States will have given South Korea almost one thousand more tanks, tripled its inventory of Tow anti-tank missiles, and bolstered its overall firepower with several hundred new artillery pieces.

Indeed, the United States has made it clear that the withdrawal of U.S. ground forces from South Korea, which, in any case, will not be completed until 1982, is dependent on the development of an indigeneous balance of power on the Korean peninsula. Should a dramatic change occur in the situation—such as a massive military buildup by Pyongyang or the introduction of Soviet or Chinese troops into North Korea—the policy no doubt would be adjusted to take into account the new circumstances. In the interim, President Carter has emphasized that U.S. obligations under the Mutual Defense Treaty with South Korea will remain intact. U.S. air and naval forces, the president has pointed out, will stay in South Korea even after the Second Division has been completely removed, not only to provide South Korean forces with the kind of close air support and naval protection that they would need in time of war, but also as an earnest of U.S. intentions in this regard. By keeping a residual force in South Korea, the United States should be able to enhance implicitly the value of the U.S. deterrent. At the same time, the remaining air and naval units will provide a continuing incentive to Peking, Moscow, and Pyongyang to reach a peaceful agreement with Seoul that will normalize the situation on the peninsula and allow U.S. forces to be completely removed from Korea.

The withdrawal of the Second Division should not, given these considerations, significantly impair the credibility of the U.S. commitment to defend South Korea in the event that it is again attacked by North Korea. Concerned primarily with the possibility of a surprise attack and with a sudden North Korean seizure of Seoul (which is, after all, only twenty-five miles from the demilitarized zone—the DMZ), South Korea has concentrated virtually all of its eighteen divisions between the thirty-eighth parallel and its capital city. One U.S. division, however well armed it may be, does not add significantly to the ability of South Korea to thwart such an attack. The forces on which South Korea would have to rely in such an eventuality would be primarily their own. Under these circumstances, the Second

Division would help, but it is doubtful that it would make the difference. Its value, therefore, is more symbolic than substantive. Yet, were the United States not to withdraw its ground forces, the erosion of public support for the U.S. commitment to South Korea would significantly outweigh the marginal advantages of keeping the Second Division where it is.

President Carter's policy of gradually phasing out the U.S. infantry presence in South Korea thus should be seen as an exercise in both prudence and preparedness. By recognizing the realities of domestic U.S. political problems, the policy is designed to make more durable the nature of U.S. commitments abroad. And by making the withdrawal of the Second Division implicitly contingent upon the completion of the force improvement program, it will ultimately strengthen the capacity of South Korea to defend itself in the future.

What are the political problems that would be created by a decision to keep U.S. ground forces in South Korea? For one thing, given the location of the Second Division, it almost automatically would be involved in hostilities should a surprise attack be launched while it is still on the front line north of Seoul. Under such circumstances, the United States either would have to commit itself to combat or withdraw from fighting. The former situation, particularly if it included heavy casualties and a need for U.S. reinforcements, would create a major political controversy in the United States. For better or worse, the memories of the U.S. involvement in Vietnam are too compelling to sustain such an undertaking for long. Yet withdrawal, particularly if it occurred under fire, would be demeaning to the United States and demoralizing to the South Koreans. And if another war does break out in Korea, the U.S. objective should be to shore up, rather than undermine, the determination of the South Koreans to resist.

But above and beyond the complications that would be created if the Second Division became involved in the fighting, two fundamental factors militate politically against a continued commitment of U.S. ground forces to the defense of South Korea. The first is that there is no reason why South Korea, given the demographic and developmental disparities between the South and the North, should not be able to defend itself effectively. The second has to do with the repressive character of the Park regime, which, in the process of stamping out democracy and dissent in South Korea, has fueled the flames of opposition in the United States. One of the reasons why the United States is so strongly committed to the defense of Japan is that the Japanese government has embraced the principles and practices of democracy. In South Korea, on the other hand, the establishment of martial law, the promulgation of emergency decrees, the imprisonment of political opponents, and the creation of a vast authoritarian apparatus has gone a long way toward totally alienating significant segments of U.S. opinion. Indeed, under existing circumstances, if the security of South Korea were not so important to Japan, the basic nature of the U.S. commitment rather than the presence of U.S. ground forces would be the major subject of contention.

If either of these two fundamental facts—the ability of South Korea in principle to defend itself and the increasingly repressive character of the Park regime—were different, U.S. policy quite possibly would not have developed the way it did. If the South Koreans really were not in a position, upon completion of the force improvement program, to deter and defeat another attack by the North, the United States probably would have to increase rather than reduce the U.S. ground presence in South Korea. And if South Korea maintained the substance and symbolism of democracy, it would be much easier to mobilize broad-based U.S. support for the presence of U.S. ground forces north of Seoul. Particularly after Vietnam, the United States is much more determined to defend democracies than dictatorships. And the nature of the continuing U.S. commitment to the Israelis, in spite of strategic attractions of a closer relationship with the Arabs, persuasively illuminates the relevance of such political and philosophical considerations in the formulation of U.S. public opinion.

The suppression of democracy in South Korea has posed a potential threat, not only to the long-term viability of the U.S. commitment, but to the continued determination of the South Korean people to resist staunchly the threat of an invasion from the North. At the moment, President Park appears to enjoy the support of the great majority of his people. But significant sectors of South Korean society have already been alienated by the increasingly repressive character of his regime. Like dry rot, disenchantment and dissatisfaction may spread, ultimately undermining the continued willingness of the South Korean people to support their own government. In these terms, the relaxation of restrictions and the reestablishment of democracy would go a long way toward enabling President Park not only to improve relations with the United States, but to secure the continued loyalty of his own people as well.

A number of those who are unhappy with President Carter's policy of gradually withdrawing the Second Division have pointed to the apparent inconsistency between the U.S. determination to keep a substantial military presence in Western Europe and the resolve to remove all ground forces from South Korea. U.S. NATO allies, after all, enjoy the same collective demographic and economic advantages in relation to the Warsaw Pact that South Korea enjoys in comparison to North Korea. Seemingly similar as these two situations may be, however, some fundamental differences still exist between them. Compared to the political disunity of Western Europe, South Korea is a model of social stability and ideological cohesion. Given the nature of the fragmented jurisdiction and domestic divisions of U.S. NATO allies, their ability to act in unison and thereby derive the full advantage of their economic and population potential is virtually nil. In this sense, the presence of U.S. ground forces in Western Europe, which constitutes a tangible manifestation of the U.S. commitment to the survival and security of NATO, provides the political glue that holds an alliance together. If the United States were to withdraw from Western Europe, NATO probably would cease to exist as a viable military entity.

South Korea, on the other hand, is not a conglomeration of countries, each with its own attitudes and adversaries, but a united nation, firmly determined to defeat any attempt on the part of Pyongyang to reunify Korea through war. Memories of the slaughter and devastation suffered at the hands of the North in the 1950s have hardened their resolve to resist another attack. It is interesting, in these terms, to note that almost all of the dissident elements in South Korea, however much they may abhor Park Chung-hee, are even more opposed to Kim Il-sung. If another war did break out, it would not be possible for South Korea to keep fighting for more than a very brief period of time without logistical assistance from the United States. But unlike U.S. NATO allies, whose ability and willingness to resist the encroachments of communism at least from a political point of view would be significantly impaired by a unilateral withdrawal of U.S. ground forces from Western Europe, there is little doubt that the South Koreans would fight hard as long as they had the ability and ammunition to do so, even without the physical presence of U.S. troops. But perhaps the most salient, and certainly the most significant, difference between these two situations is that there are 341,000 Soviet troops in Eastern Europe, while there are neither Soviet nor Chinese divisions in North Korea. If there were, the need for the countervailing presence of U.S. troops in South Korea might well be as great as the need for U.S. ground forces in Western Europe. Under such conditions, the present policy would have to be reconsidered and most likely altered to meet the changing circumstances.

Next to Korea, probably the most important issue confronting the United States in the Western Pacific is the future of Taiwan. On the one hand, U.S. global interests, no less than the cause of international tranquility, ultimately require the normalization of the U.S.–PRC relationship. On the other hand, the United States has a historic obligation to Taiwan to prevent the PRC from using force to resolve PRC–Taiwan differences.

The relationship between Washington and Peking is clearly one of the long-term keys to the establishment of a lasting peace in Asia and elsewhere around the world. As the Shanghai communiqué points out, all Chinese, whether they reside on the island or the mainland, contend that there is but one China and only one rightful government of China. Legal and political frictions aside, it is obvious that the locus of power over the destiny of the Chinese nation lies in Peking rather than Taipei. And there is a diplomatic anomaly inherent in the fact that the United States recognizes the Republic of China, rather than the PRC, as the official government of China.

Yet Peking has said, over and over again, that the precondition for normalization is a willingness on the part of Washington to sever diplomatic relations and abrogate the Mutual Security Treaty with Taiwan. In the long run, the United States will have to recognize the realities of the situation and adjust its relationship with Taipei in such a way as to make possible a more productive partnership with Peking. In the short run, however, it would be a diplomatic error and a moral mistake to repudiate the United States's obligations to the seventeen million Taiwanese who, whatever the democratic deficiencies of their particular political system, are infinitely freer than their nine hundred million compatriots on the mainland.

To be sure, substantial and significant advantages would be gained in normalizing the U.S.–PRC relationship. To the extent that the Sino-Soviet split has fragmented the forces of communism, it has been, from the perspective of the West, a highly desirable development. A rapprochement between Peking and Moscow, while not very likely, would still be a severe strategic setback. And to the extent that the normalization of relations between the United States and the PRC, on terms acceptable to Peking, remains one of the major irritants in the relationship between Washington and Peking, it would presumably make the PRC more resistant to the blandishments of the Soviet Union. At the same time that the establishment of formal diplomatic relations between Washington and Peking would make the PRC less likely to move back into the embrace of the Soviet Union, it also would pave the way for a much closer and cooperative relationship between the United States and the PRC on a whole host of other important international issues. From the future of Korea to the autonomy of Africa, a better understanding between the two nations would facilitate the effort to achieve peaceful and productive solutions to all sorts of serious political problems.

Yet, the advantages of normalization can easily be exaggerated. The ideological and territorial differences between the PRC and the Soviet Union seem so severe that it is exceedingly unlikely that a rapprochement between them will occur in the foreseeable future. In this sense, a failure on the part of Washington to normalize relations with Peking may constitute an impediment to better bilateral relations between the United States and the PRC, but it is unlikely to lead to better relations between the PRC and the Soviet Union. The key to the long-term relationship between Moscow and Peking lies in their ability to resolve the differences between them rather than their differences with the United States.

In any case, it seems safe to say that the PRC is much more concerned at the present time about the threat it perceives from its neighbor to the North than about the failure of the United States to recognize explicitly the PRC's historic title to Taiwan. The PRC probably would be much more pleased by a decision on the part of the United States to strengthen substantially its NATO forces, thereby countering the Soviet buildup in Eastern Europe and relieving Soviet pressure on the northern front, than they would by the rupture of the U.S. relationship with Taiwan. In these terms, the PRC seems more concerned about the U.S. resolve to resist the Soviet Union than about the U.S. desire to please Peking. While the proverb "the enemy of my enemy is my friend" may not be Chinese in origin, it certainly seems to be the fundamental basis for the relationship that has developed over the last several years between Washington and Peking.

Looked at primarily from the perspective of the U.S. bilateral relationship with the PRC, normalization would seem to be a very attractive alternative indeed. But viewed in the context of broader international interests and U.S. obligations to Taiwan, the preconditions set forth by Peking would require the United States to pay too heavy a political price. Particularly at a time when the United States is in the process of withdrawing its ground forces from South Korea, the unilateral abrogation of the Mutual Security Treaty with Taiwan would raise additional doubts in Tokyo about the credibility of the U.S. commitment to Japan. Given the critical importance of the Japanese–U.S. relationship, for all the reasons previously described, this is the last thing that the United States should want to do.

Those who favor normalization, even on terms advanced by Peking, argue that if Japan managed to do it, so can the United States. Indeed, they will say, the Japanese solution of severing diplomatic relations but maintaining trade and other ties to Taiwan is the way in which to do it. The problem with this proposal, however, is that the two situations are not analogous. Japan could afford to sever diplomatic relations yet continue to get the benefit of a commercial connection with Taipei, primarily because the Mutual Security Treaty between the United States and Taiwan remained intact. If the United States chose to resolve the problem in the same way as Japan, the Mutual Security Treaty with Taiwan would have to be scrapped, and the deterrent value of the U.S. defense commitment to Taipei would be significantly diminished.

This is not to suggest that the day after the Mutual Security Treaty were abrogated the PRC would launch an invasion of Taiwan. It is no secret that, even were the PRC so inclined (which is itself doubtful), it lacks the amphibious capacity to do so. Military analysts estimate that it would take sixty Chinese divisions to mount an effective invasion against Taiwan. Right now, the PRC has an amphibious ability to transport only two divisions across the ninety-mile straits separating the mainland from the island. While some scenarios for an invasion of Taiwan envision an armada of junks descending on the island, this would seem to be a most unlikely possibility. The success of such an effort would depend entirely on the ability of the PRC to achieve total air superiority over the Taiwan straits. While the number of planes in the possession of the PRC vastly outnumbers the total in Taiwan, they are not considered much of a match for the more modern fighters available to Taipei. Unless they were prepared totally to denude their northern defenses and throw almost every available plane into the fray, the chances are that Peking would not be able to achieve the kind of air superiority that such a phantasmagoric invasion would require.

The real problem, therefore, is not so much the threat of an invasion as the possibility of a blockade. The PRC, while not a major naval power, does have around one hundred submarines, giving it the capacity to interdict shipping to and from Taiwan. If the United States, following the abrogation

of the Mutual Security Treaty, chose not to run such a blockade, it is doubtful that the commercial ships of any other
nation would be prepared to run it either. And Taiwan, as an
island outpost dependent on foreign trade for its economic
survival, would in short order be brought to its political
knees.

It does not necessarily follow from this analysis that the
PRC would attempt to establish such a blockade even if the
Seventh Fleet were withdrawn from the Taiwan straits. Neither
can one automatically assume that the United States, even if
it abrogated the Mutual Security Treaty, would idly stand by
while Peking attempted to strangle Taiwan economically. But
it is precisely because the United States cannot be sure what
would happen if it severed diplomatic relations and abrogated
the Mutual Security Treaty with Taiwan that the adoption of
such a policy would be fraught with peril.

Where does this leave the United States in terms of its
relationship with the PRC? Clearly it would be in U.S. interests
to proceed with the process of normalization. But just as it
would be desirable to have formal diplomatic relations with
Peking, it would be undesirable to sever completely the relations with Taiwan. What is needed is a formula that will satisfy
the desire of Peking for the formal recognition of its exclusive
title to Taiwan, while at the same time satisfy the U.S. concern
over the need for a peaceful rather than a forceful solution to
the problem of reunification. In the short run, it is not at all
clear that such a formula can be devised. Peking has vigorously
contended that the decision as to how and when it will liberate
Taiwan is an internal matter that will brook no interference
from abroad. The United States, through the Shanghai communiqué, has committed itself to the principle of "one China,"
thereby diplomatically precluding the possibility of a German
solution to the Chinese problem. How the circle will eventually be squared no one can say, but the fate of millions of people
and the future of the U.S. relationship with the most populous
country in the world may depend upon it.

Let us, by all means, persevere in the effort to find a solution
to this vexing political problem. But let us not, in the process,
undermine the credibility of our commitments or betray the
morality of our obligations.

5

Japan's Role in East Asian Stability

Koichi Kato

I do not regard myself as an expert on the subject of Japan's role in the stability of East Asia. The niche that I occupy at present, however, is a special one. Having been a foreign service officer for a number of years until I was elected to the Diet in 1972, I have developed my own particular perspective on the topic. My present position as representative has allowed me to observe popular attitudes on foreign affairs firsthand. Although the opinions of average citizens, my own constituents included, often lack sophistication, they are honest and, above all, they are very important. No foreign policy, however brilliantly conceived and well meant, can be viable without their support and understanding. It is from this vantage point that I would like to discuss the future course of Japanese foreign policy, especially as it relates to East Asia.

First of all, I should like to outline certain conditions that must be regarded as givens in the situation. I shall then try to evaluate past diplomatic efforts by focusing primarily on Japan's relations with the United States, the Soviet Union, and the People's Republic of China. I also shall discuss the implications of recent domestic political changes for the future conduct of Japanese foreign policy. These analyses are basic to any examination of the Japanese role in East Asian stability. To prevent the discussion from becoming unnecessarily abstract, the time perspective will be confined to the next few years, that is, until the beginning of the 1980s.

I

What basic parameters in the international environment are likely to affect the conduct of Japanese foreign policy between now and 1980? First, the U.S.–Soviet relationship, the major factor defining the overall framework of international relations, will continue more or less as it is now, despite inevitable ups and downs. Neither of the two powers desires a resurgence of cold-war hostility. The gradual attainment of a high degree of progress and differentiation in the Soviet industrial structure and the potentially strong demands of the Soviet people for higher living standards contribute to this continuity. Such internal factors make it difficult for the Soviet Union to sustain a protracted arms race with the United States. The United States also would prefer to avoid arms competition at a time when the so-called Bretton Woods system, the postwar economic framework that has enabled the advanced democracies to maintain prosperity, is facing a time of trial.

Second, the Sino-Soviet dispute seems likely to continue. Both sides are well aware of the great interest with which Japan and the United States watch their conflict, and for that reason they may very well make some overt gestures toward conciliation. On the other hand, the distrust is so deeply rooted that even if it could be overcome, neither country seems to be encouraging internal conditions that would favor a reconciliation policy. If I have any reservations about this judgment, it has to do with future U.S. policy toward the Soviet Union and the PRC, and particularly with how that policy will develop within Asia.

Third, while it is still not possible to view the PRC's domestic affairs as stable, that instability is not expected to have any bearing on the PRC's fundamental foreign policy line. It is true that many of the PRC's domestic power struggles have involved disputes over the line that should be adopted in regard to diplomatic issues, but there seems to be a consensus among PRC leaders in support of the anti-Soviet tone of recent PRC foreign policy. However, the Hua Kuo-feng regime should be watched closely for signs of stability or instability.

Fourth is the heightened Soviet interest in Asian affairs. Before 1980, however, the Soviet Union probably will make no *unilateral* move to disrupt existing power relationships in that region. The expansion of Soviet naval power in the Far East and the movements of ground forces along the Sino-Soviet border will bear careful watching, but barring unforeseen circumstances, the Soviet Union is not likely to consider any action that would agitate either the United States or the PRC.

My basic assumption, then, is that three of the four factors listed above—PRC policy, Soviet policy, and the Sino-Soviet dispute—will remain more or less as they are today. Neither party will initiate unilateral moves to bring about fundamental change in the existing situation. If, in fact, such moves do take place, they will be the result of causes external to the Sino-Soviet system itself, which force the PRC or Soviet leaders to act. The most important of such active external factors is the Asian policy of the United States. Japan's Asian policy is not likely to have much effect, although there is room for Japan to have some influence.

II

How should Japan's past diplomatic efforts be evaluated? How do recent developments in domestic politics affect foreign policy? It is obvious that Japanese–U.S. relations are the most important factor to be considered in any examination of Japanese diplomacy. At the same time, Japan's relations with the PRC and the Soviet Union also provide material for assessing its foreign policy. Before addressing the above questions, however, I should like to relate my personal impressions of recent U.S. policy toward Asia.

I would be less than frank if I did not say that I have great difficulty in grasping the true intentions of U.S. policy. In particular, I wonder how Asia figures in U.S. policy toward the Soviet Union, or, more correctly, if it figures at all. My anxiety is further intensified by the impression that such policy events as President Nixon's visit to the PRC, the pullout from Indochina, and the recently announced staged withdrawal of ground forces from South Korea have been heavily motivated by domestic considerations. I am certain of the sincerity with which the United States, particularly the Carter administration, pursues relations with Japan. But what does the United States expect of Japan? To what extent do U.S. leaders realize the impact in Japan of even the slightest change in U.S. policy toward Asia? What role does the United States assign to Japan in its Asian policy? I myself cannot respond with confidence to these questions.

The Japanese people as a whole, who consider themselves the United States's foremost allies in Asia, harbor such doubts, and even people like myself, members of the Liberal Democratic Party, which has as the central tenet of its foreign policy the relationship with the United States, are deeply troubled. It is not hard to imagine how skeptical the United States's other Asian allies are. And with how much less certainty must those potential adversaries of the United States—the Soviet Union and, to a lesser degree, the PRC—be forced to make their policy judgments? Such unpredictability is a potential source of crisis.

It should be reiterated at the outset that the primary objective of postwar Japanese diplomacy has been the maintenance and enhancement of friendly relations with the United States. The majority of Japanese, with the exception of a small segment of the opposition parties, are fully aware that their present level of prosperity would have been impossible without a close relationship with the United States. The chief factor in that prosperity has been the maintenance by the United States of its commitment to Japan under the United States–Japan Security Treaty. An increasing number of Japanese realize how fortunate they are to have been able, under U.S. military protection, to devote their entire energy to economic recovery and growth.

I consider that evaluation to be completely correct. It would be impossible to understand postwar Japanese foreign relations without considering the U.S. role. It is true that Japan's relations with the Soviet Union and the PRC generally have been considered the antithesis of the Japanese–U.S. relations, and it should not be forgotten that the mending of ties with those two socialist nations occurred only as a result of popular skepticism concerning Japan's U.S.-centered diplomacy. It is no accident that the restoration of diplomatic relations with the Soviet Union in 1956 was carried out by Ichiro Hatoyama and Ichiro Kono, two men who had long been rivals of the U.S.-oriented Shigeru Yoshida. More recently, the reaction, or more precisely, the unease, of the people and the LDP when the United States began a dialogue with the PRC without prior consultation with Japan was a factor behind the normalization of Japan's own relations with the PRC in 1972.

When relations were established with the Soviet Union and later normalized with the PRC, there were moves in Japan to reexamine the conduct of Japanese–U.S. relations based on the Mutual Security Treaty. Nonetheless, they did not lead to change in the basic direction of Japanese policy. That, it seems, shows how much Japanese policies toward the PRC and the Soviet Union were conceived within the framework of Japanese relations with the United States.

In Japanese-Soviet relations, it is noteworthy that the Soviet Union has yet to abandon its consistent hostility toward the United States–Japan Security Treaty, even though the emphasis on it has altered with time. Japanese policy toward the Soviet Union, however, has always been clear. Although the return of the northern territories has always been a principal objective, Japan has consistently resisted any attempt by the Soviet Union to bring the issue of the Mutual Security Treaty into those negotiations.

From another point of view, a hostile relationship with a military superpower like the Soviet Union would be too great a burden for Japan. Japan therefore takes great pains to ensure a neighborly relationship. Until recently, the Soviet Union opened its fishing grounds to Japan; because fish constitutes the major source of animal protein for Japan, this was significant. An additional incentive has been the vast resources of Siberia, which are very attractive to a nation like Japan that has little or no raw materials of its own. The Soviet Union is a nation that Japan cannot afford to ignore.

There are many reasons why a more active development of relations with the Soviet Union is desirable, but Japan always has acted cautiously. In the cold war era, U.S. pressure was a factor. During the 1970s, Japan had to be careful not to provoke an adverse reaction from the PRC. In addition, however, Japan's own tendency to be very circumspect in its relations with its neighboring superpower cannot be ignored. Many Japanese still brood over the final days of World War II when Stalin unilaterally abrogated his treaty with Japan and declared war. Postwar Soviet behavior such as the constant, high-pressure harassment year after year of fishery operations in the Northern Pacific only adds fuel to this suspicion. The cumulative impact of these incidents has been very great. I am sure that I am not alone in believing that, although Japan is very interested in the natural resources of Siberia, it is hesitant about crossing the line to conclusive negotiations because of the fear of becoming involved in another problem as agonizing as that of the fisheries. It probably would have been impossible for Japan to maintain its stance with regard to the Soviet Union in the absence of a U.S. security commitment and popular confidence in U.S. policy.

Let us now turn to Japanese–PRC relations. Japanese emotions with regard to the PRC are very complex. On the one hand are the feelings of reverence (or awe mixed with fear) toward the nation that is the birthplace of so much Japanese culture. This aspect of Japanese sentiment also includes guilt and a need for atonement arising from Japan's invasion of that country. On the other hand is a feeling of contempt for the Chinese people, whose country was so late in modernizing. Together those feelings add up to a high degree of intimacy encompassing both respect and disdain.

As with the Soviet Union during the cold war era, Japan's relations with the PRC could not escape the influence of the U.S.–Soviet confrontation. However, the worsening of Sino-Soviet relations removed many obstacles to the normalization of relations. Just as Japan started to improve its PRC relations, it found itself brought short by the Taiwan problem; it took the Nixon shock of U.S.–PRC rapprochement to bring Japan past that barrier. Nevertheless, as far as popular feelings were concerned, the basic obstacles working against a normalization of relations with the Soviet Union were not present in the case of the PRC.

In addition to the above factors, the PRC's policy toward Japan during the past few years fundamentally has been favorable to the improvement of Japanese–PRC relations. More precisely, the correctness of the LDP foreign policy was in effect affirmed by the change in the PRC's stance toward Japan. An extreme example is the PRC's evaluation of the Mutual Security Treaty as a positive element in the stability of Asian international relations. As PRC leaders have stated on numerous occasions, relations with the United States are more important for Japan than relations with the PRC. Imagine the situation if the PRC had held fast to its earlier distrust of the Japanese–U.S. relation: the normalization of relations with the PRC might not have taken place in 1972. There has always been strong Japanese emphasis on potential economic relations with the PRC, and this will continue as a factor for improving all aspects of the relationship. I am, however, hesitant about putting too much weight on economic relations as the fundamental factor in PRC policy.

While things have gone reasonably well, some people believe euphorically that Japanese–PRC relations are completely problem-free. I believe that there is every possibility of problems occurring. The most important reason is that a relationship of mutual trust has not yet been established, as may be seen in the protracted dispute over the hegemony clause in the proposed peace treaty. That problem was provoked in part by differing Japanese and PRC attitudes toward the Soviet Union, but other more important factors were involved.

First, the PRC considers relations with Japan to have started with the joint communiqué of 1972 and insists that conclusion of a treaty of peace and amity must be the next step in developing the relationship. Japan, however, is not ready to progress further with the PRC out of consideration for Soviet relations. On the contrary, Japan would now prefer to retreat from the position established in 1972. The PRC must be wondering where it stands in Japanese policy. The Japanese, for their part, feel that the PRC is not sufficiently sympathetic to their situation in regard to the Soviet Union. Also, in view of major turnabouts in PRC policy toward Japan since 1970, the Japanese are apprehensive that another change could take place at any time. Japanese negotiators worry that if an ill-defined concept like hegemony is included in a treaty now, it could be used to Japan's disadvantage in the future.

Other elements of instability in the Japanese–PRC relationship are the issue of the Senkaku Islands and the different styles of defense policy pursued by the two nations. Nor can Japan be optimistic about the differences in approach to the Taiwan issue. Hence, while expectations must not be too high concerning Japanese–PRC relations, they can be at least more manageable than the problems with the Soviet Union. As long as the Mutual Security Treaty is operative and the United States has the ability and the will to put the brakes on Japanese military expansion, the PRC will perceive no threat to its security from Japan.

Let us now look briefly at the effect that the domestic political situation is likely to have on Japan's foreign policy. The LDP was just barely able to hold on to its majority in the recent (July 1977) House of Councillors election, and there is little reason for optimism about the future. Starting with the next election, it appears unlikely that the party will maintain a stable majority. There already exists a de facto conservative-progressive coalition in the parliament, and plans need to be made for a future coalition government.

Recently, nationalistic sentiment has been on the rise, but the opposition parties, more than the LDP, are trying to align themselves with that new force. A primary factor behind the emotional upsurge is the wave of national indignation engendered by the high-pressure tactics used by the Soviet Union in the fishery negotiations. Also, as the day of coalition government approaches, the opposition parties are seeking to find in nationalism a justification for forming a coalition with the LDP. It certainly is conceivable that this increased nationalism will give rise to forces calling for reexamination of past Japanese foreign policy, which has been based on the relationship with the United States.

By and large, the opposition parties have no quarrel with the emphasis on Japanese–U.S. amity and cooperation, and they are well aware that Japan cannot become a global power. However, support for a more autonomous Japanese role in Asia is growing. There is also a real possibility that public opinion will demand a revision of the status-of-force agreements, although this is not likely to affect the Mutual Security Treaty. But if the United States again embarks on actions in East Asian relations without consulting Japan beforehand, new tensions could enter the relationship. What seems more likely is that the growth of nationalism will bring changes in Japanese policy toward the Soviet Union, the PRC, Korea, or Southeast Asia. If the Soviet Union continues to place restrictions on Japanese fisheries in the Northern Pacific, there is a possibility that the public may demand a revision of Japanese relations with the Soviet Union and closer relations with the PRC.

What should be stressed, however, is that the near-parity between the conservative and reformist forces can exert increasing influence on Japanese foreign policy. Whether we like it or not, that factor must be kept constantly in mind as we deliberate on directions for Japan's foreign policy.

III

Now I should like to offer briefly my own views on what Japan's East Asia policy should be. The first question is, what framework for international relations will best contribute to stability in the entire region, and then how should Japan orient its relations to each of the nations in East Asia.

The U.S. and Soviet mutual deterrence in East Asia will most likely remain effective. If that is so, then Japan's role in the maintenance of regional stability need not be inconsequential. Since not only the United States and Japan, but also the PRC, are anxious to maintain the status quo, it seems that the pursuit of deeper mutual understanding among the three nations would be highly significant. For that reason alone, Japan should take on a more active role. This is important not only for the stability of relations among the three countries themselves, but also for dealing with problems of regional stability, such as in Korea, Taiwan, and Southeast Asia.

It is unlikely that any simple answer to the Korean problem will be found. There is no sign of an immediate shift in U.S. and Japanese support for South Korea or in PRC support for

North Korea. More important than that division, however, is
their common desire to maintain the status quo on the peninsula. The PRC is not wholly content with the North Korean
policy of maintaining equidistant relationships with Peking
and Moscow, but from the PRC standpoint it is certainly pref-
erable to a one-sided North Korean turn toward Moscow.
Furthermore, the PRC realizes that it cannot provide all the
aid necessary to bring North Korea out of its economic difficulties. This means that there is more of an opening now than
ever before for the United States and Japan to join the PRC in
a cooperative effort. As far as Washington is concerned, any
overtures to the Pyongyang government "over the head" of
Seoul are fraught with problems. So here also is an opportunity
for trilateral cooperation, this time among the United States,
the PRC, and Japan. On the negative side as well as from
Japan's point of view (and the United States's as well), it is
undesirable for South Korea to maintain such large military
forces that they might upset the power balance on the peninsula; the PRC, too, finds that the controls exerted on South
Korea by Japan and the United States help prevent North Korea
from leaning too far toward the Soviet Union.

The Taiwan problem is more complex. While Japan wants
the United States to maintain its present PRC policy, it has
no intention of sacrificing its own relations with the PRC.
Washington wants relations with Peking normalized but also
must consider whether it is worthwhile to go ahead at the
expense of its relations with Taipei. It must also determine
what impact the abrogation of its defense commitments to the
Taiwan government might have on its credibility with other
countries. The United States and Japan are both concerned
about preserving their economic interests in Taiwan. At least
on the surface, the PRC holds to the position that the Taiwan
issue is an internal matter, but it is not so stubborn as to force
an immediate solution at the cost of U.S.–PRC relations. The
PRC also has to consider any negative effects that its handling
of the issue might have on relations with Japan. Even if the
PRC were successful in forcing concessions from the United
States and Japan concerning Taiwan, it would have to face the
possibility of a desperate Taipei government seeking to save

itself by inviting in the Soviet Union. From the PRC's viewpoint, a U.S. presence in Taiwan is "less worse." Hence the PRC, the United States, and Japan are positioned very delicately with respect to the Taiwan issue, and there is every reason to believe that better coordination among them would contribute to East Asian stability.

I am convinced that enhanced mutual understanding among the PRC, Japan, and the United States would be very helpful to regional stability, and therefore I believe that Japan should make more active diplomatic efforts in that direction. Undoubtedly some will say that this would provide a ready target for Soviet criticism and therefore would demand great caution. In my view, that is not the most promising approach.

In the first place, as against the caution that relations with the Soviet Union would be radically worsened, I believe that there is little hope for Japan to recover its fishery rights in the North Pacific. Therefore, rather than pursuing a lost cause, Japan should recover its independent diplomatic stance vis-à-vis Moscow by devising an effective program to compensate fishermen for the loss of their livelihood and by accepting the blow with dignity. Second, as far as the argument that Japan's involvement in the Sino-Soviet conflict would endanger its security, it should be remembered that as long as the Mutual Security Treaty is fully operative and Japan is securely under the nuclear umbrella, there is little likelihood of the Soviet Union making any reckless moves. Third, the advantages of an increased ability to predict the PRC's action accurately would more than offset any disadvantages that would arise from Soviet threats, which would most likely be limited to propaganda and bluster. Fourth, in view of changing Japanese feelings, the policy of equidistance soon will seem anachronistic. A strengthened relationship with the PRC would contribute immensely to the deepening of mutual trust between Japan and the PRC, providing improved conditions for East Asian stability.

Next, let us discuss ways in which Japan can improve relations with individual nations. The Soviet Union already has been covered from that viewpoint. As for the PRC, in addition to the diplomatic moves already suggested, the least that can be done is to conclude a treaty of peace and amity as soon as possible. What conceivable benefit is there in delaying such a treaty any longer? It is next to impossible to imagine the Soviet Union responding to postponement with a favorable modification of its Japan policy. Conversely, if destabilizing factors are a concern, the possibility that further delay might have a serious impact on Japanese–PRC relations must be taken into account.

In framing policy for the Korean peninsula, heightened nationalist feelings in Japan cannot be ignored. Not only would it be constitutionally impossible for Japan to acquire a military capability placing it on a par with the Soviet Union and the PRC, but there also appears to be a national consensus that such a course would be undesirable. I agree with that view. But if there were a military threat from the Korean peninsula, the Japanese might respond very differently. Japan's relations with South Korea, for example, particularly with regard to the Takeshima Island issue, could become very tense if handled badly. Thus, with respect to Korean policy, Japan not only should strive for a better exchange of views with the United States and the PRC, but also must be careful to avoid a threat to its own security by maintaining understanding with South Korea. If a certain degree of harmony is not maintained, public opinion might demand a Japanese military force capable of standing up to South Korea.

So far I have not touched on Southeast Asia. This is because I do not believe that region has a direct bearing on Japanese security. On the other hand, Southeast Asia is economically important to Japan, and accordingly its security is of great interest as well. Therefore, I entirely agree that Japan should search out ways to make a contribution. The recent government approach to the Association of Southeast Asian Nations (ASEAN) is most welcome and should be pursued even more actively in the future. The ASEAN states expect much from Japan, and in order to keep those hopes from rising too high, the Japanese government will have to give a clear outline of what it can and cannot do. At the same time, Japan must reconsider the significant role that expanded cooperation with those nations can play in the preservation of stability in the entire East Asian region and make the maximum possible efforts as part of the Japanese development assistance program. Policy toward the Indochinese nations also is important, but I do not believe that it should be a major focus of attention.

Finally, I should like to say a word about the possibility of Japanese–U.S. cooperation in Asia. U.S. policy is the most dynamic factor in the determination of Asian international relations. Although I have treated the Sino-Soviet conflict as a given condition, I would not reject the possibility that, depending on the course of U.S. world strategy, the Soviet Union and the PRC might put aside conflict and move toward a renewal of solidarity.

I also have based my remarks about Japan's policy toward East Asia on the assumption that Japan always will be able to gain the understanding of the United States for its foreign policy efforts. U.S. policy in Asia, however, is by no means always clear. Insofar as the peace and security of East Asia are important in principle to both countries, Japan and the United States stand on common ground. But when it comes to particular policy problems, one wonders how much Japan and the United States really have tried to understand each other. Japan's economic power makes it no longer possible to apply formulas mechanically, based upon the structure of forces in the immediate postwar era. Today it would be highly unrealistic to expect the two nations to have identical interests in all fields of Asian policy. The rise of a new nationalism in Japan and the U.S. move to revise its Asian policy are only two ingredients that complicate the situation.

The need for Japan and the United States to seek mutual adjustments on policy and a continuing exchange of views on peace and security in East Asia has grown much more urgent, which makes this forum even more important. International affairs are too important to be left to government alone. More and more, it will be frank and intimate exchanges such as are being pursued in this conference that will make the greatest contribution to long-term cooperation between the two nations.

6
Groping for Korean Unification

Tamio Kawakami

Since the Vietnam War ground to its end, the focal point of Asian politics has shifted to the Korean peninsula. With that shift, Northeast Asia now has entered upon a new era of uncertainty.

It has been just ten years since the First Shimoda Conference was convened. When I look back over that period, what stands out in my mind are the important changes that took place in the Asian situation in and around September 1969, when I had the pleasure of attending the second of these conferences. Let us review the events of that year. President Nixon was inaugurated in January, and in August, right before the conference, he visited Rumania. The cessation of the U.S. bombing of North Vietnam had been announced on October 31, 1968, and in March 1969 the expanded Vietnam peace conferences began. In the PRC, the Great Proletarian Cultural Revolution was winding down, while Sino-Soviet relations worsened suddenly with the outbreak of the Damanski Island incident. The Pueblo incident had taken place in January 1968, and tension was rising between North and South Korea.

At that time, very few foresaw the dramatic contacts that would take place two years later between the United States and the PRC. Nevertheless, the atmosphere at the 1969 conference was such that harsh denunciations of the PRC by participants decreased, and a change was evident even compared to six months before. It is significant that the Second Shimoda Conference adopted a statement calling for reinstatement of the

83

PRC as a member of international society. I can remember receiving the distinct impression during a discussion with Donald Rumsfeld that President Nixon would seek to open the door to the PRC by visiting Rumania—a country unique among Eastern European nations in its maintenance of cordial relations with both the PRC and Western Europe. Later, in relating my impressions of the conference in the Japanese magazine *Ekonomisuto,* I noted that U.S.-PRC contact probably would be made before most people expected.

At any rate, 1969 marked the beginning of a reduction of tension in Asia. It was followed in South Korea by the withdrawal of 20,000 U.S. troops in 1970, the first Red Cross preliminary conferences between North and South Korea on September 20, 1971, and the publication on July 4, 1972, of the joint communiqué calling for the independent, peaceful unification of Korea. Secretary of State Kissinger's secret visit to the PRC[1] was announced on July 15, 1971, and it also was made known that President Nixon would make such a visit. The following year, the president's visit resulted in the U.S.-PRC concord announced in the Shanghai communiqué. In a very positive sense, these events led to the end of the Vietnam War in 1975, followed by Vietnamese unification in 1976. The entry of Vietnam into the United Nations this fall will bring this series of events to its natural conclusion.

As the above survey indicates, the course of events in Asia over the past ten years has been influenced heavily by a turnabout in U.S. policy. That turnabout was effected through what has become known as Nixon-Kissinger diplomacy, an approach that emphasized four points: the consolidation of détente with the Soviet Union and the PRC; the cessation of U.S. overinvolvement in Asia; the establishment of preventative measures in areas of potential conflict (such as the Middle East and Africa); and the taking of radical measures to halt the deterioration of U.S. economic power.

The end of the Vietnam War meant, first of all, the completion of nationalist struggles for independence in post–World War II Asia. Second, it also indicated an end, for the time being, of hostilities in Southeast Asia. With that, the dangers of another nightmare like the Vietnam War diminished. As for the United States, it now could turn back to its domestic issues without the distraction of war and social disorder. Third, it also brought an improvement in U.S.–PRC relations.

The problem remains, of course, of how the ASEAN states will relate to the three nations of Indochina under their new governments. The issue of how the United States and Vietnam as former enemies could normalize relations was left pending as well. The latter also is a problem for Japan, which was a former collaborator with the United States in waging the Vietnam War. On the whole, however, there is room to be optimistic about the problems left in the wake of the Vietnam War.

Unfortunately, however, we cannot be so optimistic about the Korean peninsula. On the contrary, there is ample reason to be seriously concerned. I say this because there are forces that do not welcome and even fear the changes that are now taking place in Northeast Asia. These forces tend to equate change with crisis. Hence, they may very well fail to cope effectively with those changes.

In many ways, the situation of the Korean peninsula in the seventies has moved in a direction contrary to that experienced by Asia as a whole. Although he endorsed the North-South joint communiqué of July 4, 1972, in October of the same year President Park Chung-hee of South Korea instituted an emergency system of martial law, further consolidating the *yushin* (revitalization) system and hardening his presidential rule. His government has continued to justify such actions as the August 8, 1973, kidnapping in Tokyo of Kim Dae-jung and the series of emergency presidential measures that since January 1974 have been directed against Koreans who seek a restoration of democracy. His government claims that these actions have been necessary in the face of the threat from the North. The result of such heavy-handed measures, however, can only be the further broadening of a subterranean swell of political discontent that in turn exacerbates the overall instability of the Park regime.

The advent of the Carter administration has dealt a severe shock to the South Korean government. Not only has President Carter oriented his diplomacy around the problem of human rights and in that connection called for democratization and an end to oppression in South Korea, but he also has taken steps to carry out, with some modification, his election promise to withdraw U.S. troops from the Korean peninsula. It is as yet unclear what the ultimate objectives of the Carter administration's policy toward South Korea are or how far the policy is designed to go. In other words, will it be considered sufficient merely to put pressure on the Park regime in order to force an end to the violation of human rights, or is present U.S. policy toward South Korea a signal that the United States is considering direct talks with North Korea? President Carter has announced that he will withdraw 6,000 soldiers in 1978 and the rest in a period of four or five years. He is obviously already looking forward to his second term. It appears that President Carter probably will fulfill his commitments with regard to withdrawal despite constraints imposed by public opinion, congressional moves, and reactions from both South Korea and Japan (i.e., the LDP government).

During the second JSP (Japan Socialist Party) mission to the United States which took place in 1975—the first in eighteen years—party representatives engaged in a series of animated discussions with U.S. government, congressional, opinion, and academic leaders on a variety of subjects, including post-Vietnam Asia, a nuclear weapon-free-zone centering on the Japanese archipelago, abrogation of the United States–Japan Security Treaty and its replacement with a treaty of friendship, and above all, the Korean situation. At that time, Assistant Undersecretary of State Habib, then in charge of U.S. policy toward Korea, summarized that policy in the following four principles: (1) prevent the outbreak of another war; (2) observe all commitments to South Korea; (3) support the communique of July 4, 1972; and (4) hold to the formula of cross-recognition.

The JSP delegates completely agreed with points one and three of that official U.S. policy. They could not accept points two and four, however, because the second further increases the tension between North and South and the fourth raises the danger of freezing partition; moreover, it is unacceptable to North Korea. In the course of the debate, it became clear that the assumptions behind the respective positions differed widely, the U.S. side considering partition to be desirable as a means of containing communist expansion and the JSP representatives regarding self-determination and national unification as just and appropriate wishes of the Korean people, and also desirable from the viewpoint of stability in Northeast Asia. The meeting concluded on a humorous note, with the mutual recognition that we had done very well to agree on two out of four points and with a promise to meet again in the future. The substantive differences, however, remained.

Mr. Habib, who was the Department of State spokesman for both the Nixon and Ford administrations, has been promoted to more illustrious heights by President Carter. That raises the question of how President Carter's Korea policy differs from that of his predecessors. On the surface, the policy of the Carter administration is an extension of the Nixon doctrine, and there has been no clear indication of a change in the four principles outlined by Mr. Habib. On the other hand, it seems that rather than setting certain conditions, such as cross-recognition, and then compromising in accord with concessions offered by the other side, President Carter is offering North Korea a signal that he wants to talk directly. That was the method used by the Nixon-Kissinger team from 1969 to 1972. We should also be aware of the possible significance of the parallel trips by U.S. Secretary of State Vance to the PRC and Yugoslav President Tito to Moscow, Peking, and Pyongyang, which began on the eve of this conference. President Tito may be playing the same role in fostering contact between the United States and North Korea that Rumanian President Ceausescu performed vis-à-vis the U.S.-PRC breakthrough.

How are the major actors on the Korean peninsula reacting to the Carter administration? As is to be expected, Park has made no secret of his disappointment with President Carter's policy of military withdrawal from Korea, and South Korean demands that the United States observe its aid commitments are gaining strength. The Japanese government, too, has made known indirectly its displeasure with Carter's policy by noting cooly that the issue is a bilateral one between the United States and South Korea, and therefore Japan is in no position to comment.

Chairman Kim Il-sung of North Korea recently met with a party led by the editorial bureau chief of *Yomiuri Shinbun*.[2] During their conversation, Kim said with regard to President Carter's policies of withdrawal of U.S. troops from South Korea, diplomacy geared to human rights, and removal of restrictions on travel by Americans to North Korea that "they can be viewed as indicating goodwill toward my country." While warning that Carter's continued action in a manner contrary to his campaign promise is a source of concern, Kim said, "We are not making any statements critical of the Carter administration. We should reserve judgment for a while longer" (April 23, 1977). In July 1977 Kim maintained what appeared to be a favorable attitude in his exclusive interview with Japan Broadcasting Association's chief commentator Akira Ogata. Chairman Kim seemed to see more potential in the Carter administration than some leaders of the left-wing movements in Japan who have resolutely maintained their skepticism.

North Korea's star has risen in international politics during the seventies, with ninety-one countries now giving it their official recognition. Also, the passage of a United Nations resolution supporting the North Korean position in 1975 (along with one supporting South Korea) and the recognition of North Korea as a participant at the Nonaligned Nations Foreign Ministerial Conference the same year in Peru indicate that its status is also on the rise in external affairs. The economic situation of that country is marred by some bad trade debts and a number of matters that must cleared up in the course of bilateral relationships, but these difficulties do not seem to be reflected in domestic political instability. Chairman Kim believes that, overall, world trends are working in favor of his country.

Taking a look at North Korean policy alternatives, it seems that in the long term the political, economic, and military moves of South Korea are very important factors. In the short run, however, the nature of those alternatives depends heavily on what the United States does. In terms of international politics, one can conceive of a number of possibilities, but an appeal to war at the present time would appear to be out of the question. Also, in light of the intricate Sino-Soviet dispute, it would seem impractical for North Korea to lean in the direction of either of these neighbor countries even when bolstered by the support of Third World countries. Rather, the most likely possibility would seem to be a strategic turnabout toward more flexible relationships with the United States and Japan. In that case, the order or precedence would most likely be rapprochement first with the United States, then Japan, followed finally by a softened stance toward South Korea.

In his conversations with the editorial bureau chief of *Yomiuri Shinbun* and the chief commentator of the Japanese Broadcasting Association, Chairman Kim consistently expressed a desire for direct negotiations with the United States. At the Thirty-fourth United Nations General Assembly, North Korean delegation Chief Lee Chong-mok proposed in a speech on October 21, 1975, that "Following the conclusion of a peace treaty between the actual parties to the cease-fire agreement, that is, the United States and North Korea, and the withdrawal of U.S. troops pursuant to that treaty, problems posed by the maintenance of peace in Korea should be solved at a North-South military council convened for that purpose" (retranslated from Japanese). In rejecting the North-South treaty of nonaggression proposed by South Korea, he said that such a measure is designed not to achieve unification but to legalize the existing partition of the country.

With regard to Japan in the above-mentioned discussion with the *Yomiuri* editorial bureau chief and his party, Kim said, "What we want from the Japanese government is only that it refrain from any actions that would obstruct the unification of Korea. Even if that is all the Japanese government does, we will consider it ample evidence of goodwill." His comment suggests that he does not consider negotiations with Japan as a possible means of achieving a breakthrough.

It has been emphasized from the outset of the Carter administration that the sort of secret negotiations and direct contacts with communist nations over the heads of allied nations that took place during the days of Kissinger diplomacy under the Nixon administration will no longer be contemplated. In fact, it is our impression that the extreme care and discretion with which both the United States and North Korea handled the helicopter incident earlier in this year in the vicinity of the thirty-eighth parallel resulted from anxiety over the possibility of a repeat of the Pueblo incident. It was primarily that possibility that led them both to seek talks in an atmosphere of conciliation. At least neither side seemed to want to disrupt that faint hint of conciliation.

Three divided nations were left in the wake of World War II: Germany, Vietnam, and Korea. Since that time, Germany and Vietnam have reached a modus vivendi through completely different processes. In the case of Germany, political conflict was moved toward solution through the political development of West Germany's *Ostpolitik;* in Vietnam, military conflict was resolved with the military victory of the North. The Korean solution is likely to differ from both. In order to explore the prospects for Korean unification, it is necessary to locate those points on which all concerned governments agree.

At the present time about 1,000,000 troops are in the vicinity of the thirty-eighth parallel, and their existence alone constitutes cause for tension on the Korean peninsula. The troops of the South, numbering 570,000, exceed the 490,000 of the North, but when it comes to reserve forces, the Northern Worker-Farmer Red Guard force of 1,800,000 vastly outnumbers the 400,000 maintained by the South.[3] The population of the South is 34,600,000 and that of the North 16,280,000; together they total 50,880,000. It is clear that the burden of military competition is heavy. Above all, it is the desire not only of the two Korean governments, but of the United States, the PRC, the Soviet Union, and Japan as well, that another war be avoided. In that common concern alone lies a basis for talks.

Nevertheless, while at first glance the cross-recognition formula proposed by former Secretary of State Kissinger (whereby Japan and the United States would recognize North Korea while the Soviet Union and the PRC would recognize the South) appears reasonable, it is actually the source of contention. As long as North Korea is opposed to it, the Soviet Union and the PRC will remain opposed. Therefore, it is not a useful device. Cross-recognition is opposed by North Korea because in its view the South Korean government is against the unification of Korea and supports the continued division of the Korean people. Therefore, recognition of such a government can serve as a foundation only for the freezing of the status quo of two Koreas, not for unification.

The same applies to the formula proposed by Japan, whereby North and South Korea would simultaneously become United Nations members. North Korea rejects it on the grounds that it would rigidify partition. Germany also is a divided country some people point out, yet both sides joined the United Nations at the same time; Korea should be able to do the same. But North Korea protests that the example of Germany, whose historical and political background is quite different, cannot mechanically be applied to the Korean situation. In the case of Germany, there was complete agreement between the parties, and joint entry into the United Nations was proposed on that basis. In the Korean case no such agreement exists; therefore, it is a mistake to propose joint entry as a serious alternative.[4]

The one set of principles that all parties, including the two principals, agree upon, was enunciated in the joint communiqué of July 4, 1972: independent unification on the initiative of the Koreans themselves, peaceful unification, and national solidarity. Kim Il-sung made a special point of explaining them to the *Yomiuri Shinbun* party, and they also are made clear in the book by President Park's secretary in charge of political affairs, Lew Hyuck-in.[5]

The difference is that South Korea emphasizes peace first, then unification, holding that a nonagression pact should be concluded between North and South in order to secure peace on the peninsula. Then both sides should open their doors to interchange and dialogue, leading to unification through free elections. North Korea proposes that a peace treaty be concluded between itself and the United States, thereby averting the danger of a new war. After U.S. troops are withdrawn from South Korea, the military confrontation between North and South can be dissolved, and military forces of both sides can be reduced to 100,000 or less. The initial form of government for the unified nation is to be a federal republic. The withdrawal of U.S. troops is an important point in the eyes of North Korea. Official North Korean documents are consistent in their

opposition to any proposals that arise out of policies hostile
to North Korea, but in an atmosphere of mutual trust, a flexible, no less principled, response would be fully possible. In
that sense, it would be desirable for Japan and the United States
to abandon policies based upon the concept of the "threat from
the North" and, rather than trying to contain North Korea,
make an effort to persuade that country to become a full-
fledged member of international society. To that end, it is
probably necessary for the United States to enter unconditionally into contact with North Korea. Once the ice is broken,
concrete programs can begin.

By 1977 the framework of cold war alliances in Northeast
Asia already had changed markedly and may be in the process
of dissolution. The now inoperative Sino-Soviet Friendship
Treaty is one example. An important impact on that relationship has been exerted by U.S.–PRC rapprochement. Nevertheless, the treaty structure surrounding the Korean peninsula
is still firmly in place. North Korea is party to mutual aid
treaties with the Soviet Union and the PRC, and South Korea
figures prominently in both the United States–South Korea
Treaty and the United States–Japan Security Treaty. Japan
is tied into a trilateral U.S.–South Korea–Japan defense
network through both of the above treaties involving South
Korea. Significantly, the U.S. 314th Air Wing stationed in
Korea belongs to the Fifth Air Force headquartered at Yokota
Air Force Base near Tokyo and also is tied directly to the
Kadena Air Force Base in Okinawa. While it is not a defense
treaty, the Japan–South Korea Basic Treaty also links the
two countries in a very close political and economic relationship.

The dense web of treaties centering on the Korean peninsula
constricts the freedom of both the Soviet Union and the PRC
on the one hand and the United States and Japan on the other
to change their policy with regard to that area. In that context,
the withdrawal of U.S. forces by the Carter administration is
creating quite a stir. On the Korean peninsula, a deep-seated
atmosphere of mutual distrust left over from the Korean War
impedes the pace of problem solving. By the same token, fear
of a renewed outbreak of war constrains the movement and

policies not only of North and South Korea, but of the other parties involved as well. There is little doubt that the PRC and the Soviet Union also would view any prospect of war on the Korean peninsula with great apprehension.

It has reached the point where defense commitments to South Korea are a millstone around the neck of the United States. It looks as if, with the gradual withdrawal of U.S. forces, U.S. intervention on the Korean peninsula will become a matter for careful deliberation rather than for automatic response as it has been in the past. By pursuing contacts with North Korea and at the same time focusing on problems of human rights and democratization in relations with South Korea, the United States seems to be seeking a reduction of tensions on the peninsula and the stabilization of South Korean politics.

Japan's relations with South Korea were normalized in 1965 with the conclusion of the basic treaty. By establishing relations only with the South, however, and excluding North Korea completely, the treaty actually serves, as it was designed, to bolster the relative position of South Korea. Indeed, the latter sought to make of it a solid "alliance of destiny." In view of the fact that 1965 was the year the bombing of North Vietnam began and the war reached fever pitch, it is not surprising to find that the treaty between Japan and South Korea reflects Vietnam War priorities.

The Japan–South Korea Basic Treaty should have been a voluntary effort on the part of the Japanese to settle historic accounts with the Korean people. Having once colonized the entire Korean peninsula, Japan now had an opportunity to establish a new foundation for relations between two independent nations based on equality, trust, and mutual respect. Unfortunately, under the circumstances, that opportunity was wasted. Not only was it rendered totally inadequate by its neglect of North Korea, but it failed for that very reason to provide a sound basis even for Japan–South Korean amity.

The actual effect of the treaty was to facilitate the collusion of South Korean and Japanese elites in governmental and capitalistic circles and to assign to South Korea the functions of serving militarily as a breakwater and economically as an export, cheap labor, and capital market for Japan. Relations became so cozy politically that instead of taking a resolute stance in the Kim Dae-jung case, as the West Germans did in similar circumstances, the Japanese government contented itself with incomplete investigations of the Tokyo KCIA kidnapping and left the facts of the matter vague.

Symbolic of this pattern of relations between Japan and Korea is the passage in the 1969 Sato-Nixon joint communiqué that reads "the security of the Republic of Korea is essential to Japan's own security." Known as the "Korea clause," this has been included in one form or another in the joint communiqués issued by a whole succession of Japanese prime ministers and U.S. presidents and has served as the foundation of policy toward South Korea for a number of foreign ministers.

One exception to the rule was a statement made in the Diet by Foreign Minister Takeo Kimura in 1974 to the effect that the Korea clause in the 1969 Sato-Nixon communiqué should be taken to mean that "the security and peace of the *entire Korean peninsula* is essential to Japan's own security" rather than just the security of South Korea. His statement drew a heated reaction from the South Korean government and from Japanese supporters of that government, and when Kimura left his foreign ministerial post a short time after, it was widely interpreted as a direct consequence of his indiscretion. Since that time, Japan's Korea policy has beat a hasty retreat from the Kimura statement. Nevertheless, Japan's ability to adapt to the new situation in Northeast Asia will depend heavily upon whether Kimura's understanding of the clause can be reinstated as a basis for policy formulation.

The year 1977 was the year of the 200-mile exclusive fishing zones, and on August 1 North Korea followed the United States and the Soviet Union in establishing such a zone. Japan, however, has no channel through which to ascertain the intentions of the North Korean government in that regard and therefore can provide no protection for Japanese fishermen. Although the Japanese government has engaged actively in fishery negotiations with the United States and the Soviet Union, it has not even tried to make formal contact with North Korea for fear of impairing South Korea's position.

Since 1965 Japan has been committed to South Korea politically, and economic involvement has been extremely close to
the point that the shadow of prewar days still lingers over
relations between the two nations. As a result, Japan is in
danger of being left in the lurch by the Carter administration's
new policy initiatives. The 1973 Kim Dae-jung incident was
extremely unfortunate, but it is ironical that it catapulted to
fame a former presidential candidate who had been completely
unknown in Japan and heightened concern in Japan for the
fate of South Korean democratic forces.

Following the North-South joint communiqué issued on
July 4, 1972, the Park regime proceeded to expand armaments
and further oppress democratic forces in South Korea to oppose
the North. It also adopted a high-growth policy designed to
surpass its northern rival economically. While it continues to
harbor grave contradictions, that policy of economic growth
has produced some results; it has also enabled President Park to
raise up a group of technocrats. As pointed out in the March 1,
1976 Declaration on the Restoration of Democracy, which
might be called the manifesto of democratic forces in South
Korea, it is nonetheless true that economic power is not all
there is to national strength: the foundation of national
health is a "vigorous democracy."

Another indicator of the future course of Northeast Asia will
be the manner in which the Park regime responds to the new
policies of the Carter administration. Will President Park react
to the troop withdrawals by opting directly for arms expansion,
including the development of an independent South Korean
nuclear capability, and will oppression of democratic forces
become more thorough? Or will he realize the futility and
meaninglessness of resisting President Carter's policy and
wisely opt for gradual concession in the face of demands for
democratization?

It is also important to watch the degree to which democratic
forces in South Korea grow. Will they have the wisdom to avoid
repeating the failure of democracy that occurred after Syngman
Rhee was overthrown in 1960? What sort of principles and
symbols (like the March 1 incident in 1919 that provided the
starting point for the Korean independence movement) do they

have at their disposal to deploy in the event of peaceful unification with the North? (In the case of North Korea, the heroic anti-Japanese guerrilla fight led by Kim Il-sung will be *the* symbol.) How can they achieve unification in a manner that transcends differences of social system? These are important matters from the viewpoint of North Korea as well.

No doubt the road to Korean unification will be long and beset with obstacles. Will it follow the pattern set by Vietnam? Highly unlikely. The German solution then? Or will a Korean path to unification be invented? The answer depends more than anything else on the wisdom and dedication of the Korean people and of political leaders in both North and South. However, it will depend also on the action of the four countries intimately involved—the United States, the PRC, the Soviet Union, and Japan. Japan must abandon as rapidly as possible its policy of total commitment to one side and its efforts to bolster South against North. We must become fully conscious of the existence right next door of a nation of fifty million people and learn to interact with that entire nation on the basis of equality and goodwill. At the very least, we must avoid retracing the steps of the past by forming an alliance of destiny with the Park regime.

The year 1980 will mark the end of the twentieth year of the revised United States–Japan Security Treaty. President Carter's withdrawal of U.S. troops from the Korean peninsula is due for completion in 1982. President Carter also is propounding a policy of withdrawal of nuclear weapons from Korea, so if Japan holds fast to the three nonnuclear principles, we will have an opportunity to realize the ideal of a nuclear-weapon-free zone in Northeast Asia, including both Korea and the Japanese islands. Naturally, the Pentagon and the Japanese Defense Agency can be expected to drag their feet, but for our part we must exert every possible effort to carry that ideal through to completion.

In ratifying the Nuclear Nonproliferation Treaty in 1976, the Japanese Diet adopted a special resolution demanding that the government make an international effort to establish a nuclear-weapon-free zone centering on Japan. We must persevere through any and all difficulties to extend such a zone from

Japan and Korea throughout the Asian and Pacific region, bringing it up in the United Nations, and contributing in any way possible to a relaxation of tensions throughout the world.

A resolution was adopted at the Second Shimoda Conference, in 1969, to the effect that the PRC again should be allowed full participation in international society and that such a development would be desirable for both Japan and the United States. Having weathered the storms of change that have swept the international scene in the eight years since then, it is clear now that our resolution was correct. I hope that this conference will make a resolution on Northeast Asia that will be similarly prophetic.

Notes

1. Dr. Henry Kissinger, then special advisor to President Nixon, visited the PRC to see Premier Chou on July 7, 1971.

2. The *Yomiuri* editorial bureau chief met Kim on April 23, 1977, while Akira Ogata of NHK visited North Korea in July 1977.

3. Shunkichi Murase, "Nanboku Chosen no gunji tairitsu" (North-South Military Confrontation in Korea), *Sekai*, September 1, 1977. Note, however, that Stephen Solarz, "Japan and the United States: Security Issues in the Far East," in this volume, gives slightly different figures.

4. North Korean memorandum, September 26, 1973.

5. Lew Hyuck-in, *Kankoku wa nani o mezasu ka* (What is the Republic of Korea Aiming At?) Tokyo: Simul Press, 1976.

Part 3
Political and Economic Development in Southeast Asia

7
Asian Development and the United States

Gustav Ranis

Introduction

This paper attempts to assess current trends in political and economic development in East and Southeast Asia, the U.S. interest in the area, and the likely willingness and capacity of the United States to be influential given that its interest continues. It should be noted at the outset that the influence of any outside power, using whatever instruments it has at its command, is bound to be a limited one at best. We cannot have too many reminders that without real understanding of what is happening within the countries of the region, any analysis focusing mainly on their interrelations with the hegemonic rich is bound to be beside the point. If all that is clearly understood, it is nevertheless true that the postures taken by the United States and the potential for actions by that country can continue to be of substantial importance in the region, if only in a catalytic and supportive fashion, in relation to domestic actions taken by individual countries or groups of countries.

Regions and countries are forever at some crossroad. But there can be little doubt that this conference is meeting at a time of more than usual uncertainty concerning both the definition of political and economic development objectives and the capacity on the part of the developing countries in the region to address them. This relates in part to the profound upheaval caused by the drastic change in oil and fertilizer prices plus subsequent global inflation and recession, in part to the local repercussions of the global North-South confrontation, and in part to the growing political difficulty confronting many countries that might want to sweep the "growth for whom?" questions under the carpet.

At the same time, the U.S. interest in the area and its willingness to use whatever instruments are available to pursue those interests appear less certain than at any time since World War II. In spite of recent reassurances by Secretary Vance that the United States "is and will remain an Asian and Pacific power" and that "it will continue its key role in contributing to peace and stability in the area"—followed by similar, appropriately more military-presence-tinged comments by Secretary Brown—there are those in Japan and in the less developed countries (LDCs) of the region who are uncomfortable and nervous about U.S. reliability and intentions.

Japanese statesmen are complaining about the "inscrutable West." There are those who see a return to the traditional primacy of European concerns or, as Reischauer put it, a concern with the fate of rich democracies over that of poor developing countries.[1] After all, much has happened in recent years to shake the comfortable assumptions of the first postwar quarter-century. It is not frequent that a major hegemonic power has been given as bloody a nose as the United States received in Vietnam, and the marked turning inward of the United States, if not all the way to "Fortress America," at least to an intermediate position, has not been lost on anyone. Such very current events as the Korean troop withdrawal decision and the impending discussions concerning the longer-term arrangements with respect to the PRC and Taiwan only illustrate the point. The "bottom line" on human rights in the area remains unclear and, while the new administration in Washington clearly has a different style favored by many, the anticipation of more (this time Carter) shocks is the current pervasive reality in the area. Such critical uncertainties must be viewed as the backdrop of our attempt, on the one hand, to assess the present in the light of the experience of the recent past and, on the other, to analyze what a mutually beneficial set of arrangements in the future might look like.

The Setting: Past and Prospective

It will be hard to understand where we are and where we should be heading without some minimal agreement as to where we have been. To understand what recent history tells us about the developing countries in the region, it is important to have a reasonable grasp of the diversity of the countries of South and East Asia. While a full typological approach with respect to their political and economic development is not possible here, one should note that at least four major categories need to be differentiated.

First, there is the mixed economy group that has experienced unusually rapid economic growth in excess of 10 percent annually during the last decade combined with good distributional outcomes: i.e., Taiwan, South Korea, Hong Kong, and Singapore—all culturally related to each other as well as historically related to the PRC and Japan. Second is the group of countries that also has experienced growth at a respectable rate, i.e., better than 6 percent annually, but whose internal equity problems are more serious and have worsened over time rather than improved. This includes, certainly, the Philippines and Indonesia and probably Thailand and Malaysia. Third, there is a smaller group of virtually stagnant mixed economies. Its one major member is Burma. Fourth, there are the communist countries in the region, including Vietnam, Laos, and Cambodia, as well as North Korea. Finally, of course, there is mainland China, which is *sui generis.*

There is little to say here about the performance of Hong Kong and Singapore, the laissez-faire atypical city states, or about the Indochinese countries too recently affected by war. Burma represents an interesting case of equitably shared stagnation under self-imposed autarchy. Relatively little is known about mainland China and less about North Korea, but one has the impression, certainly with respect to the PRC, of a large if not always well-coordinated development effort that has brought steady growth combined with a good measure of egalitarianism. The big question is the extent to which moral incentives can be preserved as the engine of progress in the longer run and in the absence of credible enemies. But all that is too big a question to be addressed here.

For our present, pragmatic purposes, the interesting categories are clearly groups one and two—mixed developing-economy types. While they are seeking to initiate industrialization via import substitution, the patterns of development that they have experienced are very different. South Korea and Taiwan, Type I countries, started from a very poor natural resource base but moved rather quickly from a raw-material, export-fueled pattern of industrialization in the 1950s to labor-intensive production and export in the 1960s and early 1970s. During this process, the rural sector was fully mobilized, with agricultural surpluses playing their crucial historical role—as in Meiji Japan. The name of the game was industrialization, but it was relatively decentralized and avoided some of the extreme distortions in output mix and technology choice so often typical of the consumer-goods, import-substitution era.

Once entrepreneurial capacity in these industries had been sufficiently sharpened, energies could turn outward as domestic markets were gradually exhausted. This dictated the need for accommodating policy shifts away from import substitution and toward export orientation in the area of labor-intensive industrial products—mostly consumer goods. Necessity was, indeed, continuously the mother of invention in these highly successful development situations. Not only did industrial and overall growth assume remarkably rapid proportions by any international standard, but the explosion of industrial exports at rates of 30 to 40 percent per year has astounded the experts. Taiwan's exports today are more than 90 percent non-agricultural (from a mere 10 percent in the 1950s) and are up to 50 percent of the GNP (from 15 percent in the 1950s). Perhaps less well known is the fact that this very rapid growth and structural change pattern was accompanied by an unusually favorable performance with respect to both the level and changes over time in the distribution of income. The avoidance of a conflict between equity and rapid growth was in large part due to the initially rural orientation of the development effort, not only in terms of how agricultural productivity increase was generated via a chemical/fertilizer type of technology change, but in how secondary agricultural products were encouraged (high value and labor intensive) and how industrial activity was encouraged (increasingly competitive and export oriented).

Type II countries—Indonesia, Malaysia, the Philippines, and Thailand—also have experienced what may well be called a respectable growth rate by any international LDC standard— 6 percent or above per year. However, blessed as they have been by a good natural resource base, these countries have persisted with raw-material, export-fueled industrialization, moving from consumer goods to intermediate and capital goods import substitution, thus avoiding the need for any major policy changes.[2] However, while growth rates could thus be maintained, both the level and the direction of change in equity compare very unfavorably with those in the first group. Unemployment has been growing and income distribution indices have worsened even as overall growth rates have been maintained. Output mixes and technologies have tended to be more capital intensive even as unemployment and underemployment rates have mounted.

With respect to recent political developments in the region, there has been a clear trend toward increasing authoritarianism and a predisposition toward single-party coalitions. This trend seems to be almost independent of the extent of commitment to continued direct state intervention—more typical of the Type II countries—or indirect intervention via the use of the market mechanism—as in Type I countries—and perhaps underlines the fact that some degree of authoritarianism may be inherent in transitional societies.[3] At best, it may indicate that it takes time for functioning democratic institutions of an indigenous character to be established.

Perhaps the most important phenomenon of all in the region has been the increasing power of nationalism, which exhibits itself in the resolute rejection of hegemonic intervention, whether Eastern or Western, and in the certain deliberateness and caution concerning regional arrangements requiring mutual give and take, as in the Association of Southeast Asian Nations and other regional organizations. President Marcos's efforts to strike a new deal on U.S. bases in the Philippines while seeking strengthened ties with the PRC has its equivalent in Vietnam's apparent determination to shape a foreign policy independent of PRC influence while seeking an accommodation with (and aid from) the United States. With the possible exception of Cambodia, such nationalism has been associated with the ascendancy of pragmatism and diplomatic "cool" over doctrinaire positions and messianic fervor.

During the 1950s and 1960s, the United States was heavily involved in Asia in a number of ways. Its major, transcendent motivation in those days was clearly strategic and political in character, the Asian expression of a global anticommunist containment policy. The objectives of security and stability in the area were addressed mainly with foreign assistance instruments, both military and economic, tied in with defensive alliances. Table 7.1 indicates the mix and trend in the U.S. foreign assistance package during the 1960s and 1970s. Economic assistance and P.L. 480 food aid were provided in substantial quantities, but it was always clear that the basic motivation was to shore up economies in terms of enhancing the indigenous capacity to resist both foreign and domestic threats. Econometric analysis undertaken to determine what variables affected the intercountry allocations of U.S. aid during this period clearly indicates the existence of a very large bonus for being located on the periphery of the communist bloc.

This is not to say that major long-term developmental successes were not scored during this period. In fact, it was during the early 1960s that both South Korea and Taiwan shifted from a domestic-market-oriented, import-substitution strategy to a more liberal, export-oriented type of economic growth, with foreign aid making a major timely contribution in easing the always considerable pains of policy transitions. U.S. program lending, for example, was crucial to the adoption of the famous Nineteen Points during the 1961-63 Taiwan reform period, just as budget support had been of vital importance in overcoming the initial inflationary threat in the early 1950s. But it is also fair to say that if we look at the total picture of U.S. foreign assistance efforts in East and Southeast Asia over the decade, the preponderant motivation was clearly security and stability related. Certainly, when

TABLE 7.1 U.S. Aid Expenditures in East Asia 1960, 1970, and 1975 (in millions of dollars)

	FY1960						FY1970						FY1975 (estimated)			
	Economic Aid	Defense Support	Development Loans	P.L. 480	Military	Total Expenditures	Economic Aid	Supporting Assistance	Development Loans	P.L. 480	Military	Total Expenditures	Economic Aid	P.L. 480	Military	Total Expenditures
Indonesia	10.5	–	2.6	12.0	–	22.4	34.7	–	19.3	169.9	6.1	210.8	44.1	54.9	25.1	124.1
Malaysia	–	–	–	0.2	–	0.2	–	–	–	12.5	0.2	12.7	–	0.3	5.0	5.3
Philippines	18.0	15.0	–	4.8	14.3	37.1	9.6	0.6	5.2	105.5	26.0	141.1	45.3	10.9	31.0	87.3
Thailand	23.0	18.5	–	0.06	19.2	42.2	30.7	21.4	0.3	4.2	96.8	131.7	9.1	–	54.0	63.1
Taiwan	109.3	68.0	38.9	12.6	127.4	249.3	1.6	–	1.6	88.3	130.4	220.2	–	–	74.3	74.3
South Korea	201.8	194.3	1.1	12.4	181.1	395.4	62.4	20.1	37.5	314.8	386.7	764.0	20.3	82.6	150.3	253.3
Singapore	–	–	–	–	–	–	–	–	–	2.2	–	2.2	0.6	–	0.01	0.01
Burma	1.1	–	–	0.07	–	1.1	1.8	1.1	–	5.5	0.1	7.4	–	–	–	0.6
Cambodia	22.5	20.0	–	–	2.9	25.4	0.04	–	–	0.1	8.6	8.8	98.0	47.4	267.0	412.4
Laos	42.1	40.8	–	–	13.4	55.5	48.3	39.9	0.01	3.9	74.2	126.3	27.0	3.2	29.9	60.1
Vietnam	169.9	156.0	9.7	12.3	69.6	251.8	315.6	311.1	–	27.1	1692.6	2035.3	261.1	18.9	827.6	1107.6
11-Country Total	598.2	512.6	52.3	54.4	427.9	1080.4	504.7	394.2	63.9	734.0	2421.7	3660.5	505.5	218.2	1464.3	2188.1

Sources: U.S. Aid Operations Report, various issues; U.S. Statistical Abstract, various issues; Senate Hearings Before the Committee on Appropriations, *Foreign Assistance and Related Program Appropriations FY 1977* 94th Congress, Second Session; and U.S. Aid, U.S. *Overseas Loans and Grants and Assistance from International Organizations,* 1973.

selling the program annually to the U.S. Congress, economic development as such was strictly a secondary objective in this region and was viewed as one major means of strengthening economies in the struggle against possible foreign invasion or internal subversion. Military assistance addressed the same objective directly.

In addition to the deployment of official development assistance, mostly bilateral, other dimensions of economic interaction between the United States and Asia were gaining importance during this period, especially in the latter half of the 1960s. These included an increasing volume of exports from the countries in the region to the United States on the one hand (*see* Table 7.2) and the increasing absolute importance of private investment flows into the area on the other (*see* Table 7.3).

Turning first to trade, the increase in U.S.–Asian interchange has, of course, been most pronounced in the developing countries of Type I, which, as noted, shifted toward an export-oriented growth path in the early 1960s. The 1970-75 export boom in the Type II countries is attributable largely to oil and other specific raw material booms. The Type I countries also received an increasing proportion of direct U.S. foreign investment that sought to participate in the growing industrial export orientation, both with respect to labor-intensive consumer goods and the international subcontracting of intermediate labor-intensive processes via the so-called "export platforms" of South Korea and Taiwan. The phenomenal success of these export performances was based in large part on the increasingly competitive environment that permitted low-wage labor to be combined with rapidly maturing entrepreneurial capacities enhanced by the inflow of private capital from the United States. Increased trade relations, some intra-firm and some at arms' length, between the United States and the countries of the region followed.

What, then, have been the tendencies in more recent years with respect to the U.S. presence in Asia—tendencies that are likely to continue to be of relevance in the years ahead? Clearly, there has been a diminution of U.S. willingness to participate in the form of large-scale bilateral aid operations. First military

TABLE 7.2 Export Performance (in millions of dollars)

Exports to:	A. Indonesia, Malaysia, Philippines, and Thailand					B. South Korea and Taiwan				
	1960	Inter-period Annual Growth rate	1970	Inter-period Annual Growth rate	1975	1960	Inter-period Annual Growth rate	1970	Inter-period Annual Growth rate	1975
World	2737.1	5.1%	4547.9	24.4%	15442.5	196.5	26.7%	2828.7	25.3%	10024.8
East Asia (excluding Japan)	741.6	3.8%	1086.3	19.3%	2857.7	54.2	20.2%	407.3	24.5%	1383.8
% of total	27.1%		23.9%		18.5%	27.6%		14.4%		13.8%
Industrial Countries	1647.5	6.0%	3005.9	25.4%	10697.4	119.5	28.9%	2144.9	23.9%	7089.9
% of total	60.2%		66.1%		69.3%	60.8%		75.8%		70.7%
U.S.	618.9	3.7%	892.1	27.2%	3474.0	22.6	40.2%	1260.6	19.2%	3293.1
% of total	22.6%		19.6%		22.5%	11.5%		44.6%		32.8%
Japan	356.8	13.4%	1360.6	26.0%	4993.8	82.0	17.6%	478.7	27.8%	1925.3
% of total	13.0%		29.9%		32.3%	41.7%		16.9%		19.2%
Rest of World	348.0	2.7%	455.7	28.4%	1887.4	22.6	25.0%	276.5	34.5%	1551.1
% of total	12.7%		10.0%		12.2%	11.5%		9.8%		15.5%

Source: A—IMF, Direction of Trade, various Annuals; B—Direction of Trade, various Annuals.

TABLE 7.3   U.S. Direct Foreign Investment (book value,
in billions of dollars)

	1950	1960	1970
World:	11.8	31.9	78.1
Developed	5.9	18.4	53.1
% of total	50%	58%	68%
Developing	5.9	13.5	25.0
% of total	50%	42%	32%
Latin America	4.6	10.0	14.7
% of total	39%	31%	19%
Southeast Asia	0.2	0.6	2.0
% of total	2%	2%	3%
Africa and Middle East	1.0	2.0	5.1
% of total	8%	6%	7%

Source: T. W. Allen, *Direct Investment of U.S. Enterprises in Southeast Asia*
(Bangkok: Economic Cooperation Centre for the Asian and Pacific Region,
1973), Study 2.

then economic assistance have come under increasing pressure, with the U.S. regional as well as global commitment steadily eroding in real terms. Second, there has been an increased tendency toward a multilateralization of the (reduced) volume of foreign assistance, either via the World Bank/IDA family, the use of regional banks, or the United Nations. Third, it increasingly has become donor policy to provide heavily con-cessional aid only to the poorest countries or to the poorest people in poor countries.

These recent new directions in U.S. aid policy have more or less eliminated many countries in the region from anything but P.L. 480 (food) assistance. On the other hand, since all but Indochina and Burma may be counted among the middle class of developing countries, the relative role of trade and private capital movements in the region has continued to increase. Most of the countries seem to be in a position to satisfy the demands of the United States for either industrial consumer goods (Type I) or raw materials (Type II). Most are generally considered credit-worthy, and their relative stability and lower-level confrontationism have led to an increase at the margin, relative to Latin America, in U.S. direct investment, with limited access for some to portfolio investments and bank credits. (For a summary of their substantial increase in foreign debt in recent years, see Table 7.4.) Whether this is healthy or unhealthy depends on the nature and dependability of the export performance.

In summary, by the mid-1970s the landscape shows a group of developing countries with fairly high levels of per capita income and fairly good growth rates but very different levels of success in participating in the world economy in a sustained fashion and in solving their domestic distribution problems. They are unified by their determination to find their own national paths to a better life and reject interference from both political dissenters at home and, increasingly, the superpowers abroad. On the other hand, the United States is viewed as being increasingly uncertain of its future role in Asia yet conscious of the fact that a retreat into "Fortress America" is neither desirable nor feasible in a more interdependent world.

Prospective Interests and Actions

All this brings us to one of the central questions, i.e., what *should* be the U.S. interest and posture in Asia in the years ahead, based on the events of the recent past and the realities of the current situations of the countries in the region?

Utilizing the typology advanced earlier, we would expect the Type I countries, i.e., South Korea, Taiwan, Singapore, and Hong Kong, to continue their rapid growth patterns. Having solved their labor-surplus problem and growing at rates in excess of 10 percent for more than a decade, they can be expected to move in the direction of more skill, technology, and capital-intensive production and export patterns and to be in a position, for all practical purposes, to join the ranks of the developed countries. Needless to say, such a prediction is based on the assumption of no major upheavals on the political front, especially with regard to South Korea and Taiwan. In any case, this first group has demonstrated in the course of the recent

TABLE 7.4   Foreign Debts of Selected Asian Countries
(in millions of dollars)

	1970	*1976*
South Korea	1,675	6,728
Taiwan	609	1,600
Indonesia	2,914	10,396
Malaysia	364	1,126
Philippines	646[a]	5,554
Thailand	322	825

Source: World Debt Tables, IBRD.

[a]Does not include publicly guaranteed private debts.

post-OPEC global inflation and recession crisis—deepened by
greater protectionism among the rich—that "development" is
but another word for the ability to "roll with the punches" and
be able to adjust flexibly to sudden shocks. Though growth
rates may be interrupted, even turning temporarily negative,
as was the case in Taiwan, these countries have demonstrated
that they are capable of overcoming increased voluntary and
involuntary trade restrictions, the oil crisis, and global in-
flation-cum-recession, just as has Japan. This does not mean
that their future success is guaranteed, that the adjustments
are painless, or that continued effort will not be required. What
it does mean is the avoidance of currently threatened further
restrictions in the United States and other import markets as
well as the maintenance of the flow of foreign and private
investment.

Turning to the Type II countries (the Philippines, Thailand, Indonesia, and Malaysia), the existing tension between
growth and distribution is likely to intensify as long as the
present narrow growth path is maintained. With nature having
been relatively kind to them, this group is really not "up
against it" and can be expected (as they have up to now) to
try to continue to postpone the day of reckoning by maintaining their traditional export-fueled industrial patterns. Given
their import-substitution policy syndrome, they are likely to

continue to find it difficult to mobilize their rural sectors by increasing their productivity of food-producing agriculture and absorbing their unemployed and underemployed labor forces both in rural industry, directed to the domestic market, and in labor-intensive industrial exports. As long as the growth path remains highly centralized and narrow, focusing mainly on the urban industrial sector, especially in such countries as the Philippines, Thailand, and Indonesia, and perhaps to a lesser extent in Malaysia, there are likely to be serious problems with respect to the employment and equity dimensions of growth. The pronouncedly dualistic features of these systems moving deeper into costly secondary import substitution can be expected to produce more rather than less tension and unrest. The fact is that such an outcome is, of course, by no means inevitable and that one or more of the Type II countries in the region can, with the proper changes in policy, step into the shoes of the Type I countries, whose very success finally led them into unskilled labor shortages and declining international competitiveness in labor-intensive commodities.

What is required is not all that painful—not even to the vested interests themselves in the longer run: a more decentralized public sector, creating overheads in relation to the generation of a broader, more participatory pattern of growth; greater emphasis on primary and secondary food crops rather than excessive cash-crop exports in agriculture; balanced domestic growth that includes labor-intensive production of appropriate goods for domestic rural markets; and greater "openness" with respect to exchange-rate, tariff, and interest-rate policies, permitting much greater participation in the international markets for industrial goods. All of this, of course, does not mean rejection of the comparative advantage in natural resources that some of these countries now have—Indonesia's oil being only a case in point. What is required instead is a realization that such natural resources can and should be utilized to ease the pains of transition to a greater utilization, with time, of their underutilized human resources.

Policy changes of this kind, while reformist and not radical, do require the persuasion of the vested-interest groups presently benefitting from the policies of government intervention that provide them with hothouse temperatures and windfall profits. It cannot be assumed that the ruling elites of Asia are committed to a more equitable growth path. Therefore, such persuasions must in part be based on the fact that continuation of the present path is untenable for economic as well as political reasons. But it also requires some assurance that if a new domestic order is, in fact, to be achieved the international setting for such a development will be minimally receptive; i.e., that one can count on not having import doors slammed in one's face or capital inflows dried up at critical junctures.

The really poor countries of East and Southeast Asia are, with the exception of Burma, now in the communist orbit. Nevertheless, as any comparison of recent development in mainland China and Taiwan would illustrate, the basic problems of a poor labor surplus economy are not so very different regardless of the institutional-cum-organizational tools employed to solve them under a variety of social systems. While the mainland, given its size, can be expected to focus much more inwardly for some time to come, both Chinas had to find a way to mobilize their human resources, especially in the rural areas. This was the only way to avoid a conflict between growth and distribution objectives. Burma on the one hand and most of the Indochinese countries on the other are still at an earlier stage of development; that is, requiring a good deal of technical assistance and infrastructural investments, much of which can be provided by both bilateral and multilateral aid from abroad. The poorer countries of the region are not yet in a position to be major participants in international trade or, realistically, recipients of large inflows of private foreign capital.

Given this necessarily rough sketch of the country-by-country or at least type-by-type situation in the Asian countries we are concerned with, let us now proceed to the central matters before us; that is, what are the conditions for regional stability in Asia, what is the appropriate U.S. interest, and what is the U.S. capacity to serve that interest?

Regional stability will, as already indicated, depend in large measure on the extent to which the countries in the region are able to solve their domestic development problems in the years ahead. This always will be at least 90 percent within their own hands. Much depends on the ability, especially within the Type II countries, to forge progressive coalitions for the accommodation of the required economic policy change. Just as landlords in an earlier day were persuaded of the merits of exchanging landed for industrial interests, industrialists can be persuaded that export-oriented, large-volume-based profits can be superior to domestic-market-oriented, high-margin-based windfalls. Workers similarly can be persuaded that working family incomes will be better off if more family members are employed more hours per week rather than if wages for the head of the family rise prior to the exhaustion of the labor surplus.

The best guarantee for stability is success in the national development effort plus continued rejection of intervention by the major outside powers: the PRC, the Soviet Union, Japan, and the United States. With respect to the first, the major powers can be helpful in terms of their trade, investment, and aid policies combined in different proportions for different groups of developing countries in the region. Most important for the middle-class countries is some assurance that there will be no backsliding by the developed countries concerning the liberal trade and investment policies so fervently espoused as a matter of principle. With respect to the second, nationalism, even within the communist orbit, is likely to be the best guarantor along with the continued schism between the PRC and the Soviet Union. Both can be pulled into an increasing trade and (where appropriate) donor relationship with countries in the region without posing a threat to independence.

Focusing next on the particular U.S. interest, it seems clear that the task before us is to convince Asian leaders—having thoroughly persuaded ourselves—that the United States has a global interest in development even as it withdraws from its role as global policeman. The real danger being perceived by the developing countries of Asia and by Japan is that, having been burnt by the costly act of containment, the United States will withdraw to a position of general "benign neglect" with respect to Asia while expending whatever meager LDC-related energy and resources it can muster on its traditional Latin American "sphere of influence." Just as it is important for

Japan to be viewed as being concerned with development on a global basis, i.e., not only in Asia or where important raw materials are located but also in Africa and Latin America, it is important for the United States to be viewed as wanting to be associated with this important historical process wherever it is occurring.

What does this mean in terms of the U.S. posture in Asia, given the situation of the countries in the region and given the local representation of global discussions on North-South relations, whether couched in terms of the recognition of mutual interdependence or the need for a new international economic order?

In my view, it means that the United States must cease pyramiding its grab bag of motives for being helpful in the developing world, moving from security and stability to the purchase of bases to the assurance of markets and raw material sources to an interest in economic development. We have traditionally been ashamed to admit to some basic humanitarian impulse in wanting to be associated with the process of economic and social transition. Admittedly, our interest goes beyond that. It is an interest based on long-term stability in the developing world, on the recognition of an interdependence that surely has its commercial, raw-material access, as well as on political stability—even that related to nuclear proliferation. But also, admittedly, there exists no tested positive relationship between satisfactory development performance and the absence of instability in the short run. All we can say is that successful development is very likely to telescope the period of instability as countries try to reach economic maturity and that failure does breed frustration and instability in all runs. We should clearly own up to our inability—and unwillingness—to try to orchestrate or manipulate human progress in any particular direction that is helpful to U.S. policy in the short run. There is, moreover, nothing to be ashamed of in simply wanting to be associated with the process of transition to economic maturity. Surely there is much to be gained by lowering our voices, ceasing to oversell, and being more candid with ourselves and our friends concerning our limited power to shape events.

If this is to be the posture toward which we are moving in the Asian region, massive transfers of concessional resources are not likely to be required. What is required instead is a posture not of benign neglect, but of a sometimes, somewhat passive interest in helping, when and if we are asked. As recent studies of the Overseas Development Council have demonstrated, "Main Street America" is far ahead of its politicians in the recognition that basic humanitarian and development objectives are legitimate reasons for incurring overseas expenditures in the face of large domestic needs. At the same time there has been a growing reluctance to accept the perennial exaggerated claims as to the multiple purposes served and achievements made under U.S. foreign assistance programs. In our region, LDC Types III and possibly IV could thus be the beneficiaries of modest concessional aid programs, hopefully multiyear in both authorization and appropriation and conceived not as a political tool to "show the flag" and maintain country aid levels, but as a multiyear response if and when countries approach the United States with multiyear programs that appear sensible. Such use of foreign assistance should be extended as well, if on a temporary basis, to some middle-income Type II countries if and when such assistance is clearly associated with an indigenous determination to persuade the system to shift gears on the income distribution/growth trade-off front over a three- or four-year period. In other words, the U.S. aid posture should be essentially passive but responsive, including at the point where the pains of transition may require some ballooning of concessional capital transfers.

Such an aid effort, mainly responsive to LDC initiatives, would of course constitute a U.S. response within the context of a multilateral framework in which other bilateral donors, as well as the World Bank and the United Nations family, would play their proper roles. All the above is consistent with the notion that the bilateral programs of the United States and the multilateral efforts of IDA should be directed increasingly toward the poorer countries and only occasionally toward the alleviation of the lot of the poor within middle-income countries *if* the donor community is convinced of the integrity of the largely domestic effort required to achieve that purpose. Initially rather small but, once the program shows its effectiveness, substantially larger amounts of relatively "clean" (development-oriented) water could be deployed in this fashion. Meeting the 0.7 percent of GNP aid target, to which Japan is more committed than the United States, is, in that context, much less important than the credibility of what we are trying to achieve and the posture we are willing to assume.

As already pointed out, for most countries in the region the openness of international markets is more relevant than public capital transfers. For the Type I countries, this is a requirement of continued growth within an interdependent international economy. For the Type II countries, the prospects of a lessening rather than increasing protectionism in the advanced countries is an important part of the setting required to convince them to make the necessary changes from inward-looking, import-substituting policies to outward-looking, market-oriented postures. The argument most frequently encountered in Indonesia, the Philippines, Thailand, and (if to a lesser extent) Malaysia as to what constitutes the main obstacle to the restructuring of their economies is that the success of the Type I countries cannot be imitated on a large scale, partly because of an actual or prospective increase in protectionism abroad and partly because the world just cannot absorb such a large volume of labor-intensive industrial goods, even in the absence of advanced-country protectionism.

The objective response to this kind of concern consists of four parts. First, the march of a dynamic comparative advantage means that some will move out, as labor shortage is achieved, as others move in—witness the Japan-Taiwan-Korea sequence.

Second, as the past experiences of Taiwan and South Korea have amply demonstrated, the increased flexibility that comes with a larger role for the market within an indirectly controlled economy permits the system to respond effectively even to the threat of increased tariffs or, more likely, to quotas and voluntary market restrictions.

Third, this realization does not in any way weaken the argument that the advanced countries—Japan and the United States as well as Europe—have an obligation to continue the liberalizing trend that has been part and parcel of the international economic structure since World War II, rather than give in to the currently strong and rising pressures for a reversal. An effective, well-thought-out, and possibly multi-lateralized (as to rules and financing) adjustment-assistance program in the rich countries would constitute a most effective accompaniment to any necessarily modest future foreign assistance programs. Such foreign assistance spent at home might even be included in future aid appropriations. An effective way of moving in this general direction within the global North-South negotiations context might well be to negotiate successfully within a global GATT-like framework rather than apply additional pressure for LDC preferences, the benefits of which have generally been much less than meets the eye.

Fourth, developing countries, including those in Asia, are well advised to consider not just the export of traditional commodities to traditional trading partners, but also the possibility of a substantial increase in two kinds of production: that of appropriate goods for internal markets and that of both traditional and nontraditional goods as exports to each other. The trade of the countries in the region with one another is still at a very low 18.5 percent of the total (*see* Table 7.2). If the countries in the region were to liberalize with respect to one another, perhaps via initial halfway houses of an ASEAN common market variety, the possibility for exchanging such commodities with each other is indeed very substantial. Mutual economic benefits also are likely to be of great political benefit in terms of the strengthening of interdependence within the region. Just as "real peace" in the Middle East connotes trade between Israel and her Arab neighbors, the expansion of inter-regional trade to include Vietnam and North Korea would be an important stabilizing factor politically in Asia. Outside powers such as the United States and Japan could be very helpful in easing moves that the countries in the region might want to make directly or via expanded ASEAN or other common market groupings through the provision of liberalization funds from either the World Bank or from a restructured Asian Development Bank. The argument that Type II countries in the region are too similar in structure to permit a substantial growth of trade falls by the wayside when the great diversity of quality characteristics within any particular classification of manufactured goods, such as textiles or shoes, is recognized. The countries in the region, but especially the Type II countries that are growing rapidly as a consequence of liberalization, could become major customers at the margin for each other's goods.

As international trade theory explains and as the pattern already established in the region is observed, the most labor-intensive goods are likely to be exported to the advanced countries, where the products' comparative advantage is highest and where the goods are required to overcome large transport costs. U.S. leadership, on behalf of a resumption of its own domestic growth and the rejection of protectionism, is perhaps the most important single contribution that the United States can make to stability and development in the area. The same, of course, holds for Japan—except more so, given Japan's embarrassingly large and growing export surplus.

Let me now turn briefly to the important, always highly charged subject of foreign investment and the multinational corporation. The issues of the contribution of multinationals, positive or negative, to growth, distribution, and other societal objectives in the developing world are the most controversial in the literature. Conclusions range from those who believe that any foreign corporate presence ipso facto entails the loss of independence to those who view such activity as a simple augmentation of all the "good things" at the disposal of the developing society; i.e., capital, management, entrepreneurship, and technology. The problem is that the contribution of the multinational corporation cannot really be assessed independently of time and place; nor can it be viewed as a monolithic organizational concept instead of as a very heterogeneous set of packages and organizational forms, ranging from wholly owned subsidiaries through joint ventures to licensing and management contracts. In Asia, for example, the Type I countries already have a very substantial domestic entrepreneurial capacity, which means that the multinational presence is likely to take increasingly the form of management contracts and licensing arrangements, while in the Type II countries, the transition from wholly owned subsidiaries to joint ventures would seem to be very much tied in with a gradual opening up of the economy to trade and the indigenization of the entrepreneurial contribution.

In other words, there are very few situations within the region, with the exception of Indochina and Burma, where the contribution to the brute act of saving, of getting things done, and of managing a relatively new type of activity as provided by the wholly owned subsidiary form of multinational activity, is still the dominant requirement. As a society shifts from the forced march pattern of import substitution to the more ballet-type advance of export orientation along comparative advantage lines, joint ventures become increasingly more important relative to wholly owned subsidiaries.

The style of the Japanese multinationals in Asia is more joint-venture-oriented and more conducive to export orientation than the U.S. style, which largely is focused on the domestic market via wholly owned subsidiaries (*see* Tables 7.5a and 7.5b). It is also true that the Japanese trading company pattern makes it easier to reach out to the medium- and small-scale industries within the developing country, whose activation and mobilization are so important to a reduction of and possibly elimination of the conflict between growth and income distribution objectives. Once the appropriateness of technology and output mixes in penetrating international markets becomes more important within a particular society, the potential combination of an international company's global scan of markets and technology with the growing domestic expertise based on the specificity of the local resource endowment and institutional factors can become increasingly important.

For U.S. private investment to make its full contribution to development in the region and to serve at the same time the primary interest of the investor, increased flexibility on this and other fronts will be required if the current trend toward confrontation is to be reversed. Unbundling of the multifaceted, multinational corporation's package and a more explicit set of examination and information systems as to just

TABLE 7.5a Accumulated U.S. and Japanese Direct Investments in Asia, 1971 (in millions of dollars)

Host Country	United States 1971	Japan 1971
Taiwan	133	85
Hong Kong	286	139
Indonesia	512	241
South Korea	277	33
Malaysia	307	50
Singapore		33
Philippines	719	74
Thailand	124	91
Others	691	33
Total	3049	779

Source: Y. Tsurumi, "The Multinational Spread of Japanese Firms and Asian Neighbor Reactions," in *The Multinational Corporation and Social Change,* D. Apter and L. Goodman eds., Praeger, 1976.

TABLE 7.5b   Ownership of Overseas Subsidiaries by Nationality of Large Parent Firms as of January 1, 1971 (in percentages)

Parent Firm's Nationality	Parent Firm's Ownership Percentage					
	100-95	94-51	50	49-26	25-5	Total
France	38	23	9	18	12	100
West Germany	56	22	9	10	5	100
Sweden	80	9	4	5	3	100
Canada	68	12	7	10	3	100
Japan	27	8	7	25	33	100
United States[a]	71	20			9	100

Source: Same as Table 7.5a.

[a]The U.S. data are as of January 1, 1968.

what is being transferred and what is being paid for at each stage of the development process will become increasingly important. Flexibility in terms of "fade out" and divestiture agreements, which take into account the changing contribution of local and foreign capital, technology, management, and entrepreneurial resources, would tend to provide more realistic settings for a mutually beneficial, interdependent set of relations in the future. The often used screening of foreign investments should include unbundling and full disclosure procedures, permitting LDCs to shop comparatively rather than accept or reject the "all or nothing" principle as is so frequently the case.

Some of the admitted excesses of the multinational corporation (MNC), ranging from transfer pricing to the payment of unduly high wages to the inappropriateness of imported technology to the underutilization of patents and the over-utilization of domestic credit markets and export-prohibition clauses, are not unrelated to the policy environment existing in many of the countries of the region. Many of these "crimes" are based on insufficient competitive pressure, either with other MNCs or with host-country industry. Foreign investors can be most effective if they are forced to put their energies into building the famous "better mousetraps" and into giving up the "quiet life" of satisfying behavior patterns as the policy regime is shifted to a more competitive, market-oriented one. Evidence from the export-processing zones of Korea and Taiwan as well as from other parts of the developing world indicates that multinationals are quite capable of coming up with appropriate technology and output mixes when pressures exist for them to "scratch around." Whereas in the Type II countries the "quiet life" is the norm for the large corporations, multinationals also can be expected to behave differently.

The United States can make an effort to facilitate the evolution of a mutually more beneficial relationship and one less fraught with the fictions and frictions of the past. Most important, perhaps, is an effort to move away from the image of a knee-jerk reaction in favor of U.S. multinational citizens abroad, whether they are right or wrong. The Hickenlooper and González amendments, even if not always zealously administered by the executive branch, are viewed as only slightly modernized versions of old-fashioned gunboat diplomacy and are equally ineffective. The extensions abroad of domestic antitrust, trading-with-the-enemy legislation and other forms of attempted extraterritoriality represent similarly ineffective and highly offensive instruments. Likewise, there would seem to be little reason to continue to provide U.S. foreign investors automatically with taxpayer-subsidized risk guarantees via OPIC (the Overseas Private Investment Corporation), thus implying the blessings of the U.S. government, without some effort to reassure ourselves that no unfair trade practices, exclusive market agreements, export-prohibition clauses, or other objectionable procedures are being contemplated—in addition to the purely financial flow criteria now being utilized.

Especially for the middle class of developing countries in Asia, whether of Type I or Type II, the flow of international capital, moving gradually from direct investment to portfolio and bond markets, should play an important contributing role to sustained development in the future. Since interdependence connotes a measure of symmetry, the rich countries also should be willing to consider liberalizing their current tight restrictions against the flow of unskilled labor from the developing Asian countries, i.e., beyond today's tightly circumscribed temporary agreements. The serious political obstacles to any such move are recognized, but the logic is nevertheless loud and clear.

In short, the United States needs to reassure others that it wants to be associated with the process of Asian economic development, which will be going on in any case, in a constructive, responsible, and overall sustained fashion. This, in the aftermath of Vietnam, will do more than anything else to convince jittery governments as well as ordinary citizens in the region that the United States is there to stay in a steady and low-key fashion, and is not going to pull out or act in an off-again-on-again pattern, scrambling for special deals and favors here and there as opportunity and opportunism warrant.

As far as Japan is concerned, the advice is not, of course, very different. Interdependence for Japan is not just a polite code word but a fact of life. This, however, should not find its expression in aid programs too closely related to the ebb and flow of actual or prospective raw materials shortages or in longer-term income and trade policies that appear to respond to yesterday's shorter-term crises. Most of all, to the extent that the rich countries' posture of liberalism or restrictionism with respect to trade is of one piece, the interdependence between increasing trade surpluses in Japan, increasing U.S. deficits, and the accumulation of debt in the non-OPEC Third World must be recognized.

Japan's ideal future role in the region, as viewed from the U.S. perspective, should indeed be one of an Asian policy that is part and parcel of a global posture rather than a special game played in Japan's own backyard. This, of course, does not mean that Japan may not have an especially significant contribution to make to the developing countries of Asia, since both Japan's technology and demand patterns are closer to their factor endowments and market conditions than anyone else's. But it means a bolder, broader view of the national interest in the North-South context. As in the gradual abandonment of the U.S. "special relationship" with Latin America, it means a relatively greater realization of Japan's rights and responsibilities as a major power.

In summary, the United States and Japan still have to convince others, and each other, that they understand interdependence as a longer-term "spaceship earth" proposition rather than as the short-term, self-interest euphemism for the assurance of access to scarce raw materials, military bases, or votes in the United Nations. Once the two major industrial powers operating in Asia have this basic understanding in common—leaving, of course, room for all kinds of natural differences in interpretation and specific action—there will be relatively little to fear, either from the growth of nationalist rivalries within the area or from communist expansionism into it. The PRC and the Soviet Union may well continue to give low-level support to governments and insurgent movements—just as the United States would not be expected to curtail all military and political aid in the area. But if we both put our big chips visibly where they count—on long-term development objectives of the countries in the region, shared by noncommunist and communist countries alike—Asian communism should frighten us even less than European communism. The current trend toward a more pragmatic, businesslike attitude in virtually all of the communist countries in Asia, including mainland China, should be reassuring on that score. We agree with *The New York Times*[4] that "the more . . . Vietnam and the two smaller communist powers behave as states among Southeast Asian states, rather than as the seats of victorious revolutionary movements, the greater the prospects for peace and stability in the region." An even greater contribution would be made to the same end if the United States and Japan decided to behave consistently as the two richest advanced countries on a fully interdependent globe.

Notes

1. Edwin O. Reischauer, "Back to Normalcy," *Foreign Policy,* February 1975.

2. Malaysia started her import-substitution phase much later and with less enthusiasm, but we will not follow through the differentiation here.

3. We do not wish to imply that the same box fits them all in terms of the extent of permissible dissent, freedom of the press, and other indices of pluralism.

4. Editorial, *New York Times,* July 25, 1977.

8
Toward a Reorientation of Asian Policy: The Fukuda Doctrine and Japanese–U.S. Cooperation

Toru Yano

Manila was the last stop on Prime Minister Fukuda's tour of Southeast Asia, and it was there on august 17, 1977, that he delivered his important speech on Japan's policy toward that region. Japanese news media billed the event as the epoch-making unveiling of the Fukuda Doctrine, finding deep significance in the very fact that such a speech was made. While I would not go so far as to call the contents of the Manila address a "doctrine," it is certainly the first time since World War II that a Japanese prime minister has made such a systematic presentation of views on Japanese relations with Southeast Asia.

The main points of the speech were as follows: (1) Japan is committed to peace and to the role of an economic power—it will not become a military power; (2) as "an especially close friend" of the Association of Southeast Asian Nations (ASEAN), Japan will cooperate in efforts to strengthen the solidarity of that organization; (3) Japan will emphasize "heart-to-heart" contacts, building stronger ties as an equal partner not only economically but in social, political, and cultural realms as well; (4) Japan will forge particularly close economic relations with the countries of Southeast Asia, continuing to deal with them in the context of world economy; and (5) Japan also will attempt to foster relations based on mutual understanding with the nations of Indochina. Prime Minister Fukuda phrased these points as the "pillars" of Japan's Southeast Asian policy.

No doubt the real intentions behind the prime minister's speech will be interpreted variously as time goes on, but my immediate impression is that his approach represented a compromise between two views, one advocating active, full-scale involvement in Southeast Asia, the other, rather similar to the Meiji era's "dissociation from Asia" thesis, holding that Japan must avoid deep involvement in that region. Be that as it may, the very fact that Japan should publicly announce any sort of a doctrine at all on this subject is highly significant.

A broad historical background underlies these events; the force of its logic has pushed Japan into the center stage of Asian regional politics, irrespective of the will of the Japanese people. We did not actively seek an expanded role. It has been forced upon us by history.

My objective will be to explore, from the present vantage point immediately following the announcement of the Fukuda Doctrine, several questions, including: In what manner does Japan intend to become involved in Asia in the future? What specific role will Japan seek to play? And what sort of cooperation can be expected from the United States? I certainly cannot claim to represent the Japanese people, but I shall try to explain their thinking about these problems.

A New Era for Southeast Asia

The Indochina war ended in April 1975. That event concluded a long and unhappy experience. At the same time, it inaugurated a new season of diplomacy in Asia. As the international environment surrounding Japan continues to change rapidly, partially as a result of Japan's own diplomatic participation, it is necessary to reconsider what sort of international order—or disorder—is in the process of construction.

We must begin by assessing the historical significance of the Indochina war for "post-Indochina" Asia. The conflict may now, in some sense, be relegated to the past. On the other hand, it was an international drama that brought into play such tremendous forces and had such a disruptive effect on Asian regional order that its full historical significance can only be judged over a long period of time.

At the present, the legacy left by the Indochina war during its twenty to thirty years of development, and especially of the active U.S. intervention, can be considered under the following headings.

First, its effect on U.S. policy must be taken into account. As a result of its Vietnam failure, the United States was forced to review its policy in Southeast Asia and in Asia as a whole. This, in turn, resulted in the decision to carry out a full-scale withdrawal from the Asian continent. In light of the United States's massive military and political involvement since the 1940s and its ideological justification, that was indeed an epoch-making change.

Since that time, the United States has changed to a policy of selective response in Asia, emphasizing relationships with certain key states that are deemed to be central. In his December 1975 visit to Asia, for example, President Ford chose to stop only in the Philippines and Indonesia. U.S. policy probably will continue to develop within a framework of the principle of selective response, but the standards according to which that selectivity is exercised will only become evident over a period of time.

Second, the effect on the PRC must be considered. One of the main U.S. goals in the Vietnam War was the containment of the PRC. Insofar as postwar Vietnam and Laos have remained free of PRC influence and the Indochinese peninsula as a whole bears few marks of PRC domination, the U.S. policy of containment has been successful. On the other hand, the stark fact is that after twenty years of U.S. involvement in Vietnam, the PRC's voice in international affairs is stronger than ever. The U.S. overtures toward reconciliation with the PRC bear witness to that fact. Throughout the Indochina conflict, which bore all the earmarks of a typical people's liberation war, the PRC shadow over Southeast Asia grew larger. Thus, the Indochina war had ambiguous results in respect to the original U.S.–PRC policy.

Third, the effect on the Soviet position must be considered. Traditionally, the Soviet Union had little interest in Southeast Asia. It was the August 1964 Tonkin Gulf incident that provided it with an opportunity to intervene actively. Soviet aid to North Vietnam expanded exponentially in the year or two following Premier Kosygin's February 1965 visit to Hanoi. From 1969 onward, the Soviet Union's call for an Asian Collective Security System and the continuation of the bitter Sino-Soviet dispute brought the nation more deeply into Southeast Asian politics.

Fourth, the effect on regional stability and order is a factor. Despite thirty years of international conflict, no nucleus for the formation of a stable and lasting order in Southeast Asia emerged. Despite a long war and the determined intervention of several great powers, Southeast Asian peace must still be kept within an unstable balance of power by multiple competing forces.

Fifth, the effect on the center of gravity of Southeast Asia must be taken into account. This has now shifted from the continent to the peninsular and island nations. As these latter have taken on new importance, the international status of the continental countries has fallen proportionally. This is another way of saying that the relative weight of ASEAN, including Indonesia, Malaysia, the Philippines, and Singapore, has increased. In effect, it appears possible that the future Southeast Asian order will be preserved by means of a balance between the ASEAN nations and Indochina. It is also possible that the continental location of Thailand, the only ASEAN nation so situated, will constitute a destabilizing factor.

Sixth, the prospects for the future are relevant. It is possible to identify two aspects of the legacy of the war that point in a more optimistic direction. First, Indochina is now for the first time under the stable control of legitimate authorities, so the possibility that the Indochinese situation again may touch off international tension on a global scale has faded. Second, U.S. intervention prevented the Indochina war from spreading throughout the region, thereby providing other nations with the temporal, psychological, and economic leeway that they needed to begin modernizing. Despite the radical reshuffling of spheres of influence in Indochina, neighboring countries experienced only a temporary shock from which they bounced back psychologically in a comparatively short period of time. If we follow the apparently mutual reinforcing inter-action between the two tendencies to its logical conclusion, the Southeast Asian region emerges not as a disorderly aggregation of many small states but as a combination of two loosely defined regional blocs.

In light of these effects, it is clear not only that the Indochina war had a very large effect on regional order in Asia, but that its consequences were quite unexpected in view of what the United States believed to be at stake. The Vietnam War can be regarded either as a totally wasteful detour in post–World War II history or as one route to the formation of a desirable order. On balance, however, the most tragic aspect about the war is that so few of the necessary conditions for a stable international order in Southeast Asia were provided as a result of all that agony.

It is necessary to point out something else, however, and that is the ironic possibility that the "loss" of Vietnam may have had more historical significance for Japan than for the United States. No matter how affirmative an attitude the United States might display toward nationalism in the PRC and Southeast Asia, the United States remains essentially passive with regard to the maintenance of order in Asia. Japan, on the other hand, with its important interests in the region, has been driven into taking on major responsibility in the construction of a new order. Moreover, there is a good possibility that the United States may decide to assign Japan a central role in its new Asian strategy. As these developments have taken place on the great-power level, the countries of Southeast Asia have been thrown into a new situation psychologically, and they are earnestly groping for a new status quo.

In Indochina, the union of North and South Vietnam took place more rapidly than had been expected. A political con-ference between representatives of North and South was held in Saigon in November 1975, and by the time the February 1976 ASEAN summit conference took place, the line at the seven-teenth parallel already was being erased. On April 25 joint elections were held, and in June the first unified parliament convened. As Hanoi became the capital for South Vietnam as well, arrangements for the unification of Vietnam were largely complete. In Laos and Cambodia, too, liberation governments were striving, despite difficulties, to bring their countries under control and were making concrete gains toward that end. Indochina now had reached the stage of a loosely united socialist bloc of nations. The tragedy of divided peoples had ended, and a determined search for indigenous forms of socialism had begun.

Steady efforts to adjust to new realities are also underway among the ASEAN states. Their new awareness of their problems has led to at least three shifts of emphasis: from reliance upon one particular power for security guarantees, from exclusive reliance on military might to a more flexible approach to security, and from bilateral diplomacy to a multilateral regional framework.

Let us briefly examine these trends more closely. Following Malaysia's 1974 example, the Philippines and Thailand established diplomatic ties with the PRC in June and July of 1975, respectively, and in the process they by and large accepted the treaty provision advanced by the PRC opposing hegemony by any power in Asia. Rather than what is usually thought of as "leaning toward the PRC," however, these actions constituted no more than a natural movement away from the past exclusive reliance on relations with the United States. The Philippines carried that tendency one step further by establishing relations with the Soviet Union, following a visit to Moscow by President Marcos in May 1976.

Thailand entered into negotiations with the United States in order to secure administrative control over U.S. military bases, and after brushing aside U.S. resistance, especially with regard to the intelligence collection base at Ramasoon, the Thais succeeded in securing what they have long dreamed of— the virtually complete reversion of U.S. bases. This, too, was from the Thai viewpoint an integral part of efforts to divest themselves of outdated cold war type arrangements.

Finally, the ASEAN attempts to forge a sturdier organization, which began in response to the rapid turnabout in the Indochinese situation, constitute another important aspect of their adjustment to new realities. Altogether, these trends demonstrate a vigorous search for principles around which a new order can be constructed, a search that has emerged with full force out of the confusion following the "loss" of Indochina. By and large the measures that have emerged are entirely appropriate policy adjustments helpful to the stabilization of Southeast Asia.

New Implications for Japanese–U.S. Cooperation

As Southeast Asia's importance to U.S. policy has declined, its importance for Japan has increased proportionally. This turnabout will no doubt pose new problems to be worked out in the context of the Japanese–U.S. relationship. The psychological impact on Japan has been subtle but profound. It has been somewhat of a revelation for the Japanese to discover that there is a region from which the United States, but not Japan, can withdraw at will. The end of the Vietnam War brought no reduction at all in Southeast Asia's relative weight in Japanese foreign policy priorities. While this came as a surprise to many, it was, in a way, only natural. As always, for a number of reasons Southeast Asia remains central to Asian international relations.

In the first place, while it seemed for a brief time that the United States had washed its hands of Asia, it soon became clear that it was not contemplating the complete abandonment of Southeast Asia. President Ford's New Pacific Doctrine, enunciated in Hawaii on his return from the December 1975 PRC visit (with stopovers in the Philippines and Malaysia), formally signalled the U.S. intention to continue its commitment to Southeast Asia on a selective response basis. The announcement of that doctrine gave a psychological boost to those who were apprehensive about the apparent U.S. abandonment of the region. Since then, the United States has recognized ASEAN, even though this recognition may be little more than a formality. The United States also has made diplomatic contacts with the new regime in Vietnam. These are laudable efforts from the Japanese point of view. It is still highly uncertain whether Japan is capable of pursuing an independent policy in Southeast Asia, particularly if the United States loses all interest. However, U.S. involvement so far has remained at a satisfactory level.

Second, postwar Southeast Asia has become another arena for unbridled competition between the Soviet Union and the PRC to fill what they perceive as a regional power vacuum. The Sino-Soviet dispute is being acted out not only in Indochina but in the ASEAN region as well, and with considerable ardor. Ironically, this fact alone has tended to stem any decline in the attention centered on the region.

Third, having engaged the United States in war and come out on top, Vietnam has attained rapidly the position of the foremost military power in the region. Given its peculiar brand of political ideology, the possibility seems to exist, at least in terms of international images, that it could again become a threat to neighboring states. The Vietnamese government also has maintained a slight tilt toward the Soviet Union, as is evident in the recent heightening of tension between Vietnam and the PRC over the Paracel and Spratly islands. That inclination, in turn, introduces a new element into great power relations. It is now impossible to speak of stability in Asia without taking Vietnam into account, and that adds a new and decisive factor in the continued international importance of Southeast Asia.

Fourth, Japan's own Asian diplomacy must not be forgotten. Following the normalization of relations with the PRC in September 1972, Japan has continued, especially in Asia, to strengthen its so-called independent diplomacy. Relations with North Vietnam were successfully established in September 1973, and by capitalizing on such events as the *Shosei-Maru* incident, Japan also has made contacts with North Korea that augur well for the future. Japan's Asian diplomacy has been remarkably successful, moving ahead of U.S. diplomacy on all fronts. The independent diplomatic stance first emerged with the reversion of Okinawa. The question of why it has achieved such successes only in Asia is an interesting topic for speculation, but at any rate, it is hardly surprising that the rationale for an independent diplomacy developed parallel to the stronger sense of responsibility toward Southeast Asia. Certainly, the Japanese are not immune to the belief that areas important for them also have global strategic significance; and

Southeast Asia, through which passes 80 percent of Japan's oil imports and 40 percent of its total trade, is indeed vitally important. It is undeniable, however, that Japan has been slow to recognize that fact.

The joint communiqué issued at the close of Prime Minister Fukuda's meeting with President Carter during the March 1977 visit to Washington appears to have drawn different reactions in the two countries. Paragraph five, the longest one, attracted far more serious public attention in Japan than in the United States. That paragraph included the confirmation that both the United States and Japan are "prepared to continue providing cooperation and assistance in support of the ASEAN countries toward regional cohesion and development." In Japan, this provision was interpreted as public admission that U.S. responsibility in Southeast Asia had been transferred onto the shoulders of Japan. It is unclear whether this interpretation is merely overly cynical or properly realistic. Current U.S. concern for Southeast Asia is very moderate compared to the zeal shown by Japan. Moreover, there is very little evidence that the Japanese government has tried hard to encourage U.S. interest. It appears, in other words, that just as Europe has Africa and the United States has Latin America, Japan is acquiring its own hinterland in Southeast Asia. Japan is now at the point where it must decide whether to be content with that situation or make renewed efforts to resist the tide of history. But the Japanese inability to comprehend fully the overall schema of U.S. Asian policy is causing considerable irritation. Let us now examine present Japanese images of U.S. Asian policy.

Two of the many policies announced by President Carter around the time of his inauguration drew particularly keen attention in Japan: human rights diplomacy and the withdrawal of U.S. forces from South Korea. Human rights diplomacy has been seen in Japan as a strategy concerned primarily with the Soviet Union, one that is likely to be quite effective against that nation and the Eastern European bloc. It is believed, however, that the United States has been forced to play this important trump card because of the unfavorable military balance with the Soviet Union. President Carter seems so preoccupied with the Soviet problem that he is insufficiently attentive to the impact that the policy might have in the developing regions of Asia. So while Japan acknowledges the usefulness of human rights diplomacy, it cannot, as an Asian nation, give it unconditional support.

Regarding the withdrawal of U.S. troops from South Korea, however, Japan's response is just about what one might expect. The Japanese approach to military issues, even those that directly affect its security, is to pose as an uninvolved bystander. This was reflected in Prime Minister Fukuda's dismissal of troop withdrawals as "fundamentally a bilateral issue between the United States and the Republic of Korea." At the same time, Japanese public opinion has become accustomed to thinking of Japan's security in terms of reliance on other powers and tends to welcome unconditionally any arrangement that promises to maintain a military balance in the area. Therefore, a negative reaction arose automatically against recent U.S. moves with regard to the Korean peninsula.

It is also true that anything approaching free and open debate on the issue of troop withdrawals is inhibited by the very fact that it is not just a military problem, but a Korean one as well. Public discussion on such issues is always muted and never searching. It is therefore impossible to expect a consensus to emerge. That being the case, it is all too easy for Japanese attitudes on the question to be taken by the United States as irresponsible and irrational. It is necessary to point out, however, that most Japanese are seriously concerned by what they consider a lack of clarity about how and why U.S. troops are being withdrawn from the Korean peninsula.

One also can detect a deeply rooted feeling that President Carter and those around him are indifferent to Asia and insensitive to what is happening there. This is not incomprehensible if seen as an aspect of the psychological after-effects of the Vietnam War. At any rate, the Japanese continue to believe that in principle the United States is proceeding apace to withdraw from Asia. More exactly, the Japanese generally feel that U.S. policy in Asia is limited completely to the big-power level of relations among the Soviet Union, the PRC, and Japan to the exclusion of active concern with more humble affairs. One even hears the lament that it will be extemely difficult for

Japan and the United States to cooperate in any activity below that level, such as economic development. Be that as it may, what most Japanese want from the Carter administration is some clearer statement of the U.S. vision of Asia's future. Dissatisfaction is rising in Japan over what seems to be the U.S. government's tendency to make important decisions affecting Japan without adequately explaining essential points.

The Japanese also are seriously concerned about the normalization of U.S.–PRC relations. From the standpoint of Japan's equidistance policy, the U.S. failure to enter into extremely close relations with the PRC has not been unwelcome. Yet, the recent rise of anti-Soviet sentiment in Japan has paralleled U.S. moves toward closer ties with the PRC. One is now beginning to hear about new diplomatic possibilities, including a scenario of "collusion among Japan, the United States, and the PRC." Public opinion is still split in this regard, with one side arguing that amicable relations with the Soviet Union should be stressed despite that country's recent toughness in negotiations with Japan and the other espousing cooperation with the United States in approaching the PRC and restraining the Soviet Union.

With regard to the Sino-Soviet split, most Japanese feel that the United States is interested in keeping the dispute going and will utilize all possible diplomatic means to do so. It is not surprising, therefore, that some are apprehensive about Japan's being used as a diplomatic pawn in that game. At any rate, given the apparent anti-Soviet trend of the Carter policy, Japan is confronted with another perplexing issue in its PRC policy. For that reason, too, there is a strong impetus in Japan toward a dialogue with the United States of today. In what way does the United States consider itself a Pacific power? The Japanese are seriously troubled by this question, and their fears should be relieved as soon as possible.

Japan's Policy Toward Southeast Asia

Japan's recent démarche in the realm of Southeast Asian policy was not necessarily a response to U.S. desires. Rather, it resulted from the convergence of a number of historical circumstances. Japan's foreign policy began to change in 1973 when preparations were being made for former Prime Minister Tanaka's January 1974 visit to the ASEAN nations. Hence, it is evident that even before the conclusion of the Vietnam War, the Japanese government had begun to anticipate the course of history. In fact, negotiations toward the establishment of diplomatic relations were initiated at about that time with the Hanoi government. That burst of independent diplomacy was further reinforced by the oil shock that hit the world in autumn 1973. Following that event, Tanaka's visit to Southeast Asia provided an occasion for the people of that region, who had lost all hope for the future, to retaliate bitterly against a Japan that they perceived as interested only in self-serving resource diplomacy. Rather than dampening Japan's concern for that region, however, the riots that greeted Tanaka in Djakarta served to encourage a stance that was more responsive than ever before.

The fall of Vietnam in April 1975 precipitated an overall reassessment of the conditions under which Japan could enjoy greater freedom of action. Hence, that event confirmed an approach that already had begun to emerge—freedom of action for Japan instead of total reliance on an international order constructed by the United States.

The final and decisive element in the development of an active Japanese policy toward Southeast Asia was the first ASEAN summit conference of February 1976. That conference created a situation in which Japan, regardless of past difficulties, had to have an articulate policy toward ASEAN. The Japanese understood the historical significance of the first ASEAN summit conference in a dual sense. In the first place, the meeting legitimized the ASEAN organization itself and the efforts it had made up to that time. Second, by giving concrete substance to ASEAN as a regional bloc, the conference granted credibility to the view that Southeast Asia would divide into two opposing camps. In addition, Japan was forced to take another look not only at the ASEAN nations but at the other nations of the area, including the three Indochinese nations and Burma. In effect, Japan began to formulate a systematic approach to Southeast Asia as a whole.

ASEAN itself began to make great strides following the February 1976 summit conference. Several points were characteristic of the changes that the organization has experienced in the past year or so. In the first place, its members have recovered from the psychological shock of the fall of Vietnam and have developed the confidence to preserve a system that is different from that of the Indochinese nations.

Second, ASEAN increasingly has become an economic as opposed to a political entity. Prior to the summit conference, and partially as a result of the Vietnam War, ASEAN often had spoken out in a political vein, advancing concepts of neutrality and so on. Since last February, however, concern for trade has been increasingly conspicuous. Henceforth, it is desirable when discussing issues relating to ASEAN to treat the organization as primarily being concerned with economic policy.

Third, the ASEAN countries now have greater expectations with regard to Japan. Behind this development is the increasing awareness of the U.S. departure from Asia under the Carter administration and a desire for Japanese participation and know-how in their industrialization projects. Nevertheless, the change in attitude since Tanaka's visit three years ago is very welcome from the Japanese point of view. Of course, Japan has not completed the systematic formulation of its policy toward Southeast Asia. The decision has been made, however, that Japan should respond actively to the changes that have taken place within the region. There remains a sharp divergence of views among Japanese on the subject of Southeast Asian policy, but in fact Japan's postwar Asian policy never has been based on a national consensus. Anyway, the time certainly has come for Japan to do something positive with regard to that region.

Prime Minister Fukuda's recent tour of Southeast Asia and the Fukuda Doctrine that he presented in Manila reflect in concentrated form the changes that have taken place in Japanese attitudes toward Southeast Asia. Japan first sought to respond idealistically and philosophically to the new Southeast Asia, taking up concrete policy alternatives only secondarily. The philosophy of accommodation that Japan currently has in mind is composed of various elements. The following list might seem somewhat visionary, but its components can all be found in the August 7 Japan-ASEAN joint communiqué.

First, ASEAN will have to be seen in a global context. It must be considered as one element in Japan's overall policy approach to relations with the developing nations. Last year's UNCTAD convention provided an opportunity for ASEAN economic policy to be integrated with the philosophy of a new international economic order. That organization's approach to the issue of a common fund for primary products was particularly forceful. Nine of the ten "hard-core" items included therein are relevant to the ASEAN countries, and a couple of them, copper and rubber, are for ASEAN alone. Hence, it is certainly understandable that ASEAN has become acutely concerned with the North-South problem.

Second, vast changes have taken place in Southeast Asia's expectations of Japan, and Japan finds it necessary to be responsive. The common demands of all ASEAN countries are as follows (with the main emphasis on the first three): (1) cooperation in joint ASEAN industrialization projects; (2) access to the Japanese market for ASEAN products, both primary and manufactured; (3) an export indemnity system in order to stabilize the primary product prices; (4) favorable treatment with regard to accumulated debts; and (5) access to Japan's capital market.

When economic relations with Japan are considered in the context of ASEAN's new position, and especially when the Japanese and ASEAN standpoints are juxtaposed against each other, what might be called a "perspective gap" rises in bold relief. An important aspect of that gap, of course, is the spectacular size of the Japanese economy in comparison with the ASEAN countries. From the perspective of Japan, the ASEAN nations are not very important, but from the ASEAN viewpoint, Japan is of critical importance. Trade figures clearly illustrate this disparity. ASEAN nations account for about 10 percent of total Japanese imports and exports, 15 percent of resource imports, and 20 percent of private investment. From the ASEAN side, however, Japan absorbs 30 percent of the total import and export trade that ASEAN nations carry on with many different countries and 100 percent of specific export-oriented resources.

A second important aspect of the perspective gap has to do with Japanese preconceptions. When expansion of trade between Japan and the ASEAN nations is considered a means of responding to charges concerning excess exports and one-sided trade, the assumption is that if Japan cooperates in the development of natural resources for later importation, the trade imbalances will be rectified. However, the error of this preconception finally has been realized. Japan already maintains an unfavorable trade balance with resource-exporting countries such as Indonesia and Malaysia, so when development and import of resources are further accelerated, the result is to heighten the excess of their exports to Japan over imports. Japan, in turn, tends to compensate by further exacerbating its favorable trade balance with those nations in the region that lack resources. Japan must remain sensitive to the differences between ASEAN nations that have resources and those that do not and carefully consider its economic cooperation and aid policy with that distinction in mind.

Third, in the interest of regional peace and stability, relations of peaceful coexistence must be established between ASEAN and the countries of Indochina despite the accumulated antagonisms and the differing political and social systems. Currently, Indochina is quite hostile toward ASEAN. The establishment of peaceful relations between the two blocs not only would play an extremely significant role in the maintenance of stability in the region, but also would affect the degree of independence that the three Indochinese nations are able to manifest in their relations with the Soviet Union and the PRC. Japan can play a useful intermediary role by helping to convey the peaceful intentions of the ASEAN countries to the Indochinese side. It also can keep ASEAN apprised of the true intentions and inward-looking tendencies of the Indochinese nations, thereby allaying needless tension in both blocs.

The role of facilitator in bringing about a new, open Southeast Asia will not be an easy one. Aside from domestic public opinion, Japan's diplomacy could be upset by a number of unpredictable factors such as political instability in the region and developments in the Sino-Soviet dispute. U.S. policy, which has a direct bearing on the conditions for Japan's freedom of action, must also be included. The U.S. approach to the three nations of Indochina is of particular concern. Japan must continue to call upon the United States to play a constructive role throughout Southeast Asia. Japan would welcome, very frankly, a close dialogue between Washington and Hanoi. The first step toward a constructive role for the United States in Southeast Asia must be the establishment of stable relations with Hanoi. One hopes that the United States will become more sensitive to historical change.

Japan and the United States must come to a clear understanding about Southeast Asia. That understanding should incorporate the following elements: first, that the exercise of hegemony in the region by any great power is perceived by the ASEAN and Indochinese nations as inimical to their interests; second, that all the nations of Southeast Asia, including those of Indochina, require economic cooperation from the West; and third, that although they are still under PRC or Soviet influence, the nations of Indochina will most likely escape Sino-Soviet domination and proceed along independent lines. Further, they probably will become socialist countries with a higher degree of freedom than exists in the Eastern European bloc. On these points, at least, it should be possible for Japan and the United States to agree, and on that basis they should be able to follow similar policies with regard to Southeast Asia.

The Role of the United States in Japan's Asian Policy

Four major policy issues have emerged in the context of Japan's approach toward Asia: (1) the establishment of an organically integrated strategy toward the Soviet Union and the PRC; (2) the development of scenarios for the long-term stability of the Korean peninsula; (3) the execution of a Southeast Asian policy directed toward peaceful coexistence between the Indochinese and ASEAN blocs; and (4) the development of a uniquely Japanese policy toward the North-South problem in accordance with the philosophy of a new international economic order that emerged from the fourth UNCTAD convention (1977).

The first two are matters of concern not only for Japan but

for the United States as well, and therefore they require an intimate exchange of views. Obviously, the two nations cannot expect to proceed in lock step on these two issues. Indeed, we are very much aware of the differing interests in certain areas. On the other hand, Japan is concerned that these conflicting interests might give rise to widely divergent policies. Hence, Japan will try systematically to feed her judgments and demands into the U.S. policy-making process. The latter two issues have arisen only recently, and the prime minister's visit to Southeast Asia was the first step in an effort to address those issues with full attention to their close interrelationship. Japan is still a neophyte at this sort of diplomacy but is seriously trying to make concrete progress.

No one, of course, contemplates the total replacement of the United States. Japan has a more modest goal of using economic cooperation to supplement U.S. naval power, thereby bolstering the overall resiliency of the region. The Japanese are aware that the clumsiness of their earlier forays into Southeast Asia has thus far made it difficult to establish relationships of complete mutual trust and confidence. That being the case, it would be most unfortunate for Japan if the simplistic notion that Japan is creating a hinterland or a sphere of influence in Southeast Asia should become widespread. Nonetheless, in the short run Japan will be unable to avoid the impression of having suddenly concentrated on Southeast Asia. The suspicion of another Greater East Asian Co-prosperity Sphere must be combatted continually even though under present international circumstances it is very difficult to convey accurately Japan's true intentions.

The fundamental elements of Japanese foreign policy thinking today are: the complete rejection of cold war-type thought patterns based on the assumption of East-West conflict and a serious response to the North-South problem as an international economic issue; and the encouragement of dialogue between parties still locked in cold war confrontation and the conscientious maintenance of relations of equality with all of them, aiming at the early achievement of peace formulas. Rather than continuing to remain a neutral bystander in all international conflicts, including the Korean confrontation and the Sino-Soviet dispute, Japan will most likely attempt to deepen its interaction with both parties.

As a nation unable to use military force as an instrument of diplomacy, Japan will have an increasing reliance on economic power. The problem is that previous attempts to convert economic power into effective diplomatic negotiating strength have failed. Japan's ability to unleash a torrent of exports has invited anti-Japanese sentiments, and its import patterns, especially in primary goods, have incurred extreme hostility because of the capricious buying habits of private trading companies. Japanese–Australian trade relations provide an excellent example. Japan has not yet succeeded in winning confidence, even in economic matters.

It seems likely that the U.S. image of Japan as irresponsible and lacking in confidence will continue for some time to come. Some rules and mechanisms are still left over from the Asian international order unilaterally constructed by the United States in the years after World War II that Japan has difficulty in dealing with. The United States does not appreciate the extent to which they affect Japanese policy.

Most likely, Japan will continue to refuse unilateral responsibility for any region of Asia. This is not because Japan wishes a free ride, but rather because we recognize our own limitations. On the other hand, Japan will no doubt continue to seek out new ways to make a contribution. The many new commitments made by Prime Minister Fukuda during his visit to Southeast Asia exemplify that effort. Japan certainly will continue to develop its independent diplomacy in the Asian region.

Nevertheless, Japan feels that it must persuade the United States that it is only through Japanese–U.S. harmony and cooperative efforts that Japan's Asian policy can be carried out more effectively. Japan urgently hopes that the United States will take a close look at the remaining vestiges of the Asian order that it constructed and reflect upon whether it might still be possible to do something in the interest of peace and stability in the region.

The two countries should be able to play complementary roles. Japan can do what the United States cannot and the

United States what Japan cannot. The working out of those roles requires a serious and thoughtful effort and unremitting dialogue. In other words, both parties must go beyond the transfer-of-burdens formula to a higher plane of mutual responsibility.

In conclusion, it seems to me that the crisis faced by both Japan and the United States is a crisis of leadership. We can only be apprehensive about the instability of the LDP government in Japan and the inward-looking orientation of the U.S. government. On the other hand, the crisis of leadership in both countries can be viewed as the product of an evolutionary process toward maturity in civil society in general, and in that case it is futile to attempt to reverse the tide. Perhaps the most important thing is that, crisis or not, the leaders of both nations honestly strive to maintain cool-headed judgment and reasoned dialogue on foreign affairs. Asia's future will be determined largely by the ability of Japanese and U.S. leaders to make sound decisions that are not too constrained by narrow domestic political considerations.

9

A Reformist Vision
of Southeast Asian Policy

Ro Watanabe

Prologue—Debate on an Atami Streetcorner

The Japanese newspapers feature bold headlines of Prime Minister Fukuda's visit to the Association of Southeast Asian Nations (ASEAN) summit meeting. He was welcomed warmly in Southeast Asia, they reported, and he offered $1.4 billion in aid. "Cooperative relations between Southeast Asia and Japan are now entering a completely new phase," one claimed.

The day I read this, I overheard some shopkeepers engaged in lively debate as I strolled through a shopping arcade in Atami, a hot-spring resort in my constituency. "With this recession," said one, "the number of visitors to Atami has declined. My shop is about to go broke. Instead of giving all those billions to some foreign country, they ought to give it to us, the ones who really need it." "Now come on," said another, "don't be so narrow minded. Giving the Southeast Asian countries $1 billion now helps them to develop so that some day their purchasing power will increase to $2 billion. That's in Japan's favor, and that's what the LDP says is going to happen. Mark my words, there are prosperous times ahead for Japan."

Newspaper reporters usually pay no attention to this kind of conversation. They are too busy covering the big events and the high-level government announcements to listen to what the man in the street has to say. Journalists seem to operate in another dimension, where the great abstractions like "cooperation" and "solidarity" prevail. When I heard this conversation between the shopkeepers, a light went on. Both of them, I knew, were wrong. But if I suddenly had been called upon to show where they were wrong, I realized unhappily that I would have been unable to offer a single concrete argument.

But why should I be so unnerved? The feeling is related to concerns that have been with me ever since I first became involved in Southeast Asia many years ago. So far as I can see, the opposition, of which I myself am a member, has failed miserably to come up with a viable Southeast Asian policy.

What Southeast Asia Means to Me

In 1953 I was in Rangoon, Burma. Twenty-seven years old, I had been sent to Rangoon by the Japan Socialist Party (JSP) to work on the staff of the secretariat for the newly formed Asian Socialist Conference (ASC). I spent the following two years headquartered in Rangoon, travelling in all of the countries of the region as an advisor to movements for national independence and economic development. World War II was over, and the nations of Asia and Africa either had achieved independence or were deep into nationalist movements for independence.

The ASC was established partly with the support of the democratic socialist parties of Europe, particularly the British Labour Party, for Great Britain had been involved in Asia for a long time. The countries that participated in the inaugural meeting were Burma, India, Indonesia, Israel, Malaya, Lebanon, Nepal, Pakistan, and Japan. As nations still under colonial rule or newly liberated from colonialism or occupation, all of them were full of fire and ambition. The right-left split in the JSP was at its height, but the joint conference delegation worked in harmony. (It was not until late 1959 that Suehiro Nishio and his associates bolted the JSP and formed the Democratic Socialist Party (DSP)).

As I mixed with the leaders of the various Southeast Asian national movements, I must confess that I felt a dilemma: in trying to relate Japan to Southeast Asian nations and their aspirations, there was always a bottleneck. The bottleneck was the attitude of the Japanese people, for whom that region always held great fascination though it remained something of another world. The reaction of the Japanese to my work was usually, "Interesting, but what's the purpose?" The left-wing parties, who could pay attention to nothing but the domestic power struggle, had little interest in what was going on in Southeast Asia.

The ASC was organized at the height of the cold war by Asian political parties committed to moderate, noncommunist socialism. Through its institutional framework, Asian leaders debated such questions as whether a socialism based on democracy, freedom, and nationalism could serve as the guiding ideology for national independence movements, and how democratic socialism could be helpful in nation-building and economic development for countries that had achieved their political independence.

As a result of the Marshall Plan, Europe was making rapid strides in recovering from the war. In Asia, however, the Kuomintang had been defeated by the communists despite massive U.S. support and driven out of Mainland China. In 1950 the Korean War broke out, bringing the United States into full involvement in Asia. Because it came into being just at that critical juncture, the ASC was the focus of much expectation from the emerging nations of the Third World as well as the developed Western countries.

Asia's leaders were groping for a way to achieve autonomy and to develop without adopting communism or falling under U.S. control. They envisaged a system of mutual economic assistance encompassing all nations of Southeast Asia. Politically, they would pursue a policy of nonalignment and seek to bring together a third force of nations. This concept proved an inspiration to many Asians among both the intelligentsia and the people at large.

Eventually, however, the ASC was dismantled before it was able to realize its goals. After the 1957 Katmandu Conference, all official activities of the organization were terminated. With the October 1958 military coup in Burma, the Burmese Socialist Party, ASC's leading force, was outlawed. In December 1960 conflict between King Mahendra and the cabinet led to the suppression of the Nepali Congress Party led by Koirala, and in Indonesia, Sukarno prohibited the Socialist Party from carrying on any political activities. Thus, most members of the ASC were either outlawed or not permitted to function. Even where repression is not the rule and political freedom is guaranteed, democratic socialist parties had somehow lost momentum and remain out of power to this day. This is the case with the JSP and the DSP in Japan, one of the few nations in Asia where full political freedom exists. Many countries in the region are still in the grip of authoritarianism.

At the end of the 1960s, a movement began calling for a new regional organization of democratic socialist parties. The Asia and Pacific Socialist Organization (APSO) was formed in 1972 and held its inaugural meeting in Singapore. Members who had not participated in the original ASC included the People's Action Party of Singapore and the Labour parties from Australia and New Zealand. Also present were the Indian Socialist Party, the Israeli Labor Party, the Malaysian Democratic Action Party, the Korea United Socialist Party, and Japan's JSP and DSP. APSO was chartered as a regional association of political parties devoted to democratic socialism. This organization, which rejects communism, seeks affiliation with the Socialist International. Unfortunately, APSO has not met again since its inception, although plans are now underway for a convention in 1978. While we may still look forward to a revitalized APSO, I have grown increasingly pessimistic about the future of democratic socialism in Asia. I realize that this may seem a rather curious statement for the vice-chairman of this organization to make, but it is based on many years of personal experience.

So much for my personal involvement with Southeast Asia. Nine months before this conference, in December 1976, I was elected to the lower house for the first time, after working on the staff of the JSP Secretariat and then serving as international secretary of the DSP for fifteen years. In Japan, foreign affairs will not get you elected. Perhaps that is one reason for the lateness of my Diet debut. Now everyone tells me that if I am really serious about getting reelected, I should not get involved in international affairs. The message is that a Diet member should instead devote his time to working for the benefit of his constituency. Despite these hard political realities, I chose, with no hesitation whatsoever, the Foreign Affairs Committee as the base of my activities in the Lower House.

One thing I have learned in my limited experience with the committee: Asian problems rarely come up for attention. Most of our attention is given to the United States, particularly concerning trade and security matters. The list has grown somewhat larger in recent months to include greater notice of the energy question; relations with the Soviet Union, particularly concerning the northern territories, fishing rights, and economic cooperation; relations with the PRC, most notably the hegemony clause of the proposed peace treaty; and relations with the European Community, primarily concerning trade. With the sole exception of Korea, there is no heated controversy over Asia between the government and opposition parties.

When I was asked to present my views on Southeast Asia to this conference, it occurred to me to wonder whether Japan really has a policy. If the region is virtually neglected by the House Foreign Affairs Committee, who else in the national legislature can possibly be concerned about it? The situation is truly appalling; the apathy is past the critical point. I will not place the responsibility for this negligence solely on the government and the LDP, for the opposition parties, including my own party, must also accept the blame for their lack of policy and even of interest.

The question to which I address myself is simple: what does Southeast Asia mean to Japan? What does Japan mean to Southeast Asia? What can Japan do *in* and *for* Southeast Asia? What should be the role of the opposition parties in improving our Southeast Asian policy? And, in light of whatever conclusions we reach, how can Japan and the United States cooperate in Southeast Asia? What I say here represents my own views, not the official views of my party.

What Southeast Asia Means to Japan

Tenshin Okakura was a man who left his imprint on the pages of history; a brilliant man, active during the Meiji period from the end of the nineteenth to the beginning of the twentieth century. He was appointed curator of oriental art at the Boston Museum of Fine Arts in 1904. There he rose to worldwide renown as an art critic. His book, *Ideals of the East,* exerted considerable influence on Japan's prewar Asian policy. Although not directly responsible, his notion that "Asia is one" provided one of the ideological foundations for Japanese militarism in its march through Korea, Manchuria, China, and Southeast Asia. Okakura's ideas contributed to what became known as the Greater East Asian Co-prosperity concept.

In prewar Japan, the relationship with Asia was that of ruler and ruled. Japanese in other parts of Asia did not think of themselves as being in independent foreign nations, but in a Japanese dependency or colony. I, too, was raised in a Peking that was then under Japanese control. I spent my early years in a place where Chinese people spoke Japanese and worked for the Japanese. After World War II, the Japanese colonialism ended. With U.S. aid, a decimated Japan headed out on the road to recovery to the tune of the slogan "catch up with Europe." A popular injunction was "learn from foreign countries," but for us that meant the United States and Europe —the advanced industrial nations. For a long time after the war, Southeast Asia receded to the fringes of popular awareness. Meanwhile, a powerful nation took Japan's place in Southeast Asia: the United States. There is little need to go into the reasons for the U.S. presence in Southeast Asia, but that turned Japanese attention again to the region.

Less than one quarter of a century after military defeat, Japan, again riding the crest of rapid economic growth, sought to do business in Southeast Asia. Despite the absence of a clearly formulated government policy for the region, Japanese corporations made steady economic advances. No matter where you go now in Southeast Asia, the signs of Japanese business are plainly visible. This rapid incursion is a major reason for the anti-Japanese movement in the five ASEAN nations, a movement against the Japanese overpresence. A capitalist country like Japan cannot sit back while its industries are being boycotted, so it has to send what it calls aid, which in fact is an attempt to buy off or pacify the Southeast Asians so that

Japan, Inc., can conduct business as usual. As far as Japan is concerned, Southeast Asia represents essentially a site of Japanese industrial expansion, a market for Japanese goods, and a recipient of Japanese aid.

Prior to his recent trip to Burma and the ASEAN nations, Prime Minister Fukuda stated that the visit had little to do with "money or goods. What we seek is increased mutual understanding through heart-to-heart communication." This is an approach designed to appeal to the emotions, yet the prime minister might be interested to know that the peoples he has visited are far more concerned about the money and the goods than about heart-to-heart understanding.

Like the government and the intellectuals, most Japanese have their eyes glued to what goes on in the United States and Europe. They esteem highly the history, culture, and people of the West, but the number who believe that there is anything to be learned from Southeast Asia is miniscule.

These days, because of the enormous accumulation of surplus dollars, there has been an unprecedented boom in foreign travel. In 1976, 2,850,000 Japanese travelled abroad, and the largest portion of them, 630,000, visited Southeast Asia. With so many people exposed to the actual conditions and lifestyles of other countries, one might expect some new attitudes and understanding toward the region to emerge. Sad to say, however, the old-fashioned prejudices linger on. The majority of Japanese continue to want to know more about the United States and Europe; their interest in Southeast Asia is virtually nil. This attitude is likely to continue for some time.

Yet, there has never been greater need for mutual understanding and cooperation. The day when the government, the opposition parties, businessmen, and the general public come to understand Asian problems is a long way off. Most shocking of all is that the mass media, whose job it is to help shape public opinion, is equally guilty of this narrow-mindedness.

What Japan Means to Southeast Asia

The attitude that "Asia is one" is still part of the popular ideological baggage. Even now Japanese steadfastly refuse to abandon the preposterous notion that Southeast Asia is a single entity. In history, culture, and lifestyle, each of these nations is unique, each exemplifying the diversity of value systems and world views. Multiethnic societies such as Singapore, the Philippines, and Malaysia have problems that are very different from those of Japan, whose society is more or less ethnically homogenous. We must realize that we cannot use the same criteria to judge each country and each people. Needless to say, the attitudes of people in Southeast Asia toward Japan differ from nation to nation and from generation to generation, as I know from my own, sometimes quite painful, experience.

The attitudes of Southeast Asians toward Japan vary according to whether the particular nation has or has not experienced Japanese colonial rule. When I visited areas that had, I was very aware that many people could not forgive Japan's imperialism. On the mild side were remarks such as, "I know you're not responsible, but there are things Japan did to us during the war that I will never forget." There was also another type of people who had been educated in Japan before 1945 and are now in their forties or fifties, often in some position of leadership. They would comment, "I admire Japan. Your country has done exactly what I hoped it would. Despite defeat, it has sprung back to complete recovery and is now numbered among the great industrial nations of the world. The Japanese devotion to the work ethic is something we Southeast Asians would do well to learn." To such people, Japan is the model for nation-building.

I also met members of the government elite in Indonesia, the Philippines, and Malaysia, people who had studied in the United States and who were not as enthusiastic about Japanese economic growth as the Japan-trained group. Although they asserted the need for cooperation, I sensed that they preferred to maintain a certain distance and a cooler approach to contact with Japan.

Students whom I met in Singapore and Thailand were very displeased with the way in which Japanese corporations and Japanese citizens, including tourists, behaved in their countries. For a good sample of the opinion of youth, one need only recall the anti-Japanese riots and the demonstrations against

Prime Minister Tanaka's 1974 visit. Observing the attitudes of Southeast Asians toward Japan cannot fail to convince us that we are separated by a tremendous gap.

While Southeast Asia is just beginning to emerge from its agrarian economy toward industrialization, Japan has completed its industrialization and is now plagued by the problems of pollution and environmental destruction. The disparity in national development, not to mention the differences in value orientations, do not make for many points in common. The differences are extreme, and part of the reason is the inadequacy of communication, which perhaps is even more serious than that between the United States and Japan. Between Japanese and the ordinary man in Southeast Asia, the gap is much greater, since there is almost no opportunity for the two sides to communicate.

Aid without a Philosophy

Often, the participants in the dialogue with Japan are an elite educated in the United States who envision the modernization of their nation along European or U.S. lines. Just as the Japanese government's policy toward Southeast Asia does not have full domestic support, neither do the Southeast Asian governments reflect the understanding support of their people in their dealings with Japan.

Southeast Asian leaders are sensitive about the overpresence of Japanese industry and goods, but their need for economic relations with Japan is nevertheless pressing. For Japan, despite the low level of awareness of Southeast Asia from the top layers of government down to the ordinary citizen, the region will become of even greater importance in the coming years. Japan's aid to Southeast Asia will have to have the support of the Japanese people and will have to be truly helpful in raising the living standards of the people in the recipient countries.

Nations with major social or economic inequities are potentially unstable or prone to crisis. The same may be said for the relationship between nations. A world with great differences and inequalities among nations is crisis-prone.

Real peace in Asia depends on how successful we are in correcting these disparities; and, needless to say, stability in Asia will further the cause of world peace.

Aid to any region must be granted on much broader criteria than whether or not it will help Japan obtain markets and resources. The largest portion of Japanese assistance goes to Southeast Asia, but the impression cannot be avoided that our aid policy is makeshift. Certainly, the aid has no clear philosophical base capable of answering the question of why we offer aid at all, or why cooperation is necessary. During his recent trip, Prime Minister Fukuda suggested that his $1.4 billion assistance pledge might help us "escape international censure." I find it curious that international opinion should be the the sole determinant of how Japan conducts its aid program. It behooves the opposition parties, the government, and the LDP to do some serious thinking about the basic premises of Japan's Southeast Asian policy.

Before Prime Minister Fukuda visited the United States, all the opposition leaders were invited for consultation. Meetings like this are becoming established procedure prior to any major move in relation to the United States. But before Prime Minister Fukuda's Southeast Asian trip, there had been no consultations. On the other hand, even if there had been, it is doubtful that anything productive would have resulted, since the opposition views on Southeast Asia are so insubstantial that they would have had no realistic alternatives to offer. Whatever opposition shadow policy does exist is superficial; as far as foreign relations are concerned, almost all attention is concentrated on the United States, particularly the Mutual Security Treaty. If there is a policy for Southeast Asia, it is purely coincidental.

The opposition, the government, and the LDP have begun recently to pool their forces in support of the aid slogans: "Increase official assistance rather than private loans" or "Raise government aid to 0.7 percent of the GNP" (the present rate is 0.24 percent). This is all well and good, except that this new approach was not decided on its own grounds but rather in response to external pressure: "The EC countries are criticizing us" or "The recipient nations are hostile to Japan."

The opposition has a tendency to use a fixed set of political formulas and slogans in attacking government policy: foreign aid is too tied to corporate interests, official assistance is far too low, and so on. One thing that always bothers me about Japanese political parties is the extreme difference between what they say and what they really mean. The opposition demand for an increase in official assistance is just a pretense. In fact, both the government and the opposition are playing the same tune: "Let's not do anything that brings us criticism or embarrassment in the eyes of the world." If you will permit me a slight, but only a slight, overstatement, Japanese political parties are all essentially isolationist. They are all protectionist at heart. Protectionism still prevails because the parties advocate only those programs that will ingratiate them with the voters, carefully avoiding anything that might be unpopular. It is the popular opinion that giving $1.5 billion of the taxpayers' money to foreign countries is unnecessary, particularly in view of the present domestic recession. Not one political party seems to have the strength of conviction to try to educate or persuade the silent majority. Even those who call themselves progressives are often vehement advocates of an ultraprotectionist trade program.

During the 1960s, there was a great deal of international pressure on Japan to liberalize its imports. The left-wing parties were even more vocal than the conservatives in opposing additions to the liberalization list in fear of the collapse of some industries and the growth of unemployment. Today's talk of more aid and cooperation to help ASEAN nations modernize has made workers anxious about their jobs. I doubt that the parties on the left can offer any persuasive rationales to persuade the people that aid is necessary, despite its potential disadvantages for them.

What is needed for a viable reformist policy toward Southeast Asia is a clear recognition of the following: (1) The modernization of Southeast Asia will force drastic changes in Japan's industrial structure. If the opposition is to be persuasive to both labor and business, the inevitability of the structural change must be clearly acknowledged. (2) Cooperation with the ASEAN countries must give greater emphasis to trade than to assistance, encouraging them to develop through their own efforts. As Japan imports more from them, it must absorb shocks harmful to agriculture and certain industries. To that end, preparations must be made for reshuffling the labor force and industrial facilities into other sectors.

Proposals for Opposition Action

A plan for Japan's future relations with Southeast Asia cannot be premised on the present conditions in those countries. It must be calculated in the expectation of a much higher level of development; this may be achieved more quickly than is usually assumed because Southeast Asian nations have a good deal of resiliency and a fairly high level of modernization. The nationalists of Southeast Asia aim to build modern industrial states, whether after the Western European, the PRC, or the Soviet model, not to continue as pastoral or agrarian societies. Competition and friction with the advanced industrial nations will be unavoidable, as the experiences of Japan and the United States, Japan and the EC, and Japan and South Korea show. The Japanese must prepare themselves for the eventual decline or destruction of various industries as Southeast Asia industrializes—textiles is the most obvious example. We must anticipate major social changes. Once restrictions are lifted, as they must be, on rice imports from Thailand, Burma, and Vietnam, where the cost is one-tenth of Japan's domestically produced rice, our own rice growers will have been dealt a fatal blow.

Near Shimoda is one of the world's largest producing areas of the *mikan* or mandarin orange. When Japanese started to eat oranges and grapefruit from California, the farmers in this area were forced to cut down their *mikan* trees. It is not hard to imagine many similar situations resulting from the growth of Southeast Asia. Southeast Asia must be considered in a context not just of changes in structure but of evolving shifts of popular taste and lifestyle. The postwar generation, raised on bread made from wheat flour imported from the United States and Canada, eats very little rice. The agricultural cooperatives have been trying to reverse this trend with a campaign that tells women that rice will make them beautiful. So far, the campaign does not seem to be very effective.

Because Southeast Asia is becoming so important to Japan, enormous social change can be expected, and we must start preparing the social, economic, and cultural conditions capable of accommodating this change. This endeavor urgently requires competent political leadership. Social reforms are bound to arouse the opposition of specific interest groups; in the worst case, they might even invoke a strong nationalistic outburst. Our parties have not yet learned how to persuade people that reform is necessary, and they have shown a consistent tendency to yield to the forces of nationalist reaction.

Here, I would like to present some proposals for an opposition aid policy:

1. Appeal to the people with an idealistic philosophy of aid, even if at first it may seem ineffectual. Try to convince them that assistance to Southeast Asia is necessary to create a global welfare society, to universalize the "welfare society in one country" concept.
2. Cultivate our own channels of aid activity while at the same time pressing for improvements in the government's development assistance programs and in the private sector's economic cooperation. For example, they can encourage labor unions and other nongovernmental organizations (NGOs) to participate actively in cultural exchange and technical assistance programs. They can send young workers and engineers as volunteers for technical assistance, organize youth exchange programs, and sponsor a variety of educational activities. The reform parties should be ready to raise funds for these programs from among the people, but they also should demand that half of the government budget of 1 percent of GNP be allocated for use by NGO channels.
3. Push forward with preparations for the expected changes in the industrial structure and in society at large. For example, the opposition can propose an adjustment program for industries that will be most heavily affected by the changing industrial structure. A

better, more expanded system of financial assistance and job training for workers in those industries will be provided.

4. Produce concrete plans for dealing with Southeast Asian security problems. These must take into account the necessity of the continued military presence of U.S. forces in Asia, based on treaty commitments between the United States on the one hand and ASEAN, Japan, South Korea, and Taiwan on the other. Japan's role will be limited to nonmilitary areas. Rather than a military commitment, economic cooperation of the type outlined in this paper must be provided. Japan also must extend economic assistance and cooperation while maintaining a friendly relationship with the communist governments of Indochina, the PRC, North Korea, and the Soviet Union. Japan's military power will be restricted exclusively to defense, and its extent will be determined by the custom of expending not more than 1 percent of the GNP for equipping this force. (As we embark upon the era of the 200-mile limit for exploitation of the seas, it will be necessary to bolster our naval forces in the near future and strengthen our antisubmarine capability.

If a consensus can be created effectively by the reformist parties on the basis of these proposals, it will be possible for the government to support a forward-looking policy in Southeast Asia. And I believe that this will be possible even if the conservative-reformist "reversal" that political analysts talk about occurs in the not-too-distant future.

Part 4
Japan and International Politics

10
The Transformation in Japanese Domestic Politics and Japanese–U.S. Relations

Tokusaburo Kosaka

The Changing Pattern of Politics

To assess the outlook for Japanese–U.S. relations it is essential to understand the domestic political changes underway and see where they are likely to lead. The December 1976 House of Representatives election and the July 1977 House of Councillors election have reduced the ruling Liberal Democratic Party (LDP) seats in the Diet very close to the opposition level. Along with this neck-and-neck race between government and opposition is a new trend toward even greater party fragmentation, a reflection of the increasing differentiation of publics and values. The major effect of these developments has been to destroy completely the pattern of politics that has obtained since 1955.

The recent transformation of the political landscape has altered the relative weight of the administrative and legislative branches. This situation is beyond the experience of Japan's officials. In this respect also, Japanese politics appears to have entered upon an entirely new era. One can only speculate whether the political system will be able to maintain its historic stability under these new conditions. It is even open to question whether the present configuration will hold. If not, what kind of change can be expected? What will the transformation of political structure mean for the decision-making process? Will Japanese democracy function properly and continue to mature? Finally, what are the domestic and international factors that might radically alter the overall trends?

Any attempt to outline the future of Japanese–U.S. relations must make some assumptions about these fundamental issues of domestic political change. In this paper I shall touch upon them from the perspective of one personally involved, attempting to place them in the context of developments since the First Shimoda Conference was convened over ten years ago. My fundamental concern is the sort of political foundation upon which a true Japanese–U.S. partnership can be founded.

The Era of Absolute LDP Majorities

In 1968, the year after the First Shimoda Conference, Japan's GNP topped that of West Germany, and we became the number two economic power in the Free World. That year has a symbolic significance with regard to the current transformation in Japanese politics.

Japan adopted a new constitution following its defeat in World War II, and Article Nine renounced one element of national sovereignty—the right of resorting to war as a means of settling international disputes. The United States–Japan Security Treaty not only guaranteed the security of an unarmed Japan but freed it from the burden of making complex choices on the rough-and-tumble stage of world politics. Moreover, with abundant supplies of low-priced oil and other resources from abroad, in an international system of free trade supported by the IMF and GATT Japan was able to throw the full energies of its people into the task of economic development.

From the Meiji restoration in 1868, Japan's national goal and the central theme of its modernization policy have been to catch up with and surpass the advanced nations of the West. In the 1960s that tradition again emerged in the extremely down-to-earth policy objectives of Prime Minister Hayato Ikeda's income-doubling plan.

Against that background, 1955 was to become an extremely important turning point. In that year the two conservative parties, the Liberal and the Democratic, joined to form the LDP, and the right- and left-wing socialists merged to form the Japan Socialist Party (JSP). The relative strength of the two new parties in the House of Representatives stood at 299 seats

for the LDP and 120 for the JSP, and in the House of Councillors at 120 for the conservatives and 68 for the socialists. This
configuration inaugurated the era of two-party politics with
the LDP retaining an absolute majority, a pattern that lasted
for more than twenty years. In labor relations, 1955 also saw the
beginnings of the spring wage offensive as an annual ritual
for determining wage levels.

The efficiency of the decision making and the broadly
acceptable income distribution that developed, along with the
broad national consensus that they reflected, made possible
very close teamwork between the LDP, the bureaucracy, and
business. The success of that cooperation manifested itself in
annual growth rates during the 1960s that averaged 11.1 percent. Today Japan is the number two power in the Free World
and is number two or three in the entire world. It should be
noted that, even in comparison to other advanced industrial
nations, the fruits of that rapid development were very equitably distributed among all strata of society. According to a
comparative study of income distribution among OECD member nations, published in 1976 by the OECD, Japan ranked first
in equitability of income distribution, followed by Australia
and Sweden, in that order (*see* Table 10.1). The report based
its findings on declared cash income after taxes, dividing each
nation's households into income brackets of 10 percent each.
In the bottommost two deciles, Japan ranked highest in the
total income earned by members of these two groups—3 percent for the lowest and 4.9 percent for the next. The averages
for all member nations were 2.1 percent and 3.8 percent,
respectively.

Underlying that relatively equitable income distribution
are several factors: the workers' bargaining strength, which
has resulted from the spring offensive, and the special price
subsidies for staple foodstuffs, which maintain farmer incomes
at levels approximating those of industrial workers. At any
rate, it is possible to assert that largely as a result of these
circumstances the Japanese people began to believe firmly
that Japan's economic growth and the free economic system
upon which it was based were directly related to welfare
expansion and improvements in their own income. They also

TABLE 10.1 OECD Countries, Distribution of Income After Taxes by Income Bracket (in percentages)[a]

		I	II	III	IV	V	VI	VII	VIII	IX	X
Australia	(1966-67)	2.1	4.5	6.2	7.3	8.3	9.5	10.0	12.5	15.1	23.7
Canada	(1969)	1.5	3.5	5.1	6.7	8.2	9.7	11.2	13.1	15.9	25.1
France	(1970)	1.4	2.9	4.2	5.6	7.4	8.9	9.7	13.0	16.5	30.4
W. Germany	(1973)	2.8	3.7	4.6	5.7	6.8	8.2	9.8	12.1	15.8	30.3
Italy	(1969)	1.7	3.4	4.7	5.8	7.0	9.2	9.8	11.9	15.6	30.9
Japan	(1969)	3.0	4.9	6.1	7.0	7.9	8.9	9.9	11.3	13.8	27.2
Netherlands	(1967)	2.6	3.9	5.2	6.4	7.6	8.8	10.3	12.4	15.2	27.7
Norway	(1970)	2.3	4.0	5.6	7.3	8.6	10.2	11.7	13.0	15.1	22.2
Spain	(1973-74)	2.1	3.9	5.3	6.5	7.8	9.1	10.6	12.5	15.6	26.7
Sweden	(1972)	2.2	4.4	5.9	7.2	8.5	10.0	11.5	13.5	15.7	21.3
England	(1973)	2.5	3.8	5.5	7.1	8.5	9.9	11.1	12.8	15.2	23.5
U.S.	(1972)	1.5	3.0	4.5	6.2	7.8	9.5	11.3	13.4	16.3	26.6
Average		2.1	3.8	5.2	6.6	7.9	9.5	10.7	12.6	15.5	26.3

[a] If we neglect the minor differences among nations from group III on (because the differences are mostly statistically insignificant), we could concentrate our attention on the figures in columns 1 and 2. These figures show that Japanese groups I and II receive the highest income among twelve nations, which could be interpreted as subtle indication of equal income distribution in Japan.

took a great deal of pride in Japan's achievement of the second highest GNP in the Free World. It was this broad, positive consensus among the Japanese people that permitted the LDP to hold an absolute majority in the Diet and provide a degree of continuity in regime unprecedented among democratic nations.

The Response and Role of the Opposition

The reaction of the JSP and the Japan Communist Party (JCP) to LDP policy was symmetrically contrary. Whereas the LDP took Western Europe and the United States as models and pursued radical reform in a very practical manner, the opposition parties took the socialist nations as their models and criticized the LDP's modernization policy from an idealistic point of view. As for security policy, particularly in contrast to the government's support of the United States–Japan Security Treaty and reliance on the U.S. nuclear umbrella, the opposition espoused unarmed neutrality and reliance for security on the "justice and faith of the peace-loving peoples of the world," to use the words of the Preamble of the Constitution. In 1960 part of the right wing of the JSP broke away to form the Democratic Socialist Party (DSP), and in 1964 the Komei Party was formed under the aegis of the Soka Gakkai, a lay Buddhist organization. These new minority parties also oriented their policies around opposition to the LDP and the United States.

To simplify greatly, the focal points of contention between conservatives and progressives during that era were the LDP policies of modernization and support for the United States–Japan Security Treaty. The opposition parties represented those ideologically dissatisfied with the LDP and looked out for the interests of labor unions and other interest groups. They also established channels for interchange with socialist countries and functioned to check the excesses of LDP policy.

The opposition parties were aided greatly during that period by the U.S. policy of full-scale intervention in Vietnam. Their charge that the powerful United States was waging a "dirty war" to deprive the Vietnamese people of the right of self-determination was on the whole quite convincing to the Japanese. The treaty, they argued, was a military alliance in support of the Vietnam War, thereby aggravating tensions in the Far East. This propaganda was a persistent thorn in the side of the LDP, for whom the treaty constituted the fundamental framework for Japanese–U.S. relations.

In about the mid-1960s, however, just as the fruits of rapid economic growth were spreading among the people, the Soviet Union, and China, which had been constant and bitter critics of the treaty up to that time, began to change their views. They began to value the treaty as a means of maintaining the status quo and refrained from frontal attacks. Also, there was considerable confusion in the socialist world, including the rebellion in Czechoslovakia, the Sino-Soviet dispute, and the Great Proletarian Cultural Revolution. These events, along with the stagnation of the socialist economies, highlighted the advantages of a free economic system. The opposition critique began to lose its credibility.

System Change and Political Multipolarization

The 1970s brought to the surface some tendencies that during the 1960s had only been latent. The first of these was the new international environment symbolized by the Nixon shocks of 1971 and the oil shock of 1973. The Nixon shocks made Japanese aware of the relative reduction in the formerly preponderant economic and military power of the United States. They also brought home the necessity for Japan, which formerly had moved internationally within the framework of the Mutual Security Treaty and U.S. world strategy, to make clear what role it intended to play. The "special" Japanese–U.S. relationship no longer existed. The message of the oil shock was that Japan's energy problems would become very serious as early as the mid-1980s. The condition of unlimited cheap resources, which had supported Japan's rapid growth from the Ikeda era onward, was a thing of the past.

Also newly apparent was the fundamental social change that had taken place in Japanese society as a result of accelerated economic growth. In the twenty-year period between 1955 and

1975, fully one-third of the Japanese population, or thirty-seven million people, left rural areas and moved to the heavily urbanized Pacific coast. The effect of this migration was to dissolve the rural society that had served both as the power base of the LDP and the foundation of a truly Japanese social order. Not only was there now a general sense of transiency, but the heavy influx of population to the cities touched off an urban nightmare stemming from inadequate development of transportation, housing, running water, and other public facilities.

Also, not only did the development of the heavy chemical sectors of industry cause environmental pollution, but consumer prices soared, principally for goods and services provided by the agricultural and small- and medium-sized enterprise sectors where productivity was low. Runaway inflation, which reached an extreme following the oil shock, fostered an antibusiness mood and lent fuel to residents' and consumers' movements that demanded the rectification of social injustice.

To the changes in the climate of opinion must be added the metamorphosis in attitude brought about by the across-the-board wage hikes achieved through spring wage offensives. Some sociologists hold that a transformation of values occurs once the $1,500 level is crossed in per capita real national income. This benchmark was passed in Japan between 1969 and 1970, and sure enough, the tendency of values to shift away from economics grew markedly.

All in all, then, the national consensus that formed around the drive for rapid economic growth may be said to have quickly disintegrated in the wake of several developments: Japan's goal of economic growth had been reached in the form of the second highest GNP in the free world; the international environment had changed; and a metamorphosis had occurred in national values as a result of wholesale domestic social change.

The oil shock in particular profoundly shook the people's hard-won sense of satisfaction with life. According to a survey on living conditions carried out by the prime minister's office, the percentage of those expressing satisfaction with their lives,

which before the oil shock had advanced to about 60 percent,
fell after that event by January 1974 to 54 percent; by November
of that year it was down to 50 percent. From the opposite
perspective, whereas 37 percent expressed dissatisfaction before
the shock, that figure became 45 percent in January 1974 and 48
percent by November (*see* Figure 10.1). In other words, in that
year the proportion dissatisfied was almost the same as the
proportion satisfied. The impact of this rising discontent
appeared in concentrated form in the results of the 1974 House
of Councilors election, which saw LDP support ebb to the
point where the opposition gained nearly the same number
of seats. It also revealed a further acceleration of a trend toward
a multiparty system and an increase in the number of voters
who refused to support any party at all.

The Rise of the New Middle Class and Conservatism

As a result of the oil shock, Japan's real economic growth
in 1974 stood at a minus 0.3 percent, the first time that real
growth was negative since the desperate immediate postwar
years. The shock was gradually overcome in 1975, with a
growth of 3.4 percent, and in 1976 with a 5.8 percent growth.
During the recovery period, consumer prices leaped 21.4 percent in 1974, were down to 10.4 percent in 1975, and by 1976
had levelled off at a rate of increase of 9.4 percent. Unemployment, on the other hand, despite slight percentage increases,
was kept by Japanese labor management practices to a real-
number level of only slightly more than one million individuals, or about 2 percent of the labor force. This is usually
low for an advanced economy (*see* Table 10.2).

Hence, Japan was able to overcome the oil shock without
transferring very much of the burden onto the population. But
the secrets of that success were deficit financing by the government and lower profit growth rates for private enterprise. The
government's reliance on public bonds in proportion to its
general accounts budget was 11.3 percent in 1974; by 1975 it
had risen to 26.3 percent; and in 1976 it was up to 29.9 percent.
Also, it is noteworthy that the rate of increase in business
profits (on an all-industry basis) fell from 60.9 percent in 1973

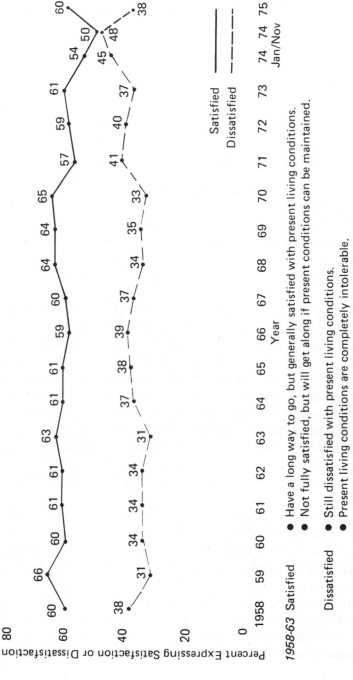

FIGURE 10.1 Level of Satisfaction Regarding Living Conditions

TABLE 10.2   Japanese Economic Growth, Consumer Price Increases,
and Unemployment Rates, 1973-1976 (in percentages)

	1973	1974	1975	1976
Economic growth rate (in real terms)	6.4	0.3	3.4	5.8
Consumer price increases	16.1	21.8	10.4	9.4
Unemployment rate	1.5	1.9	2.0	—

to 2.9 percent in 1974, and from there to minus 28.8 percent in 1975 (*see* Table 10.3). What this means is that Japan tided over the oil shock by putting the government in the red and lowering corporate profits, thus avoiding any substantial harm to the average citizen.

As a result, the index of satisfaction with living standards, which had fallen to 50 percent right after the oil shock in 1974, by 1975 was back up to 60 percent; the degree of dissatisfaction, too, that had reached 48 percent in 1974 turned back down to 38 percent in 1975. Hence, both dimensions had largely recovered their former levels. This means that Japan's success in weathering the oil shock restored popular confidence in the security of its own livelihood and restored social stability. In order to understand this strong resiliency, it is necessary to look into Japanese attitudes and values.

According to surveys conducted by the prime minister's office, in 1958 only 37 percent of the population rated their own living standard in the "middle of the middle" class. From then on, however, this proportion increased steadily, until in 1973 it had reached 61 percent. When this category is grouped with those who rated themselves "upper middle" and "lower middle," we reach a total of about 90 percent of the population identifying themselves as "middle class" in the 1970s (*see* Figure 10.2).

While the members of this large group do not usually have large accumulated assets, they receive an income sufficient to guarantee their basic life needs. That being the case, they are for the time being satisfied with the status quo and anxious to

TABLE 10.3 The Reliance on Bonds Relative to the General Budget and the Rate of Increase for Corporate Profits, 1973-1976 (in percentages)

	1973	*1974*	*1975*	*1976*
Reliance on bonds as part of the general accounts budget	11.9	11.3	26.3	29.9
Rate of increase of corporate profits	60.9	2.9	-28.8	—

preserve their position. Indeed, their basic characteristic is an instinct for self-preservation, or what might be called conservatism. However, the perceived self-interests of this huge, self-defined middle class are far from uniform. There is within this broad stratum a wide range of value orientations and splits between urban and rural, between one industry and another, and so on. Moreover, according to specialists, they generally fall into one of two types with regard to political action: those who are attentive to regional and national problems and those who focus inward on their own little worlds.

This vast middle class holds the key to the future of Japanese politics. One source of information on middle class attitudes is a survey of Tokyo and Yokohama youth, carried out by the Japan Broadcasting Corporation (NHK) in November 1976. It was found that 49 percent of the lowest age group, eighteen to twenty-two, expressed "support of conservative government"; in NHK's 1972 survey the figure was 38 percent. And the proportion supporting "progressive government" fell from 47 to 38 percent (*see* Figure 10.3). This is the first survey to show higher youth support for conservatives than for progressives. What is particularly striking is that the survey was carried out in the midst of the Lockheed scandal and among the most fully urbanized segment of the population. The degree of conservatism within that age group is therefore all the more striking. The LDP, however, thus far has been unable to offer this group a sense of meaning or of worthwhile life goals, and in consequence has been unable to win the group's full support. This

FIGURE 10.2 Class Identification

Total Middle	Upper Middle	Middle Middle	Year	Lower Middle	Lower
72	3	37	1958[a]	32	17
73	3	37	1959	33	17
77	4	41	1960	32	13
76	4	41	1961	31	13
			b		
87	7	50	1964[c]	30	8
86	7	50	1965	29	8
87	7	52	1966	28	7
88	6	53	1967	29	7
87	8	51	1968	28	8
88	7	52	1969	30	8
90	8	57	1970	25	7
89	7	56	1971	26	6
89	7	58	1972	25	7
90	7	61	1973	22	6
91	7	61	1974/Jan	23	6
91	7	58	1974/Nov	23	5
90	7	59	1975	23	5

[a] 1958-1961, the question asked was, "How well off is your household against the nation as a whole?" The upper category was 0% for this period.

[b] 1962-63, no survey taken.

[c] 1964-75, the question asked was, "How would you rate your standard of living from the viewpoint of society?" The upper category was 1% in 1964.

FIGURE 10.3   Individuals Agreeing With NHK Survey Statements, 1972 and 1976 (in percentages)

NHK Survey Statements	Age:	1972 18-22	1976 18-22	23-27
Conservative government must continue.		7	8	8
It would be better if a conservative government were to continue.		38	49	45
		31	41	37
It would be better if a progressive government were to be formed.		32	29	30
A progressive government must be formed		47	37	43
		15	8	13

failure is one of the reasons the recent election ended in such a delicately drawn balance between the LDP and the opposition.

The Age of LDP-Opposition Parity

These developments were reflected clearly in the 1976 general election. In 1976 the Lockheed scandal, Japan's counterpart to Watergate, dominated the horizon. It was held up as evidence of the corruption, almost inevitable, in a party that remains in power for so long. Inside the LDP it touched off a furious debate over party reform and a serious sense of crisis. One result was the New Liberal Club's (NLC) decision to bolt the party.

The outcome of the 1976 general election, carried out under the pall of Lockheed, brought resounding defeat to the LDP: twenty-two seats fewer than it had won in the preceding election. At the same time, however, the JCP—the LDP's principal attacker during the Lockheed incident—also unexpectedly went down to crushing defeat, and the JSP barely held steady.

TABLE 10.4   1976 House of Representatives Election Results

	Post-Election Seats	Seats Won in Previous Election
LDP	249	271
JSP	123	118
JCP	17	38
Komei	55	29
DSP	29	19
NLC	17	0
Independent	21	16
Total	511[a]	491

[a]The statutory number of Diet seats was increased by 20 over the preceding election.

The most striking success was achieved by the NLC, with seventeen seats, and the so-called "middle of the road" parties —the Komeito and the Democratic Socialists (*see* Table 10.4).

One way to interpret the outcome is to say that the people definitely wanted the LDP and the opposition to be roughly equal, but that their support for the NLC, which is a reform/ conservative offshoot of the LDP, and for the Komeito and the DSP showed that they preferred gradual and moderate reform. What appears to be at work here is the desire of the new middle class to preserve its vested interests.

Following the election, Prime Minister Takeo Miki was replaced by Takeo Fukuda, and Japan once again turned to deal with the difficult domestic and international problems facing it. First was the elusiveness of economic recovery, which plagued Japan as it did the other advanced industrial countries. Japan was under intense pressure to take the lead as an "engine country" in pulling the world out of the economic doldrums. At the same time, the likelihood had increased that protectionist trade measures would be adopted in various countries. Second, the growing trend toward the establishing of 200-mile exclusive fishery zones made public opinion particularly sensitive to the tough Soviet stand in the bilateral fishery negotiations. As a result, tension between the two nations rose. The third problem was the Carter administration's demand for a halt in Japan's reprocessing of nuclear fuel. Since Japan intended the plutonium processing for peaceful purposes, primarily to secure its future energy supplies, the U.S. demand introduced a note of disharmony into Japanese–U.S. relations.

According to a 1977 NHK survey, 40.7 percent of the Japanese felt that Japan should take steps to obtain resources while considering the position of other countries, even if it meant bearing a fairly heavy cost; fully 32.5 percent believed that Japan should reduce living standards in order to proceed in the direction of self-sufficiency. Those who in one way or another felt insecure about Japan's future resources totalled 84.8 percent.

Hence, the Japanese headed into the July 1977 House of Councillors election strongly at odds with the superpowers— the Soviet Union and the United States—over problems directly related to their livelihood, such as energy and food. While they basically were satisfied with their lives, they harbored a sense of uneasiness about the future. The focal point of the election was whether the opposition parties would win more seats than the LDP.

The election, however, did not bring the awaited dramatic changes: the status quo remained more or less unchanged. The LDP continued its slow decline, the JSP stagnated, and the JCP went down to stunning defeat. The Komeito and DSP continued their modest gains, and while the NLC fought a good fight, the other new political forces were soundly beaten (*see* Table 10.5).

While the LDP and opposition forces ended in a dead heat, it is important that an overall reversal was averted and that the Komeito and the DSP made gains. These facts suggest that the Japanese people were not in favor of radical political change, and that despite severe pressures, both domestic and international, they strongly preferred political stability. Moreover, the defeat of the JCP and the indifferent showing of the JSP indicate that their policies were unconvincing to a middle-class electorate bent on maintaining its standard of living.

TABLE 10.5   Results of 1977 House of Councillors Elections
(as of end July 1977)

	Present Strength	Pre-Election Strength
LDP	124	126
JSP	56	61
Komei	28	24
JCP	16	20
DSP	11	10
NLC	4	1
Niin Club	4	4
Independent	8	3
Vacancies	3	3
Totals	254	252

The Elements of Stability and Instability

What do these developments reveal about the future stability of Japanese politics? Although an LDP overthrow was barely averted, the difference between the LDP and the opposition was whittled down to a mere two seats. As a result, out of a total of sixteen standing committees in the upper house, the LDP has been able to maintain secure control over only two—the Steering Committee and the Budget Committee.

In Japanese parliamentary structure, parity between the ruling and the opposition parties in both houses of the Diet can mean virtual paralysis of the policy-making process. After more than twenty years of the LDP-ruled "1955 framework," Japanese political and administrative leaders no longer know how to handle the problems of legislative management in the new situation. The comfortable system of the past, when the government, with its absolute LDP majority, was able to monopolize the process of legislative initiative and management, has come to an end. At the same time, on the opposition side, the traditional gap between their oppositional rhetoric and their actual performance is no longer tolerable. From now on the opposition will have to take part, and responsibly, in the making of policy. It is obvious, then, that the entire postwar pattern of confrontation between conservative and progressive forces has collapsed, both in terms of public opinion and the actual power balance in the Diet.

To put it another way, over the past twenty-odd years, Japanese politics have been basically administrative—the government bureaucracy taking the lead in policy formation and the LDP following. From now on, however, the center of decision making is shifting from the administration to the legislature; that is, from the bureaucracy to the Diet. Bureaucrats can no longer get by with consulting only the LDP. To create the consensus that they need for their policy proposals, they must now take account of opposition views as well. Nor is the LDP any longer able to operate unilaterally as the government party. It must now give increasing attention to coordinating policy not only with the administrative system but with the opposition parties as well.

These changes are actually desirable from the standpoint of Japan's democratic development. The emergence of a multi-party system reflects the diversity of values in the nation as a whole, and the equalization of strength between the LDP and the opposition is one result of that development. The practice of formulating policy objectives in the rarefied heights of government and officialdom and then passing them down for implementation probably will not work much longer. Increasingly, the establishment of goals will require the participation of broad strata of the population through nationwide debate.

The will of the people also will have to be consulted in the determination of Japan's long-range role in international society. A nation without military power will have to expand its economic aid and cooperation to developing countries and contribute actively to the formation of a new order in international society. For these goals, a national consensus will be indispensable. Indeed, the solution of all of the serious problems facing Japan, such as energy, requires the broad agreement of the people. While the new political situation has weakened the ability of the LDP to rule single-handedly, if the LDP learns to cooperate with the other parties in the Diet, it will have an opportunity to reestablish its own credibility. Furthermore, it is apparent that the people are seeking participation and that they are demanding an open political system when possible. This mood requires a change in approach to political management on the part of all parties; it also creates the atmosphere in which such a change can take place.

The first step toward a new approach must be to dismantle the entrenched structure of confrontation between the government party and the opposition. Beyond that, efforts must be intensified to discover a policy consensus that will turn the political system toward stability. A prerequisite to that effort is for both the LDP and the opposition to recognize the fundamental national consensus that has existed throughout the thirty years of postwar history. That consensus has had three aspects: the preservation of parliamentary democracy; maintenance of a free enterprise system based on a market economy; and thorough pacifism based on the United States–Japan Security Treaty. The degree of agreement on these three points among the LDP and the opposition parties is now broader than ever before, and that increases the possibility of greater cooperation among the various parties on the concrete policy issues now confronting the nation. If an atmosphere of reconciliation prevails, the LDP will follow a new method of prior solicitation of opinions from the opposition even with regard to such matters as the budget and foreign affairs, which were until now unilaterally controlled by the government. With that, Japanese democracy will have reached a new level of maturity.

Let us take a closer look at how the existing political parties may be expected to change in the near future. Beginning with the LDP, a vigorous effort at self-rectification aimed ultimately at fundamental party reform was stimulated by the bitter public outcry over the corruption revealed in the Lockheed scandal. At its April 1977 extraordinary party convention, the LDP decided to dissolve the factions that were considered to be hotbeds of corruption, revise the rules governing the election of the party president in such a way that all party members could participate, modernize the party organization and public information procedures, and take other measures to assure a clean and open party.

Factions in the traditional sense of the word no longer exist in the LDP. In their place, a number of policy research groups are becoming active. They have emerged to supplement the LDP's Policy Affairs Research Council, whose major function traditionally has been the ratification of policy proposals drafted by the various governmental ministries. These groups seek to respond to the pluralization of values in the nation as a whole, and they are intended to strengthen the party's ability to take into account the broad range of demands being articulated by the public. By holding policy discussions in a public forum and opening up the policy decision-making process to the people, these research and discussion groups can play an extremely important role in eradicating the popular impression of politics as something carried on in closed, smoke-filled rooms. Also, in order to correct what is known as money-power politics, it is essential that the party clearly establish its integrity by publicly revealing the private assets of politicians and by dispelling suspicions about Japan–South Korea relations. At any rate, the most urgent business facing the LDP is reform and rejuvenation, restoring the party's vigor and opening its affairs to the public. In addition, the party must be deliberately attentive to the new middle class. The newly announced policy of "taking care of those who work hard and live honest lives" is one sign of movement in that direction.

Turning to the JSP, the entire Executive Committee resigned over the election debacle and was replaced by a new leadership under Ichio Asukata, the former very popular mayor of Yokohama. Nevertheless, the confrontation between the Socialist Association faction (Shakaishugi Kyokai), which professes Marxism, and the anti–Socialist Association faction, which is anti-Marxist, is as serious as ever. Although the Sohyo labor federation, the JSP's major support organization, is attempting to play a mediating role, real unity does not appear to be in the offing. Far more likely is a split. There is no way of knowing when that will occur, but most informed observers feel that the present situation cannot last indefinitely. What is most important, however, is that a movement promoting dissociation from Marxism is gaining strength within the largest opposition party, and its impact on JSP domestic and foreign affairs policy will bear careful attention.

At the same time, the possibility is increasing that movements of the Komei and Democratic Socialist parties will have an important influence on the course of Japanese politics. Both are middle-of-the-road and not very far apart in policy. They appear to be in the process of negotiating joint action in the Diet. Recent developments suggesting the adoption by both parties of a more liberal stand on the United States–Japan Security Treaty are highly significant.

The New Liberal Club made rapid gains in the 1976 election, but so far its policy is not entirely clear. Judging from its origins, I do not think that it will differ markedly from the LDP, but there is some possibility that it will fall in step with the Komei and Democratic Socialist parties. What with the LDP's efforts to reform itself and broaden the basis of policy formation, plus the realism with regard to policy and the tendency toward mutual cooperation displayed by the opposition, particularly by the middle-of-the-road parties, there would seem to be increasing scope for consensus between the government and the opposition.

In the course of the eightieth ordinary session of the Diet, which was held following the general election last year that brought the opposition parties almost up to parity with the LDP, the government achieved the passage into law of 85.5 percent of the seventy-six policy proposals that it introduced. The secret of that success was a turn from confrontation to cooperation on the part of both the opposition parties and the LDP, making possible the revision of a number of important bills, including the unusual case of a budget revision occasioned by an additional ¥300 billion in tax reductions. Twenty-one, or 32 percent, of the sixty-five bills passed were revised, and when this is compared to the 10 percent revision rate during the 1970 Diet session, the change is readily apparent. It is particularly noteworthy that outside of the normal channels for legislation handling, which center on the Diet Policy Committee, meetings have taken place between LDP and opposition party members responsible for policy to make adjustments in the content of important bills on tax reductions, the antimonopoly law, territorial waters, and so on. It is dangerous to generalize regarding Japan's political future on the basis of these examples, but they at least indicate the possibility of achieving political stability with the LDP acting as coordinator, even under conditions in which the opposition is roughly equal in power to the government, or if the LDP should lose its majority.

It would seem that even if the future should bring thorough-going realignment among the various parties, the people could never support a government that passed too far beyond the bounds of the three points of consensus mentioned above. A certain transitional confusion is unavoidable, but nothing alters my confidence that Japanese politics will move down the road to stability and maturity.

Political stability, however, is not determined by domestic factors alone. Economic stability is absolutely essential to political stability, and changes in the interdependent world environment have immediate effects on Japan's domestic political stability. Some obvious possibilities are: first, a rapid deterioration in trade and international economic relations; second, a price rise or a partial or complete cutback in Japanese energy imports; third, a drastic alteration of the power balance in Northeast Asia that appears to threaten Japan's security.

Domestic Political Change and Japanese–U.S. Relations

First, how can Japan's new political situation be expected to affect Japanese–U.S. relations? In the past, those relations on the Japanese side have been under the control of the LDP, particularly of the government leadership. Now that legislative cooperation is more necessary than it used to be, Japanese–U.S. cooperation and the stability of the relationship require a larger role for the opposition parties, particularly for the Komeito, the DSP, and the NLC. These middle-of-the-road parties are in favor of preserving and developing Japanese–U.S. harmony and cooperation, and there are signs of similar sentiments in the right wing of the JSP as well. The signs are favorable for a stable Japanese foreign policy, particularly in relation to the United States.

In the thirty years since the war, the United States has been the most important foreign nation in the world to Japan both in terms of security and economics. That importance is un-likely to decrease in the future. As Japan's economic influence expands, President Carter's policy of emphasis on trilateral relations among the United States, Western Europe, and Japan takes on added significance, and it is becoming increasingly desirable for Japan to play an important role in the formation of a new international order. On the other hand, it seems that Japanese–U.S. relations are now entering a period of trial.

The most urgent single problem is trade. There is no guarantee that the textile conflict of 1969 and early 1970 will not reappear in a different form, perhaps in color television, steel, or autos. A look at overall Japanese–U.S. trade figures confirms the urgency of some sort of solution to this issue. At the end of the first half of 1977, Japan had a favorable trade balance with the United States of $2.33 billion, while the United States was running a current-account deficit of more than $10 billion. As interdependence in Japanese–U.S. economic relations has increased, so has friction and conflict.

How can these problems be minimized? If relations between these two countries, which together account for 40 percent of the free world's GNP and whose trade totals $26 billion, were to deteriorate, it is impossible to predict the impact that this would have on the world. With interdependence among all countries on the increase, harmony and self-restraint between the two countries are even more essential for the sake of world stability and development. Moreover, it is clear that purely bilateral solutions to the trade imbalance problems may lead to reductions of overall world totals; therefore, such an approach should be avoided. What is most desirable is for Japanese–U.S. difficulties to be dealt with in the context of the acceleration of world trade as a whole.

By expanding domestic demand through a large-scale supplementary budget and a variety of other measures, Japan is now striving to achieve the 6.7 percent growth rate that the world expects without relying on exports. That goal is the highest of any advanced industrial nation. For countries with a payments surplus to expand domestic demand and reduce surpluses through increased imports, and for deficit countries to expand exports for the opposite effect is an extremely important element in the achievement of an overall multilateral balance in world trade.

Japan's exports, which last year totalled $67 billion, are only 7.4 percent of the world's total. It is a far smaller figure than that of the United States, of course, and even than that of West Germany, whose total was $102 billion. The problem for Japan, however, is the rapid increase in exports of certain products to particular regions. For example, Japan's exports to the advanced nations last year increased 34.8 percent over the previous year, and as part of that increase, Japan sold nearly 2.5 times as many color television sets to the United States as the year before. When this happens, movements to impose import restrictions inevitably arise in the recipient country. Japan must increase domestic demand and expand imports while taking care not to allow an export drive.

It is often pointed out that Japan imports a smaller volume of manufactured goods than other advanced countries because of the nature of its industrial structure and the peculiar configuration of its distribution system, but improvements also are going to be necessary in this regard. Part of the reason has to do with the need to help developing countries, particularly those without oil, to expand export of their products. In this regard, plans are progressing to establish in Tokyo a Center for Expanding Imports of Manufactured Products, with funds provided by both private and government sources. Trading firms themselves are beginning to turn from their excessive export emphasis to a more balanced approach. Hence, there is reason to hope that the situation will be rectified. Moreover, as part of an effort to liberalize and expand the domestic market, Japan must continue to do everything possible to relax restrictive measures against imports in areas such as agricultural products, an area in which Japan is criticized abroad for maintaining nontariff barriers to trade.

Not only is the maintenance of free trade the common interest of Japan and the United States, but it also is indispensable for the expansion of the world economy. It is all the more important, therefore, for the two countries to eliminate obstacles to free trade as they continue their close cooperation.

A consensus on Japan's role in the world economy and on the resultant constraints on the Japanese economy is in the process

of forming, not only in industrial circles but among citizens
at large. The complete fulfillment of that responsibility
inevitably involves the reform of certain aspects of the Japanese
industrial structure and will therefore require effective political leadership and a considerable period of time.

The recent upward revalution of the yen already has dealt a
serious blow to several industries, including textiles, that
employ some 1.8 million workers. Revising the industrial
structure so that it can cope with the effects of a strong yen will
take a good deal of time. And while it is desirable to revise
Japan's import-export structure in such a way as to achieve
horizontal specialization in production among the nations of
the world, it is impossible to ignore the plight of some 9
million workers in the mining, shipbuilding, machine, agricultural, and fisheries industries. If policies are not backed by
thorough spadework and broad agreement, they are bound to
lead to widespread social disorder. All of this requires skilled
political leadership.

In that sense, the emerging pattern of domestic politics need
not necessarily have a negative effect on the process of
consensus-building with regard to such complex issues. By
itself, the LDP no longer has sufficient persuasive power
among the people. But if the parties representing a broader
cross section of the population, including labor unions, were
to take policy decision-making responsibility, the persuasive
power of government could be greatly enhanced. It is important, however, that change not take place in the form of a
response to sudden external pressures. Constant communication and understanding in Japanese–U.S. relations is essential
to avoid that eventuality.

The real life-or-death issue for the Japanese economy is
energy. Whether Japan can continue to secure a stable supply
of energy, particularly oil, has an important bearing on
domestic political stability. Japan presently depends on oil for
73 percent of its energy needs, and virtually all of that is
imported. Japanese government and industry are now carrying
out a full-scale examination of ways to conserve and develop
energy alternatives to reduce reliance on oil. Nuclear energy
figures importantly in that effort.

According to preliminary calculations, if we assume that the real growth rate in GNP now and in 1985 will be 7 percent per year, and that labor productivity will rise at the rate of 6 percent, the projected number of unemployed in 1985 comes out to only eight hundred thousand; should the growth rate fall to 4 percent, however, with an annual productivity growth of 6 percent, that figure rises to twelve million individuals, or a 20 percent unemployment rate. Even if productivity were to expand at only 5 percent, there will be eight million, or 14 percent, unemployed. That being the case, it is clear that a rate of growth of at least 6 percent per year is an indispensable element in Japanese social stability. It appears that Japan must maintain a quite high rate of real growth not only to serve as an engine country in the achievement of a worldwide trade balance, but also to preserve domestic stability.

By 1985, to maintain that rate of growth will require the equivalent in energy of seven hundred million kiloliters of oil. Projecting on the basis of present conditions, Japan would have to rely on oil for up to four hundred million kiloliters worth of that energy. The dilemma, however, is that in the future era of limited resources, that sort of reliance on oil will be impossible. In that case, Japan will have no choice but to reform its heavily oil-dependent industrial structure to conserve energy while relying upon the development of nuclear power and other alternative energy sources.

It should be clear, therefore, why the reprocessing halt came as such a shock not only to Japanese industry but to the general public. Japan has ratified the Nuclear Nonproliferation Treaty (NPT), and public opinion polls show that the Japanese would never support a decision to build nuclear weapons and march down the road to becoming a military power. Further, nuclear reprocessing is provided for in the United States–Japan Nuclear Energy Agreement, which is in force between the two governments, and Japan has developed medium- and long-range plans for energy on the basis of that agreement. Japan as a nonnuclear-weapon state is already among those discriminated against within the NPT framework; a further distinction with regard to peaceful use of nuclear energy is unacceptable. When it is realized that reprocessing is permitted for nonnuclear-weapon states who are members of the European Atomic Energy Community (EURATOM), the feeling in Japan of being doubly discriminated against becomes understandable. The Japanese accepted the disadvantages of NPT because they understood it to be a step toward nuclear disarmament and important for constructing a basis for the peaceful use of nuclear energy. U.S. policy not only contradicts the spirit of the treaty but is also extremely prejudicial. Therefore, it seems that in the interests of stability in Japanese–U.S. relations, the United States should seriously reevaluate the Japanese position on the peaceful uses of nuclear energy and take immediate steps to rectify the situation.

Another problem in the near future is that of fishing. Compared to the Soviet Union, the United States presently is displaying a high degree of goodwill toward Japan and should be given full credit for that. Nevertheless, it was frankly very thoughtless of the United States to allow the Congress to establish a 200-mile exclusive fishing zone, thus triggering the worldwide trend in that direction even before the development of an international law of the sea. Not only did that action make the discussions at the International Law of the Sea Conference virtually meaningless, but by extending resource nationalism into the open sea, which has always been free to all, this action will have lasting negative consequences. It is true that within the framework of the new order, fishing quotas were established this year to the satisfaction of both sides; therefore, no damage was done to Japanese–U.S. relations. Beginning next year, however, quotas will be set by U.S. coastal fishing committees, and there is every possibility that selfish provincial interests will prevail. In view of the fact that the role of fish as a protein source in the Japanese diet is equivalent to that of beef for the United States, and that a large number of people depend for their employment on the fishing industry, a little more understanding from the U.S. side on this issue would be appreciated. Be that as it may, however, from a long-range perspective it is advisable for both Japan and the United States to cooperate in an effort to avoid making political issues out of economic ones.

While these economic issues are of great importance, they are not the whole story. No treatment of the prospects for Japanese–U.S. relations would be complete without taking mutual security into consideration. It is clear that President Carter's policy is one of gradual military withdrawal. Such a withdrawal presents problems that are extremely perplexing and unpredictable, particularly with regard to the maintenance of peace in Northeast Asia. It is certainly true that, as U.S. Secretary of State Cyrus Vance has pointed out, a gradual withdrawal has been made possible by the remarkable economic development and military expansion achieved by South Korea. Nevertheless, the principle explicitly acknowledged in the Sato-Nixon communiqué and more recently elsewhere that "the security of the Republic of Korea is essential to Japan's own security" is still operative, and nothing about the situation has changed to alter its applicability.

It is true, of course, that the withdrawal of U.S. forces from South Korea is fundamentally a bilateral matter to be worked out between those two nations. But I feel strongly that the United States should evaluate the pace and the ramifications of the action more carefully in order not to upset the balance of power in Northeast Asia. Moreover, we have reached the point where Japan can play a role in making sure that North Korea does not make a miscalculation injurious to peace on the Korean peninsula. Economic relations already have been established between Japan and North Korea on a private basis, and exchanges by Diet members from both the LDP and the opposition parties, among newspaper reporters, and so on, have developed quite well. On the other hand, Japan maintains extremely intimate political and economic relations with South Korea. It seems that for the United States and Japan to work through Japan's position vis-à-vis both Koreas and to cooperate in formulating policy in the nonmilitary realm to ensure the peace and stability of the Korean peninsula would form a useful adjunct to U.S. military withdrawal.

Japan should respond to the situation created by the gradual U.S. pullback by developing its basic defensive strength. Particularly in preparation for the era of 200-mile fishing zones, Japan must increase its antisubmarine and antiaircraft capabilities centering on the Japan Sea and build a Self-

Defense Forces structure that could actually function effectively if an incident should occur. It is possible to see a broad national consensus already forming in support of such a program. According to a poll taken by NHK in June 1977 (*see* Table 10.6), 31 percent of the people support a policy of "increasing defense power in a manner consistent with Japan's overall national strength while maintaining the United States–Japan Security Treaty." This option drew a higher percentage of respondents than any other alternative. Moreover, those who selected this response not only were LDP supporters but included a number whose sympathies generally lie with the opposition parties. If we include those who opted for autonomous defense combined with a policy of neutrality, or of self-defense in normal times with reliance on the United States in grave emergencies, it is clear that nearly 70 percent of the citizenry supports an expansion of the Self-Defense Forces, while only 9.3 percent supports unarmed neutrality. Japan should continue to increase its basic defense capability and at the same time further Japanese–U.S. cooperation by shouldering a greater share of the maintenance costs of U.S. bases.

Also important from the viewpoint of preserving peace in Northeast Asia are Japan's relations with the PRC and the Soviet Union. The U.S. military and political withdrawal from Asia leaves Japan face to face with these two great powers, and as an unarmed country, it would be extremely unwise to become involved in a confrontation with either one. We are called upon to exercise not a simplistic form of equidistant diplomacy but rather an intelligent autonomous policy of balanced relations. The escalation into serious political controversy of the so-called hegemony clause in the proposed Japan-China Treaty of Peace and Amity must be seen in that context. There is quite a difference between the Japanese and U.S. positions on that issue, even though it touches on the very foundations of the United States–Japan Security Treaty. Japan as an unarmed country has no choice but to get maximum mileage out of its economic power. It must cooperate with the Soviet Union in the development of Siberia and at the same time make an all-out effort to help stabilize the living conditions of the Chinese people, thereby increasing the degree of dependence of both

TABLE 10.6 Individuals Agreeing with NKH Survey Statements by Party, 1977 (in percentages)

Questions	Total Response	Respondents' Party Affiliation[a]											
		LDP	JSP	Komei	JCP	DSP	NLC	SCL	PLL	JWP	Other Groups	No Party	DK; No Answer
Total number responding:	2,644	1,149	468	145	109	129	99	8	4	3	3	429	98
1. Maintain the United States–Japan Security Treaty and increase self-defense power in proportion to Japan's national strength.	31.1%	42.8	18.2	20.0	13.8	30.2	37.4	37.5	25.0	33.3	0.0	24.2	15.3
2. Revise the United States–Japan Security Treaty, get rid of U.S. bases and forces stationed in Japan, and create a system whereby Japan can defend itself in normal circumstances.	25.7%	26.1	31.4	26.2	19.3	41.1	22.2	12.5	25.0	33.3	33.3	20.0	9.2
3. Abrogate the United States–Japan Security Treaty and plan a system of armed self-defense combined with neutrality.	11.4%	6.3	17.1	15.4	28.4	10.9	17.2	25.0	25.0	0.0	33.3	12.1	8.2
4. Abrogate the United States–Japan Security Treaty and institute unarmed neutrality.	9.3%	4.4	13.9	13.8	30.3	7.8	15.2	25.0	0.0	0.0	33.3	10.5	6.1
5. Other (be specific).	0.2%	0.1	0.2	0.0	0.0	0.8	0.0	0.0	0.0	0.0	0.0	0.2	1.0
6. DK, no answer.	22.3%	20.4	15.2	24.1	8.3	9.3	8.1	0.0	25.0	33.3	0.0	32.9	60.2

[a]LDP = Liberal Democratic Party, JSP = Japan Socialist Party, JCP = Japan Communist Party, DSP = Democratic Socialist Party, NLC = New Liberal Club, SCL = Socialist Citizen's League, PLL = Progressive Liberal League, and JWP = Japan Women's Party.

of those nations on the Japanese economy. In other words, Japan must engage in a diplomacy that carefully encourages these countries to rely on economic cooperation with Japan and not to feel threatened in any way. Japan must strive to build a framework of peace in Northeast Asia, centering on the Korean peninsula, and maintain it firmly. It appears that efforts to realize a peaceful, multilateral balance in Northeast Asia through economic means would in the long run be consistent with U.S. interests. At any rate, the most important thing is to avoid disrupting the balance in Northeast Asia and to maintain the status quo.

In late August 1977 Secretary of State Vance went to the PRC to draw up a new blueprint for U.S.–PRC relations. It is difficult to predict what kind of relationship the United States and the PRC will settle on as a result of that visit, but I hope, from the viewpoint of Asian stability, that nothing is done to damage substantively the status quo of Taiwan.

As the international situation becomes more fluid, it is eminently desirable that ever-stronger efforts be made to forge harmonious ties of cooperation between Japan and those countries with similar economic and political systems, such as the United States and the nations of Western Europe. The time is approaching when Japan can play an important role in that regard. For that reason, in our bilateral relationship we must strive to minimize friction arising from misunderstandings and prejudice.

That is not a simple task, and an edifice of perfect harmony cannot be built in one day. We have maintained a relationship of friendly cooperation for the past thirty years, however, and undoubtedly the desire to enhance that relationship remains strong on both sides of the Pacific. As Japan's pattern of politics now goes through a period of flux, we must preserve those sentiments and continue to translate them into action in a changing environment.

Part 5
Japan, the United States, and the World Economy

11
Free Trade Under Siege

Barber B. Conable, Jr.

Introduction

My first visit to Japan was in 1971. At that time legislation was before the U.S. Congress that would have done some damage to the free trade system. My long belief in and support of free and open trade compelled me to travel to Japan to convey to members of the Diet my concern that existing Japanese trade policies were working to fan the flame of protectionist pressures supporting that legislation.

Today, again, I stand here as a member of Congress and as a long-time advocate of a free and open trading system to deliver the same message. I emphasize my support of free trade philosophy because my discussion may at times appear alarmist or antagonistic. But I assume that we all share a common interest in the United States continuing its traditional role as a leading proponent of trade liberalization.

The fact of the growth of protectionism in the United States can neither be denied nor overstated. The threat is real. Fortunately, however, the pressures still can be contained, if not completely reversed. But it must be understood by major developed U.S. trading partners that the key to containment of the threat, for the most part, lies outside the United States. Herein, then, is my message: The growth of protectionist sentiment in the United States is closely associated with the policies and practices of major U.S. trading partners that have had, of late, an unacceptably disruptive impact on the U.S.

economy. This impact is felt intuitively by the U.S. public, and it is objectively demonstrable as well. The containment of the protectionist pressures, therefore, is very much dependent upon what course these policies and practices take in the future.

I propose here to deal with four issues: first, the nature of the attack upon free trade; second, the perceptions of the U.S. public with respect to import competition; third, the causes of the growth of protectionism; and fourth, recommendations for relief from this pressure.

The Free-Trade Environment and the Threat of Protectionism

Since Ricardo and his fellow classical economists in the late eighteenth and early nineteenth centuries, it has been well understood, though not always followed, that a system of commercial intercourse should seek efficiency over the long-term rather than the short-term accumulation of wealth. Commercial relations among nations undertaken without impediment afford to all an increase in the public welfare greater than what can be attained if barriers to trade are imposed. This is true in at least two theoretical respects: the situation allows countries to acquire indirectly what they cannot efficiently produce themselves or otherwise acquire by direct means; and if each country limits its production to what it can produce most efficiently, production costs can be minimized, production levels maximized, and prices reduced to their lowest practical levels. Thus, in general, the unencumbered flow of trade has a stimulating and broadening effect on domestic economic systems as well as on the general welfare.

Since the Reciprocal Trade Agreements Act of 1934, U.S. trade policy has been based on this view. It was not until 1947, however, that the prevailing systems of individual bilateral, liberalized trade agreements expanded into a multilateral system. The birth of the GATT marked the institutionalization of free-trade philosophy as a fundamental precept in the trade relations among the major trading countries. Through successive efforts over the years, the contracting parties to the GATT have undertaken further to liberalize trade practices in an effort to approach the best practicable approximation of the classical economists' free-trade model, as refined over the years.

The United States supported such an effort in 1963, and, despite the gathering clouds, is committed to carrying through the current negotiations in Geneva. Nevertheless, there have been rumbles of growing impatience in both the United States and Europe with the trade-liberalizing Geneva efforts. There is even a growing resistance to many trade-liberalizing features that already have been achieved. In the United States, considerable pressure is being marshalled to oppose further growth of textile imports. Similar efforts have been made and continue with regard to, among others, shoes, television sets, steel, honey, and sugar. In Europe, even greater pressure is being exerted against textile imports, and imports such as ball bearings, foreign automobiles, television sets, and steel are being controlled. Indeed, recent reports indicate increasing pressure in the European Commission[1] itself to retreat somewhat from the community's embrace of free trade as the model for the trading systems.

These cries come both from domestic producers seeking increased protection for their domestic markets and from labor seeking more protection for their jobs. Every month some new campaign gets underway in some additional sector of the U.S. economy. In recent weeks the microwave oven and motorcycle industries have joined the chorus, while the automobile industry is standing in the wings.

Owing to the sheer size of the United States, the high elasticity of demand for imports, and its traditional leadership role, ripples in the U.S market can create waves in the international trading system. Thus, it follows that the growing pressure for protection in the United States is a matter of great concern not only to the United States but to the world community. Although the major causes are not especially difficult to identify, what seems to have evaded many is an understanding of the dynamics underlying the resurgence. This must be grasped by developed U.S. trading partners if we are to reverse the tide and restore a receptive environment within which the free trade philosophy can thrive and further liberalization efforts can succeed.

There are objective causes for this growth of U.S. protectionism, but the subjective factors are even more important. It is becoming a routine matter to hear my colleagues, both on and off the floor of the House of Representatives, point with concern to the import-threatened state of U.S. industry and labor. Virtually without exception these concerns are linked to the perception that U.S. industry and labor are being victimized by a massive onslaught of foreign imports. This view of a substantial number of members of Congress is only an echo of the growing howls of complaint from their business and private constituents. Such a perception of the state of U.S. industry and the character of foreign competition is significant in several respects.

First, in a representative democracy and market economy such as ours, it is largely perception, however intuitive and subjective it may be, that influences behavior and structures opinion. Clearly, a governmental free-trade policy cannot long survive in an atmosphere in which a siege mentality exists with respect to imports. Second, these perceptions are not born of a sense that U.S. industry and labor are suffering from their own inadequacies. To the contrary, the view is widely held that U.S. industry and the U.S. worker in a fair competitive environment could hold their own. But therein lies the rub. The perceived problem is that foreign producers and even foreign governments employ predatory practices, set artificially low prices, and use other devices unfairly to undermine markets for U.S. products both at home and abroad. Third, almost without exception in this connection, Japan is perceived as the leading antagonist. Of late, the list from the sectors complaining of serious harm from precipitous flows of low-cost Japanese imports has been growing. With that growth, perceptions of the onslaught become entrenched, further pressure for protection rises, and Japan becomes more firmly the primary focal point of hostility. And finally, whether or not objective data support the intuitive sense of the rectitude of the U.S. competitive posture and the perniciousness of the foreign, the fact remains that the sentiment is being expressed with increasing intensity. It is fast becoming a proposition the truth of which is proven by its repeated assertion.

Of course, if these perceptions existed in clear contrast to objective data, one would not need to be overly concerned with their impact on trade policy and on the survivability of the free trade doctrine. But recent trade data are not all that reassuring to the alarmists. While U.S. imports over the past year have grown by approximately 30 percent, U.S. exports have only enjoyed a 7 percent growth. Indeed, the overall U.S. trade deficit for this year could well exceed $25 billion.

Regarding the view that Japan is the primary source of the import onslaught, trade data can be used to support the popular impression. The U.S. trade deficit with Japan last year was $6.8 billion, or 47 percent of the total U.S. deficit. This year the deficit is likely to exceed $10 billion out of a total deficit of $25 billion. In 1976 imports from Japan grew by 38 percent, faster than from any other area. With respect to particular sectors, the figures are even more difficult to explain to alarmists. Japanese exports of new passenger cars to the United States increased 74 percent in 1976. Exports of color television sets were up by 173 percent and black-and-white televisions by 136 percent. Exports of steel to the United States increased by about 30 percent.

Market penetration has grown with equal rapidity. Market penetration (by volume) of Japanese color television sets was approximately 15.4 percent in 1975 and reached approximately 40 percent in 1976. In 1974 Japanese steel represented 39 percent of all imported steel; in 1976 it was 58 percent; and in the first quarter of 1977 it was about 57 percent. Overall, the United States imported 13.4 percent of its steel requirement in the first quarter of 1977, of which over half came from Japan. Of the passenger automobiles sold in 1973, Japanese cars held 6.5 percent of the U.S. market (by volume); in 1976 their share had risen to 9.5 percent.

Japan's performance with respect to the rest of the developed world is not substantially different. Its trade surplus for 1976 was approximately $2.5 billion, and the Finance Ministry recently reported the trade surplus for the first six months of this year to be a record $6.6 billion, riding atop a 22 percent increase in exports over the same period last year. Much of this surplus, particularly that part relating to trade with developed countries, results from an interesting structural characteristic. Japanese imports tend to be overwhelmingly agricultural commodities and raw materials, primarily from LDCs and OPEC countries. At the same time, Japan has the lowest per capita imports of manufactured goods of any major developed country. The combination of these two structural features substantially accounts for the consistent and large traditional surpluses that Japan has with its developed trading partners.

The point is that the U.S. public's intuitive perceptions of the disrupting effects of rising imports alone are troublesome to the conduct of a liberal trade policy. Yet, when trade data can be marshalled that support this prevailing wisdom, the potential for resistance to liberal trade policies is magnified considerably. Because Japanese imports occur in highly visible sectors of the U.S. economy, Japan attracts particular attention and becomes the chief target of the resisting forces.

This litany of gloomy trade statistics is not meant to suggest that Japan and its trade policy are the only causes of the re-awakening of the forces of protectionism in the United States. Indeed, despite the fact that the Japanese recovery, insofar as trade matters are concerned, has been dramatic over the past one and one-half years, despite the fact that it has been stronger by far than any other developed country with the exception, perhaps, of West Germany, and despite the difficulty that this disproportionally strong recovery has caused in Japan's trade relations with its developed trading partners, to single out Japan as the source of all evil is, indeed, to oversimplify the complexity of the problem facing trade liberalization.

It is without question that a system of smooth, unencumbered trade is as much, if not more so, in the interest of Japan as it is in the interest of the United States and the other developed countries. It is inconceivable, therefore, that Japanese trade policy has been formulated to frighten its developed trading partners. What is more likely is that Japan continues to underestimate its own status and importance in the trading world. In formulating trade strategies, it continues to underrate the impact of its aggressive and effective tactics on its trading partners. It would seem that Japan has become a significant trade power not yet fully appreciative of the strength of its emergence.

The Causes of Protectionist Resurgence

The identification of what does account for the reawakening of the forces of protectionism in the United States, of that which lies at the heart of the prevailing perceptions about imports, becomes essential if the trend is to be reversed and if further liberalization is to succeed. There is a tendency for free-trade ideologues as well as U.S. trading partners to point the accusatory finger in this regard at the Trade Act of 1974. At the time of its passage, the Trade Act was identified by some as the greatest triumph of protectionism since Smoot-Hawley. The prophets of doom quickly predicted a surge of antiliberal trade actions under the Trade Act that would significantly change U.S. trade law and policy and, thereby, reverse the long and hard efforts to liberalize world trading practices.

One could argue that the predictions of the Trade Act's detractors have come to pass. Since its signing into law on January 3, 1975, over 150 actions have been brought by concerned and affected groups. Of those, 27 complaints have been filed under Section 201, the "escape clause," alleging that increased imports have caused or threatened serious injury to U.S. industry. Another 19 complaints have been brought under Section 341 (regarding Section 337 of the Tariff Act of 1930), alleging unfair trade practices against like or competitive U.S. products. Section 301 actions, seeking relief from unfair trade practices by foreign governments, have numbered 12. Plainly, the expanded opportunities for invoking protective measures against competition from imports have not been ignored by the import-impacted community. But to infer from this heavy use of the various relief provisions available that the Trade Act of 1974 stimulates or facilitates protectionist pressures is to misread its role in the formulation and execution of U.S. trade policy.

The Trade Act of 1974 represents a difficult and delicate effort to balance the interests of two antithetical communities. Considering that this legislation was vigorously debated

during a very difficult economic period, the extent of its
balance is remarkable indeed. While it clearly expands and
institutionalizes access to administrative procedures that can
put U.S. markets significantly out of reach, the act also offers
effective relief for those suffering legitimate injury from unfair
trade activity. For practical purposes, previous law created
demands for rigid legislated (as opposed to flexible administrative) remedies for frustrated businesses with legitimate
trade grievances. Also, the new act grants broad authority to the
president to undertake agreements substantially liberalizing
the international trading system and thereby serving to reduce
the need for relief actions.

Furthermore, the Trade Act greatly enlarges the role of
government in providing assistance to labor, industries, and
communities that have suffered from import competition. In
this light, then, this measure should not be characterized as
providing a forum for protectionist advocacy or for inciting
protectionist sentiment. In allowing for expanded but struc-
tured opportunities for redressing import-related injuries, this
balanced provision seeks to provide a channel for the forces of
protectionism. It redirects efforts away from solicitation of
rigid and retrogressive legislation and, instead, channels
energies to disciplined and sober advocacy, itself becoming
part of the final policy determination on the matter.

Moreover, the relief, assistance, and negotiation provisions
of the Trade Act of 1974 have been successful in venting and
diffusing what could otherwise have been very destructive
protectionist pressures. Note, for example, the solutions
reached in the heated matters involving shoes, sugar, mush-
rooms, and television sets in contrast to what might have
happened without the provisions and structure of the Trade
Act. Further, the act has served as a useful and rational early
warning system for the trade policy community. On balance,
then, the Trade Act of 1974 has introduced into U.S. trade a
policy-making flexibility where rigidity threatened, rationality
where irrationality existed, and broad-based consideration
where myopia was once the order of the day.

If not the Trade Act, what then is the objective source underlying the growing protectionist pressure in the United States?

Without question, both in the United States and in Europe the starting point for this most recent rise in protectionist sentiment is the quadrupling of oil prices since 1974 and the consequent worldwide recession. The impact of these events on the domestic economy continues to plague us. But although the sluggish recovery makes fertile ground for protectionism's growth, the events of 1974 and 1975 are only catalysts. Had certain other forces not been at work, or if they did not now continue to operate, the progress of worldwide recovery would perhaps not be so sluggish. Indeed, had the trading system been operating effectively, the depth of the recession itself might not have been so low, production not so depressed, unemployment not so high, and protectionism not in such ascendancy. The events of 1974-75 aggravated and exposed existing but heretofore unacknowledged weakneses in the trading system that have made us less able to cope with the strain generated by the precipitous rise in oil prices and the equally abrupt changes in the movement of capital. These systematic weaknesses generally fall into two categories: international structural problems and chronic problems of practice.

International Structural Problems

From the trade perspective of the United States, the structural problems aggravated and exposed by the recession involve two elements: the differences between the U.S. tax structure and those of developed U.S. trading partners, and the different treatment given different systems under international trading rules. Specifically, in view of the GATT treatment accorded some tax systems, the differences that exist among the various systems can, in an aggravated environment, have an important impact on trade.

Under the GATT, indirect taxes such as sales and value-added taxes can be adjusted at the border on the destination principle. Under this principle, goods are taxed only where they are consumed. The impact on trade is clear. Indirect taxes are levied on imports and rebated on exports. On the other hand, direct taxes such as property and income taxes (corporate and individual) cannot be adjusted at the border because of the origin principle. This principle places a tax on goods on the basis of where they are produced. Thus, direct taxes are neither applied to imports nor rebated upon export.

What is plain from the operation of existing rules is that domestic tax systems relying upon indirect taxation enjoy a considerable advantage in international trade (assuming relatively equal competitive positions) over those systems relying largely upon direct taxation. In those times when the indirect and direct tax systems had different effects on prices, the different treatment accorded the systems at the border had a negligible impact on trade flows. But today it is widely recognized that the difference in effect on price between direct and indirect systems is largely conceptual.

Thus, in those sectors where price and quality competition is keen or where circumstances place a premium on export volume, the marginal advantage enjoyed at the border by a product from an indirect tax system can often result in a significant influence on trade flows. In theory, the operation of free-floating exchange rates ultimately will balance whatever advantages might be enjoyed. But the operation, or lack of operation, of the free float is itself a systemic problem making a major contribution to protectionist pressures.

The U.S. tax system relies heavily on direct taxes for revenue. Insofar as impact on trade is concerned, great reliance is placed upon corporate and property taxes. In contrast, both of the major developed U.S. trading partners, either in whole or in certain key sectors, heavily rely upon indirect taxes. One need only look at the Zenith or U.S. Steel cases to appreciate the impact of this divergent treatment of taxes on the forces of protection in the United States. This sentiment is strong not only in the private sector. Notwithstanding protestations of the administration on the matter of the Zenith case, there is substantial support in the Congress for the Customs Court ruling, now narrowly reversed on appeal.[2] Eventually, Congress may have to resolve the matter should the administration lose the battle in the Supreme Court.

But the border tax adjustment matter is not the only trade-related problem area associated with the differences among the various domestic tax systems. The conflict over deferral practices and the acceptance or rejection of the territoriality concept can have grave trade-related consequences. The battle raging now in the GATT Council over the special panel reports on the Domestic International Sales Corporation and the tax practices of France, Belgium, and the Netherlands speaks rather clearly to what is at stake. Again, the point is that in times such as these, in highly competitive markets, within highly competitive sectors, the marginal advantage gained by virtue of domestic tax policies is having increasingly important consequences on trade flow, which in turn serves to fan anti-trade liberalizing sentiments.

Chronic Problems of Practice

The chronic problems highlighted by recent events that are considered here are neither new nor complex. But in these already difficult times, their impact on protectionist pressures in the United States is great.

Of immediate concern in this connection is the continuing and growing trade deficit with Japan. But what is of concern here is not so much the abundance of Japanese goods entering the U.S. market; rather, it is the relative dearth of U.S. goods entering the Japanese market. Greater access for U.S. products to the Japanese market could go a long way in deflating perceptions of unfairness, reducing the dramatic deficit, and thereby diffusing the growing focus of protectionist sentiments on Japan and Japanese products.

Despite considerable progress by Japan over the past several years to reduce its barriers to imports, a number of obstacles to market entry for U.S. products still remain. The obstacles exist in the form of both tariff and nontariff barriers. Regarding tariffs, in November 1972 and again in April 1973, Japan undertook unilateral tariff reductions of 20 percent on selected items. The result, in general, was to make Japan's duties on raw materials and essential agricultural products such as soybeans and feedgrains very small or zero, while making duties on manufactured goods, processed foods, meat, and fresh fruits and vegetables relatively high, if not, in some cases, virtually prohibitive.

Treatment of U.S. photographic film is a case in point. During the immediate postwar period, the Japanese film industry was an infant, struggling one. Accordingly, it, along with many other such industries, enjoyed considerable non-tariff, capital investment and tariff protection. Over the years, however, as all industries began to grow, these protections were gradually reduced. Quantitative restrictions on imports of film were eliminated in 1970. In May 1976 the film industry became the last industry to undergo capital investment liberalization in compliance with Japan's OECD obligations.

As for tariffs, the reduction of obstacles to trade has not been satisfactory. The Kennedy Round left Japanese photographic tariffs unchanged. Since that time tariffs on color film have been unilaterally reduced from 40 percent to 16 percent in four steps. But despite the fact that the industry has grown 40 percent in the last five years, plans even faster future growth, and has marketed a high-speed color film representing a major technological breakthrough, tariffs on imports still remain at 16 percent. Considering only the fact that the Japanese film industry is the second strongest in the world, and a close second at that, the tariff level is rather high. Though lower than the bound figure,[3] this tariff level is even high by Japanese standards and is over three times the comparable U.S. tariff. Indeed, it is the highest such tariff of all industrialized countries. The comfortable protection of this high tariff accounts for Japan's considerable film trade surplus with the United States, and this surplus will continue to grow.

Regarding nontariff barriers, substantial progress by Japan in recent years to reduce import restrictions still has left a number of barriers that concern U.S. exporters. The administration of Japanese automotive, environmental, and safety standards, for example, causes considerable delays in the approval of sales of U.S. automobiles. These delays sometimes extend for six months after the introduction of a new model. This is significant because approval for entry generally occurs at the time of introduction, when maximum sales potential exists. Japanese automobile manufacturers are subject to the same restrictions but are able to bring their product to market on time because relevant information is available to them and unavailable to importers.

Government procurement practices provide another example of difficult nontariff barriers to the Japanese market. The Japanese government frequently relies on unpublished internal regulations to favor the purchase of domestic over foreign goods. Procurements generally are made on the basis of private negotiations involving no competition or, as 90 percent of Japanese government procurement is made, on the basis of bids tendered by selected suppliers. Foreign suppliers are rarely invited to submit bids.

Although Japan was singled out here as an example of how tariff and nontariff measures act as barriers to U.S. trade and thus foster retaliatory attitudes with respect to access to the U.S. market, much the same can be said about trade practices of Europe. Of particular importance in the tariffs area is the variable levy exacted on agricultural imports. This system works considerable hardship on the export of U.S. agricultural products to Europe. It is virtually impossible to know price levels in advance, and the levy operates specifically to negate the qualitative and price competitive advantages enjoyed by U.S. products. Regarding nontariff barriers, European Community and member states' procurement practices are, in effect, not unlike those of Japan. Quantitative restrictions and licensing practices are additional nontariff barrier problems.

A second chronic problem, which has been exacerbated by the recent recession and which has a measurable effect on protectionist pressures in the United States, is the matter of "reflation" of economies and revaluation of currencies. In order for the trading system to reapproach equilibrium and restore stability to weaker economies, surplus nations need to stimulate the weaker economies. Such stimulation, in turn, expands domestic demand, which reduces the pressure to export and fosters the consumption of imports. Both West Germany and Japan, the two developed countries with the largest trade surpluses, have been reluctant to make this contribution to restoration of equilibrium in the trading system. Both countries also have been reluctant to revalue their currencies. Revaluation would accelerate the restoration of equilibrium, which is normally accomplished by the market through adjustment of exchange rates to the surpluses and deficits in trade accounts. By failing to take these rather simple steps, West Germany and Japan prolong systemic disequilibrium, extend the considerable U.S. trade deficit (which is serving to fuel other economies that have not been as successful in their recovery), and raise protectionist pressures.

A final chronic problem is the sluggish pace of the multilateral trade negotiations. Trade liberalization efforts in Geneva offer the promise of expanded trade opportunities to important sectors in the U.S. economy. The longer the negotiations are delayed, the more impatient the U.S. trade community becomes with the one-sidedness of existing trade practices and the more fertile the environment for protectionist influence becomes.

Remedies

The remedy for the very troublesome problem of protectionism in the United States seems as predictable as the underlying causes of its resurgence. A proper, long-term prescription benefitting the entire trading system has at least five essential features:

1. A timely and substantial conclusion to the multilateral negotiations is needed. As a minimum, the final package should include significant harmonization and reduction of tariffs and significant reduction of nontariff barriers that would include meaningful guidelines on subsidies/countervailing duties, government procurement, safeguards, and quantitative restrictions. Also, there must be significant improvements in the terms under which agricultural trade will be conducted.
2. A timely and substantial effort by Japan to reduce its trade surplus with the United States (and, for that matter, with the European Community) is needed if stability across the system is to be attained.
3. Continued reductions in both tariff and nontariff barriers to the access of manufactured products to the Japanese market independent of efforts at the MTN are important.

4. A timely and significant stimulation of the West German and Japanese economies directed at import expansion is necessary. Also, both countries should undertake a revaluation of their respective currencies.

5. There should be a multilateral conference of OECD nations to explore and attempt to reconcile the distortion of trade flows caused by the differing domestic tax practices and the different treatments that they are accorded under prevailing international rules.

With these actions, the attack on free trade and trade liberalization in the United States can be repelled, the trading system can be returned to fluidity, and the welfare of the world economic community can be returned to growth. Without these or equivalent actions, there is certain to be a return to the chaos in the world trade system characteristic of the pre-GATT period. Unfortunately, the choice in this matter is not, in the main, the United States's to make.

Notes

1. One of the six institutions of the European Economic Community (EEC). Its primary mission is to propose and supervise the execution of the laws and policies of the EEC.

2. The U.S. Customs Court ruled in April 1977 that the Japanese commodity tax procedure in the electronic field constitutes a subsidy under U.S. law. The ruling was reversed by the U.S. Court of Customs and Patent Appeals and is expecting to come before the Supreme court in summer 1978.

3. A tariff level established as the result of GATT negotiation. Once a country has given a concession for a particular tariff rate, all GATT members are bound by it. If a country increases its tariff, it must compensate all others for whatever financial loss they incur.

12

Some Considerations for Japan and the United States in Developing an Energy Strategy

John Sawhill

Background

The world economy suffered a severe shock following the rapid escalation of oil prices in the wake of the 1973 Arab oil embargo. Some of the industrial nations—particularly the United States, Japan, and West Germany, the so-called engines of the world economy—were able to withstand these shocks and, after temporary recessions, resume economic growth at near historic rates while containing inflation at moderate levels. On the other hand, many of the OECD countries have been unable to return to satisfactory economic growth rates, and the nonoil producing LDCs have experienced a mounting burden of external debt and in some cases an actual decline in real per capita net income.

That these changes occurred in the aftermath of a fourfold increase in the world price of oil is not surprising. What is surprising, however, is that so little has been done to find solutions to the energy problem. This inactivity has led some observers to ask whether "modern industrialized governments have the political will to face the truth and to act" and whether "these governments have the strength to avoid unilateral and nationalistic action and work together in international forums for the common interest."[1]

It would be a mistake to conclude that nothing has happened to improve the energy position of the non-OPEC world since 1973. Oil and gas production has expanded in the North Sea and promises to add about 3.5 million barrels of oil per day to

OECD Europe production by 1980. North Slope production began flowing through the Alaskan pipeline in June 1977 and will add about 1.2 million barrels per day to U.S. production by 1979 and possibly as early as late 1978. U.S. coal production has expanded marginally, and plans are underway to step up the pace of that expansion. European and Japanese nuclear programs are proceeding, albeit more slowly than previously forecast, and some countries have begun serious efforts to implement energy conservation programs. Unfortunately, the United States (the world's largest energy wastrel) is a laggard in this regard. Moreover, the International Energy Program has been signed by sixteen OECD countries. And, while the International Energy Authority (IEA) probably falls short of former Secretary of State Kissinger's claim that it is "one of the great success stories of the last decade-and-a-half," it is having some success in coordinating the development of individual country policies for handling emergency shortages. For example, it is encouraging that the United States finally has— after considerable delay—enacted an oil storage program and appears now to be moving ahead with accelerated implementation plans.

In spite of these positive signs, the response to higher oil prices and rising imports has been weak and inadequate. Governments, by and large, have not shown that they understand the magnitude of the problem, nor have they defined with any degree of clarity how they intend to deal with it. And this failure to move forcefully, either at a national or a multinational level, has been disappointing. Thus, the call for the development of a common energy strategy and rough national production goals largely has gone unheeded. Few coordinated efforts have been made to achieve the energy conservation goals that were set forth by the IEA, and only limited progress has been made in developing the international mechanisms that could ease the financial strains caused by higher oil prices. At the same time, relations between consuming and producing countries continue to be strained, as was evident in the breakdown of negotiations at the recent Council on International Economic Cooperation (CIEC) meetings, and the Arab–Israeli conflict remains unresolved and could escalate once again.

Such a turn of events would have profound impacts on consumer-producer relations.

The results of this inaction have been predictable. Oil prices have continued to escalate and did so again in July 1977 when Saudi Arabia and Abu Dhabi matched the 10 percent increase put into effect by the other OPEC nations earlier in the year. And the debt burden of the consuming nations—particularly of the nonoil-producing LDCs as well as of such developed countries as Spain, Portugal, Greece, and Italy—is becoming less manageable. The need for an international financial mechanism to provide some type of financing vehicle to meet the current account deficits of the developing nations until more permanent international monetary system reforms can be put in place is becoming increasingly clear.

On this latter point, the evidence is mounting. While it is true, as shown in Table 12.1, that the current account deficits of the nonoil-producing LDCs are expected to decline from the $28.7 billion peak of 1975 to about $17 billion this year, these deficits will continue at historically high levels. Equally disturbing, the deficits of the LDCs with the lowest per capita incomes are expected to increase. Private financial institutions now hold over $35 billion of LDC long-term debt—up from $13 billion in 1973; and banks hold $76 billion of total debt— up from $33 billion in 1973. Given this rate of increase in LDC borrowing from the private sector, it is difficult to see how the private banking system can continue to handle the future LDC debt requirements without some support from governments and multilateral agencies such as the IMF.[2]

Current Outlook for World Oil Supplies

Recently, a number of major studies have been published that reemphasize the seriousness of the energy problem by presenting a series of world oil supply and demand forecasts based on alternative assumptions about economic growth and the forcefulness of government action.[3] The conclusion in each case is the same—there will be major supply shortages leading to sharp and unmanageable oil price increases unless governments act quickly to reverse existing production and

TABLE 12.1 World Distribution of Current Accounts (in billions of dollars)[a]

	1970	1971	1972	1973	1974	1975E	1976E	1977P	1978P
Oil exporting countries[b]	.5	2.5	2.6	4.8	62.8	31.7	36.7	33.3	25.1
Seven major industrial countries[c]	6.2	7.8	- .1	- .7	-22.6	5.9	- 9.6	-14.6	- 8.8
Other developed countries[d]	-3.4	-2.8	3.2	4.1	- 7.6	- 6.9	- 9.2	- 5.2	- 2.5
Semiindustrial Mediterranean countries[e]	-1.3	- .2	1.0	.4	- 8.8	-10.4	- 7.8	- 5.7	- 3.8
Nonoil LDCs[f]	-6.5	-9.0	-6.6	-5.5	-20.6	-28.7	-17.9	-17.0	-17.3
High income	-3.0	-4.5	-3.9	-3.7	-15.2	-16.8	-11.8	- 8.9	- 8.7
Medium income	-1.5	-2.1	- .9	.4	- 2.6	- 6.9	- 5.4	- 4.8	- 4.4
Low income	-2.0	-2.4	-1.8	-2.2	- 2.8	- 5.0	- .7	- 3.3	- 4.2
Communist countries[g]	-3.0	-3.0	-3.0	-4.0	- 5.0	-11.0	-10.4	- 9.3	- 8.6
Other countries and residual[h]	7.5	4.7	2.9	.9	1.8	19.4	18.2	18.5	15.9

Source: Citibank estimates.

[a] E = Estimates; P = Projected.

[b] Consists of OPEC plus Trinidad and Tobago.

[c] Consists of the United States, Japan, Canada, the United Kingdom, Germany, France, and Italy.

[d] Consists of South Africa and the smaller OECD countries with the exception of Spain, Greece, Portugal, and Turkey.

[e] Consists of Greece, Israel, Portugal, Spain, Turkey, Yugoslavia, and Malta.

[f] The three subgroups of nonoil LDCs are based on whether 1973 per capita income was $400 or more; $201-399; or less than $200.

[g] Convertible currency trade of COMECON countries (excluding Cuba) and the PRC.

[h] Includes a statistical discrepancy arising from differences in countries' timing, coverage, classification, and valuation of transactions and possibly from biases introduced in projecting the various regions' current account balances.

consumption trends. Taking their cue from these forecasts of sharply rising prices, leading spokesmen from the world financial community have expressed growing concern about the ability of the private banking system to finance mounting oil deficits and have called for strengthening the IMF and, specifically, for activating the so-called $25 billion financial safety net proposal first put forward by Henry Kissinger. In the United States, the president has called the quest for a solution to the energy problem "the moral equivalent of war" and has given it a priority second only to maintaining peace.

In April of 1977, the U.S. government announced a major new energy initiative designed to reverse the trend of rising U.S. oil imports. The Carter administration's National Energy Plan proposes a complex regulatory scheme under which some additional incentives would be provided to domestic oil and gas producers in the form of higher (although still regulated) prices. These price incentives are intended to lead to increased U.S. oil production (including natural gas liquids) from the current level of 9.7 to 10.6 million barrels per day in 1985. While achieving this gain (which will require a high exploration rate and a better-than-average success rate) will be difficult, it is within the range of forecasts made by various industry economists and others. It is worth noting, however, that such a production level implies that over one-half of U.S. domestic oil production in 1990 will have to come from reserves yet to be discovered.

The National Energy Plan establishes a specific target for imports (including natural gas liquids) of almost 7 million barrels per day, or slightly less than the 7.3 million barrels per day that the United States imported in 1976 and substantially less than the 11.5 million barrels per day of imports that the U.S. government projects would occur in the absence of the plan. The government acknowledges that the achievement of these goals is only possible through major improvements in conservation and an unprecedented increase in coal production from the 1976 level of 665 million tons to 1.0 billion tons by 1985. The magnitude of this increase can be appreciated by comparing it with U.S. coal production since 1971, which has grown at an annual average increment of about 22 million tons. To achieve the 1985 goal, the average annual increase in production will have to be 42 million tons.[4]

Most analyses of the Carter plan have concluded that it is overly optimistic about the ability of the U.S. government to implement the mix of tax, price, and environmental policies necessary to achieve the supply increase and demand growth-reduction targets implicit in the 1985 import goals. This conclusion was made independently by two major congressional agencies—the Congressional Budget Office and the Office of Technology Assessment—in reports issued over the summer, and it tends to be supported by congressional action and debates on the program thus far. Furthermore, the OECD's recently completed *World Energy Outlook* shows U.S. oil imports in 1985 at a minimum of 3 million barrels per day above the goals of President Carter's plan and possibly even greater, depending upon the assumptions made about GNP growth and the implementation schedule for conservation policy initiatives. At the same time, total OECD demand for imports is estimated at 24.4 to 38.8 million barrels per day based on alternative growth scenarios.[5] According to the OECD analysis, four scenarios are possible:

- With continuing consumption and production trends and the maintenance of existing energy policies, the net OECD imports would be about 35 million barrels per day by 1985, assuming a GNP growth in OECD European countries of 4.1 to 4.3 percent.
- On the basis of a slower GNP growth of 3.6 to 3.8 percent, OECD import needs would be 31.9 million barrels per day.
- With a faster GNP growth of 4.6 to 4.8 percent, OECD import requirements would jump to 38.8 million barrels per day.
- And, in the Accelerated Policy case—in which maximum conservation is achieved, indigenous oil is developed rapidly, and all alternative fuels expand significantly—OECD import needs fall to 24.4 million barrels per day.

These projections can be compared with the production and

TABLE 12.2 OPEC Production Capacity Projections,
Excluding Saudi Arabia (in million barrels per day)

	March 1977	*1980*	*1985*
Algeria	1.0	1.0	0.9-1.1
Ecuador	0.2	0.2	0.2
Gabon	0.2	0.2	0.2
Indonesia	1.7	1.9-2.1	1.6-2.1
Iran	6.7	6.5	5.5-6.1
Iraq	3.0	4.5	5.0-6.0
Kuwait	3.5	3.0	3.0
Libya	2.5	2.5	2.0-2.5
Nigeria	2.3	2.3	2.0-3.0
Qatar	0.7	0.6	0.5
UAR	2.4	2.5-3.2	3.0-3.5
Venezuela	2.6	2.2-2.4	2.2
Total	26.8	27.6-28.3	27.5-29.4

Source: U.S. Central Intelligence Agency

export capacity of the OPEC countries outside Saudi Arabia shown in Table 12.2.

Except in the Accelerated Policy case, the 1985 net OECD import requirements are well above the current and projected capacities of OPEC. Furthermore, once the exporting capacity of these countries is reduced by 3.5 million barrels per day to account for local consumption, and by a further 0.8 million barrels per day to reflect Kuwait's self-imposed limit, the pivotal role of Saudi Arabia becomes even more apparent. For, between the non-Saudi production capacity of 23 million barrels per day and OECD import needs in a moderate growth scenario, there is a difference of about 12 million barrels per day, which is about the current production capacity of Saudi Arabia.

The critical question that must be answered in order to project future oil supply and demand levels is the extent to which the Saudis will be willing to continue to maintain production above the 8.5 million barrels per day level that they previously set as a limit in an effort to ease the upward pressure on price. There is strong opposition within the Saudi government against raising production further because of the lack of need for current revenues and the feeling that high production rates only exacerbate the strong inflationary pressures currently prevailing within the country. At the same time, there is a recognition on the part of many Saudi leaders that they are ultimately dependent on the West to provide an economic climate in which their surplus funds can be invested safely and a political climate in which progress toward a Middle East settlement can be achieved. For this reason, the Saudis generally have acted as a moderating force in OPEC price negotiations. The recent attempt to hold the 1977 crude oil price increase to 10 percent is only the latest in a series of similar moves since 1973. Yet, it is difficult to envision a policy of continued unrestrained increases in production without definite indications on the parts of the governments in the industrialized countries that this claim on Saudi resources will be limited in time. And, in the short run, the progress (or lack thereof) in resolving the Arab-Israeli conflict will have an important impact on the Saudis' commitment to current high levels of production.

Some of the other recent world oil supply-demand analyses have reached conclusions that are in the same range as those of the OECD secretariat. One study, however, conducted by the U.S. Central Intelligence Agency (CIA), has made a decidedly more pessimistic forecast. The CIA projection, shown in Table 12.3, estimates a required 1985 OPEC production of between 47 and 51 million barrels per day. In effect, this means that Saudi production would have to rise to 24 to 28 million barrels per day, which would, at current prices, push Saudi annual revenues to more than $100 billion—or about ten times the value of all of Saudi Arabia's current imports.

The principal discrepancy between the OECD and the CIA forecasts is the CIA's estimate that the Soviet Union will shift from a net exporter of nearly 1.0 million barrels per day now to a net importer of 3.5 to 4.5 million barrels per day by 1985. The other major difference is the buildup in the consumption of non-OPEC developing nations. Both analyses, however,

TABLE 12.3   OECD Imports (in million barrels per day)

	1976	1985 (CIA)	1985 (OECD)
United States	7.0	11.2-15.6	9.7
Western Europe	12.7	10.8-14.2	14.7
Japan	5.2	8.0-8.7	8.7
Canada	0.4	1.4-2.2	1.1
Other developed country	0.7	1.5	2.0
Non-OPEC developing country	3.0	3.0-4.0	-0.8[a]
Communist	-1.1[a]	3.5-4.5	-0.8[a]
Other	0.9	0.0	0.6
OPEC domestic consumption	2.1	3.5-4.5	3.5-4.5
Required OPEC production	30.9	46.7-51.2	38.6-39.6

Source: U.S. Central Intelligence Agency

[a](-) indicates export rather than import.

point to the large and growing role that the United States and Japan play as major consumers (and importers) of petroleum supplies. Whereas these two countries today account for slightly less than 40 percent of OPEC exports, this figure could grow to almost 50 percent in the CIA worst-case scenario. Thus, it is clear that with U.S. and Japanese imports accounting for an increasingly larger proportion of required OPEC production, the commitment of these two nations to expand domestic supplies and curtail demand growth will be critical to the success of any program designed to moderate the upward pressure of world energy prices.[6]

The recently published report of the Workshop on Alternative Energy Strategies (WAES) tends to support the more pessimistic conclusions of the CIA study.[7] This report, which focuses more on the 1985-2000 period than on the period up to 1985, concludes that available supplies of oil will fail to meet increasing demands well before the year 2000 and most probably will occur between 1985 and 1995, even if energy prices rise 50 percent above current levels in real terms.[8] Additional constraints on oil production, such as environmental restrictions in the United States and the reluctance of the Saudis and certain other exporting nations to expand capacity, could hasten this shortage and thereby reduce the time available for action on alternatives. The WAES report, like those of the OECD and the CIA, underscores the important position of Saudi Arabia, the United States, and Japan in the world supply-demand picture and cites "the critical interdependence of nations in the energy field" as requiring "an unprecedented degree of international collaboration in the future" as well as "the will to mobilize finance, labor, research, and ingenuity with a common purpose never before attained in time of peace." The authors point out that "failure to recognize the importance and validity of these findings and to take appropriate and timely action could create major political and social difficulties that could cause energy to become a focus for confrontation and conflict."

Implications of World Oil Outlook

Considering the seriousness of the coming supply-demand imbalance and the failure to date of governments to take sustained action in dealing with these forecast shortages, it is appropriate for the Shimoda conference to consider some of the issues raised by the world energy situation, especially since Japan and the United States have such an important stake in the outcome. The objective for both nations is to avoid the kind of sharp energy price rise that might lead to a serious worldwide recession, cause increased unemployment in the industrialized world, and have a very severe impact on the economies of the developing countries. The problem is not so much the level of price as the rapidity and size of the change that might occur. As the WAES report points out, "in itself, a high-cost energy world could be as prosperous and appropriate for economic growth as a low-cost energy economy; it is the rapid transition that leads to the problems."[9]

One difficulty in getting governments to anticipate the problem and provide for an orderly transition to higher energy prices is the long lead time required to expand supplies. The record of the past one-half century suggests, for example, that it is becoming increasingly difficult and expensive to find and produce oil and gas supplies. More than thirty-five years elapsed between the discoveries in the East Texas field and the next major find in the United States—Prudhoe Bay on the North Slope of Alaska. And the lead times in bringing new production onto line are lengthening. Prudhoe Bay was discovered in 1968, and output will not start until 1977. In a more accessible place like the Gulf of Mexico, it will be at least five years between the discovery of Shell's Cognac field and the start of production in 1980.

These lead times are not confined to North America. The North Sea and the Middle East have experienced similar five- to ten-year lead times and the frontier areas even longer. Coal mines take four to eight years to bring into production; nuclear power, six to ten years in Europe and Japan and ten to twelve years in the United States. Thus, an electric utility that wants to have a major new plant on line and smoothly operating in 1990 must make the decision to proceed with the project within the next several months.

Given the existence of these lead times, it is important for governments in the highly industrialized countries (and particularly in the United States and Japan) to take steps to control energy growth, expand supplies from alternative sources, and develop indigenous resources of oil and gas well in advance of actual supply-demand imbalances. Otherwise, when the "crunch" comes, little can be done short of curtailing economic growth to prevent the rising demand for oil supplies from pushing prices rapidly upward. Yet, many of the actions that are required to bring supply and demand into better balance necessitate changes in consumer life-styles and living habits. These actions are difficult for politicians to take as long as the general public remains unaware of the seriousness of the problem. Clearly, that is the case today in the United States, where a recent survey found that 50 percent of the U.S. public did not realize that the United States was importing petroleum.[10]

In the current situation, it is likely that world oil supplies will remain in rough balance at current prices at least until the early 1980s, unless Saudi Arabia decides to cut production sharply. The most probable scenario is that North Slope oil will add 1.2 million barrels per day to U.S. production in 1978-1979 and that the North Sea will add 3.5 million barrels per day to Western Europe production by 1980. These additions should be adequate to meet rising demand and offset declining production from older fields, with the net result that the call on OPEC oil for the next five years will remain relatively stable.

Sometime in the 1982-1984 period, virtually all of the OPEC producers except Saudi Arabia will be producing at capacity, and the world will have to look to the Saudis to provide the incremental supplies. The remaining OPEC members—faced with these production limitations—will press even harder than they are today for price increases, since higher prices will be their only avenues for increased revenues. With OPEC oil today priced well below the price of alternative fuels, it is entirely possible that prices in the 1982-1984 period could rise rapidly and still be below the price of most alternatives. For example, an annual increase in real prices of 5 percent plus an additional increment for inflation would not be out of line with the supply-demand scenarios presented earlier. Of course, it is possible that such an increase will not occur, but for that to happen, one or more of the following would appear to be necessary:

- An extended period of slow economic growth or recession in the industrialized countries.
- Unprecedented success of conservation programs throughout the world and particularly in the United States.
- A series of major new discoveries in the 10-billion-barrel-or-over recoverable reserves category.
- A willingness on the part of Saudi Arabia to expand production to 20 to 25 million barrels per day and thereby accommodate vast excess reserves of cash.

The first alternative is obviously highly undesirable and could result in serious social unrest; the probability of the second is highly unlikely in view of the unwillingness, so far at least, of most Americans to accept the reality of the energy problem; and the chances of the third occurring seem somewhat remote when one considers that only nineteen such fields have been discovered in the last 100 years. About 60 percent of the world's oil reserves outside of the communist bloc is concentrated in the Middle East. Most of the remaining regions that might yield such results have been evaluated by sophisticated seismic techniques or exploratory wells, with no evidence of another Middle East yet found. Thus, it is clear that there is a need for broad and well-coordinated strategy among the industrialized countries to accelerate efforts to expand indigenous supplies, curtail demand, and take the diplomatic initiatives to ensure that the Saudis continue their moderate stance on oil prices by increasing production.

Some Considerations for Japan and the United States

Japan and the United States, industrialized and heavily dependent on imported energy, have as their principal energy objective the maintenance at reasonable prices of adequate and secure supplies of energy resources to meet their socioeconomic goals while maintaining some flexibility to act independently in world affairs. This broad energy objective might be further refined to include the following subobjectives:

- To maintain sufficient supplies of imported energy to meet the expectations of rising standards of living on the part of the people in each country.
- To secure these supplies of imported energy—oil, natural gas, uranium, and coal (Japan)—in a manner that reduces the risk of disruption to the extent possible; and to ensure that the economic impact of any politically motivated supply interruptions that might occur is minimized.
- To secure energy at prices that permit orderly and sustained economic growth and that minimize the risk of severe economic recession.
- To develop alternative sources of energy in sufficient quantities so that there can be an orderly transition to the period when liquid hydrocarbons are no longer readily available as an energy source.

It is obvious from the analysis in the preceding section that self-sufficiency in energy is largely irrelevant for either country or, for that matter, for any of the OECD nations except possibly Norway. Therefore, policy options to achieve these energy objectives fall into two general categories:

- National programs designed to reduce domestic vulnerability to the vagaries of overdependence on uncertain foreign supplies. Such programs would include conservation, enhanced domestic production, emergency storage, research and development of alternative sources, etc.
- International initiatives designed to create an environment favorable to supply security and reasonably stable energy prices. These initiatives might include multinational consultations, cooperative emergency-sharing programs, mechanisms for financing energy-induced balance-of-payments deficits, multinational energy research and development projects, etc.

A global energy strategy must incorporate a mix of both national programs and international initiatives and recognize both the short- and long-range implications of the current oil supply-demand situation.

- Short-range: There is every reason to believe—based on the analysis presented earlier—that the world will face an oil crunch in the early 1980s, and in the absence of major policy changes, the resultant oil price increase could be sufficient to undermine seriously the political and economic systems of some industrialized countries and a number of the nonoil-producing LDCs.
- Long-range: Even if the oil-importing nations "manage" the oil crunch of the mid-1980s, a major effort will be required to shift the word's economies away from oil and gas to other energy resources.

Toward a Japanese–U.S. Energy Policy

During the summer of 1977, the Japanese yen strengthened against the U.S. dollar to a point where it is now approaching the peak level that it reached in the year before the 1973 oil crisis. To many observers, this situation is difficult to understand, since it seems contrary to what might have been expected when OPEC oil prices were quadrupled and commodity prices elsewhere in the world soared to levels not seen since the Korean War. Japan, almost entirely dependent on external sources for a variety of critical natural resources, might have been expected to suffer by the dramatic shift in terms of trade against the manufactured goods that it exports and in favor of the natural resources that it must import. Yet today the yen is among the world's strongest currencies. Far from suffering the five- or ten-year balance-of-payments deficits that were envisaged in 1974, Japan has returned to balance-of-payments surpluses that have persisted despite the appreciation of the yen from 310 to the dollar to about 265 to the dollar. How is such a paradox to be explained, and what are the implications for a Japanese–U.S. energy policy?

The explanation is relatively straightforward. The balance of payments is fundamentally a monetary problem, not a problem of resources. Given the fact that Japanese monetary authorities have taken a relatively more conservative stance since 1973 than other monetary authorities, it follows that consumer spending, investment spending, additions to inventories, and growth in government expenditures have been lower in Japan than an easier, more expansionary policy would have allowed. And, while it may be premature to judge the future by extrapolating some recent fragmentary indications of a downturn in the month-to-month rise in Japanese consumer prices, the evidence of the longer-term relation between commodity and wholesale prices on the one hand and consumer prices on the other is at least consistent with the view that the outlook for inflation in Japan over the next few months is for a definite slowing down. A rather dramatic illustration of this is the fact that one major Japanese company is now doing its 1978-1979 forecasting on the basis of an exchange rate of 250 yen to the dollar.

Obviously, these economic factors have placed some severe strains on Japanese–U.S. relationships. The U.S. government has called on the Japanese to reflate their economy in an effort to stimulate additional imports and help the United States as well as certain European countries (Spain, Greece, Portugal, Turkey, and the Scandinavian countries) and a number of the nonoil-producing LDCs to shoulder the roughly $40 billion in income that the richest OPEC nations are collecting over and beyond what they are able to spend on imports. The hope is that by expanding internal demand and in the process increasing imports, Japan (along with West Germany, the Netherlands, and Switzerland) will fuel economic expansion in the remainder of the world and provide the deficit nations with the foreign exchange to pay for oil imports. Many Japanese have objected to this scenario and argue that excessive stimulation of Japan's economy would aggravate worldwide inflationary pressures and lead, in the end, to a further slowdown in world economic growth.

Unfortunately, these economic differences are dominating the Japanese–U.S. dialogue and tend to obscure debate on some of the more pressing energy matters facing the two countries. Therefore, in view of the critical nature of the energy situation, it is essential that the Shimoda conference attempt to reach some conclusions on an appropriate economic policy for the two countries. One possible area for compromise might be for Japan to assume a larger role in expanding the resources of the IMF by $10 to $15 billion. In this way, Japan could shoulder a greater share of the burden of funding the oil deficits without necessarily upsetting an orderly growth of its economy.

On the narrower question of a Japanese–U.S. energy strategy, it is important that the discussion begin with a recognition of the key roles that both countries play as major oil importers. It is vital for the two nations to pursue policies that will limit imports, curtail demand, and step up domestic production.[11] Of immediate concern on the supply side of this equation is the role of nuclear energy and coal in each country, and, for Japan in particular, nuclear energy. Unlike the United States, Japan depends almost solely on imports for natural uranium, but if spent fuel can be reprocessed to create plutonium, the effectiveness of uranium as an energy source is increased severalfold. Therefore, the Japanese have tended to view plutonium as a semidomestic energy source.[12]

Japanese government officials and industrialists have expressed growing concern over the Carter nuclear initiatives. They fear that any limitations on the development of spent fuel reprocessing facilities or the breeder reactor will worsen Japan's already high dependence on foreign oil. They assert that in 1974 the U.S. government encouraged Japanese reprocessing and use of plutonium in return for extending uranium enrichment services to Japan. Further, they argue that for the United States to withhold consent for the Japanese to reprocess spent fuel domestically or to commission overseas agencies to do it for them—a consent that they are required to obtain under the U.S.–Japan Atomic Power Energy Cooperation Agreement—is a violation of the spirit of the Nuclear Nonproliferation Treaty.

The U.S. initiative is designed to reduce the motivation of nations to acquire nuclear weapons as well as their technical ability to do so. The International Atomic Energy Agency (IAEA) safeguard system has been successful in the case of the current generation of nuclear reactors in that it provides a warning signal sufficiently far in advance so that diplomacy can work in the event of the deliberate diversion. But, as the U.S. representatives pointed out at the International Conference on Nuclear Power and Its Fuel Cycle at Salzburg, "for certain facilities such as reprocessing, a safeguards system, even if technically perfect, does not prevent the spread of direct weapons-useable material that results from normal operations . . . our present dilemma is how to cope with developments in commercial nuclear energy which threaten to empty safeguards of their central political meaning."[13] In response to this dilemma, the United States has taken a number of domestic and international initiatives, including a decision to defer domestically, and not to export, commercial reprocessing facilities. And, to alleviate the concern of other countries for the security of their fuel supplies, the U.S. government has made a commitment to expand enrichment capacity and reopen its order books. Concurrently, President Carter has called for all interested countries to join with the United States in an International Nuclear Fuel Cycle Evaluation Program (INFCEP) to examine current problems associated with the fuel cycle, such as reliable fuel supply and means of storing spent fuel, and to study alternative future fuel cycles, including future generations of reactors and institutional arrangements for reducing proliferation risks.

Clearly, nuclear policy is emerging as a major point of contention between the United States and Japan, and it is equally clear that both countries must move forward with aggressive nuclear power programs if the oil crunch scenario is to be avoided. The Shimoda conference must, therfore, consider the merits of each country's position and attempt to reach a common understanding upon which future policy can be based. The questions to be addressed include: Should Japan be encouraged to participate meaningfully in the INFCEP? Should the United States, on the other hand, modify its position and encourage the Japanese to proceed with breeder and reprocessing technologies even as the INFCEP is conducting its studies? What modifications might be made in U.S. policy that would make it more acceptable to Japan without enhancing the risks of weapons proliferation?

The Shimoda conference also may want to deal with some of the issues surrounding U.S. coal exports to Japan. Both countries have embarked on programs to make greater use of steam coal under industrial and power plant boilers. For Japan, where current annual coal production of about 20 million tons has reached the limit of known reserves, the policy will necessitate a sharp increase in steam coal imports from a negligible 0.5 million tons in 1975 to between 6 to 16 million tons by 1985 and perhaps as much as 40 million tons by 1990.[14] Since the United States is seen as one of the primary suppliers of Japanese coal, it is important to begin developing long-term agreements under which the Japanese can have assured access to western U.S. coal at competitive prices and perhaps can participate in the development of these resources. At the same time, both the United States and Japan currently lack the facilities to convert coal to cleaner burning gas and liquids— facilities that will be necessary if coal is to replace imported oil in any major way over the next twenty-five years. It would seem appropriate, therefore, for the two countries to develop joint research and development programs for coal conversion technology and perhaps participate in one or more jointly funded demonstration plants. Over time, these research efforts, if successful, could be broadened to include other technologies such as solar energy, an area in which the Japanese Project Sunshine is currently moving ahead. It would be appropriate for the Shimoda conference to consider under what circumstances it might be appropriate to encourage joint Japanese–U.S. research on energy technologies.

Beyond these strictly national programs, both Japan and the United States have an important stake in continuing the North-South dialogue with the objective of ensuring the economic stability of the LDCs, particularly of those without oil or other exportable natural resources. The dismal end to the North-South conference in Paris[15] has left the world still searching for a successful formula for bringing rich and poor nations together at the negotiating table in the quest for a new international economic order. The Paris Conference was the third major international negotiating session in barely over one year to achieve much less than the developed countries had originally hoped for—others being the May 1977 UNCTAD meeting in Nairobi and the abortive Common Fund negotiating conference in Geneva in March 1977.

There were some positive achievements that came out of the twenty-seven-nation Paris Conference on International Economic Cooperation. The eight industrialized participants pledged themselves to increase financial and technical aid; a joint text was agreed to on a new Common Fund to stabilize commodity prices; and the Western nations agreed to subscribe to a $1 billion special fund to help the poorest LDCs. But no progress was made with the pressing problem of debt relief, and the West failed to receive an agreement to continuing consultations on energy.

The dialogue will, of course, continue in the multitude of international organizations dealing with economic matters, but neither side finds that mode of operation totally satisfactory. The West hesitates to conduct serious negotiations in bodies such as the United Nations or UNCTAD, where the developing countries are in the majority. The developing nations, on the other hand, are critical of such organizations as the GATT, the IMF, and the World Bank, which, they say, are dominated by the rich Western nations. And the wealthy countries can never be expected to take the poorer countries' interests into account, say the developing nations. It is for these reasons that attention is now being focused on what is known as restructuring the United Nations to turn it into an effective negotiating body on economic issues. Starting on September 13, 1977, there is to be a special four-day final session of last year's United Nations General Assembly, which recessed in December, to review the results of the Paris Conference. The debate will then be continued in the new session, which starts on September 20.

The more crucial test of North-South relations will be the resumed November negotiating conference in Geneva on the Common Fund to stabilize commodity prices, which the developing countries continue to regard as the key symbol of the West's willingness to reform the world economic system in their favor. Since the outcome of that conference is obviously so important to future North-South relationships, it might be well for the Shimoda conference to consider whether it is possible for Japan and the United States to agree on a common position toward both the developing nations and OPEC in advance of future negotiating sessions. For example, could the two countries agree on a strategy whereby OPEC would be encouraged to raise prices in relatively manageable annual increments rather than run the risk of sharp and economically damaging increases in the early 1980s? Should Japan encourage the United States to continue to strengthen its special relationship with Saudi Arabia as a means of assuring access for both countries to increased quantities of Saudi crude? If these and other questions can be resolved and the key elements of such a Japanese–U.S. position developed, and if a better understanding can be reached between leaders in the two nations on nuclear and coal policies, then we might be able to mark another milestone in the strengthening of Japanese–U.S. relations and in the emergence of Japan as an increasingly important factor in multinational negotiating forums.

Notes

1. Trilateral Commission, *Energy: A Strategy for International Action*, 1974, p. 10.

2. As W. W. Clausen, president of BankAmerica Corporation, pointed out in a recent talk before the Bank of America New York Board Luncheon in Tokyo on April 28, 1977, "the current debt servicing problems of higher income, non-oil LDCs won't disappear even though the volume of world trade recovers from the 1974-75 recession. . . . Governments of the industrialized countries—and this includes both Japan and the United States—should provide increasing financial support to multilateral financial institutions including the World Bank Group, IMF, and regional development banks. These financial institutions have the ability—and for a number of LDCs the sole ability—to provide long-term credit so that these countries can refinance their debt and bring it to manageable proportions."

3. *World Energy Outlook*, OECD, Paris, 1977; *The International Energy Situation: Outlook to 1985*, U.S. Central Intelligence Agency, 1977; Carroll W. Wilson, ed., *Energy: Global Prospects 1985-2000, A Report of the Workshop on Alternative Energy Strategies* (Cambridge, Mass.: MIT Press, 1977).

4. For the most part, the U.S. National Energy Plan fails to address the environmental issues raised by the higher coal and liquid hydrocarbon production targets. For example, according to the Congressional Research Service, with the projected increased use of coal, annual amounts of nitrogen oxides produced are predicted to reach nearly 28 million tons more than today's level, even with the application of the best available control technology to all new sources. While it is true that the fluidized-bed method of burning coal is a promising way of reducing nitrogen oxide emission, only small units are commercially available at present, and there is little prospect for their commercial use in electrical generation by 1985. Furthermore, according to a report delivered to the United States National Academy of Sciences in late July by a panel studying the atmospheric effects of burning fossil fuels, the longer-run outlook for coal is questionable. No technology now known can eliminate carbon dioxide, the main combustion product of coal. Yet, the report anticipates a 25 percent increase in atmospheric carbon dioxide over national levels by the end of this century and a doubling in the next, assuming current population and energy consumption trends. If this happens, the "greenhouse effect" of carbon dioxide interfering with infrared radiation into space would warm the earth by about 11 degrees Fahrenheit by the latter part of the twenty-second century The consequences of such a change could include radical disruption of agriculture and a melting and breakup of polar icecaps with a twenty-foot rise in sea level and widespread flooding.

5. Since the OECD forecast was published in spring 1976, most analysts have increased the estimate of the 1985 OECD Europe import requirements by a minimum of 2 million barrels per day to compensate for the slower than anticipated buildup in nuclear power capacity.

6. Recent analyses by the Japanese Institute of Energy Economies are not encouraging in this regard. Projections of nuclear power capacity have been cut back from 40 million kilowatts to 26-33 million kilowatts, with a resultant increase in the demand for imported oil.

7. Wilson, *Energy*.

8. The specific year in which shortages occur depends upon assumptions about economic growth, energy prices, the strength of government policies in pursuing alternative strategies, OPEC production limits, etc.

9. Wilson, *Energy*, p. 5.

10. CBS–*New York Times* survey, fall 1977.

11. It is probably true that Japan, which consumes less than one-third the energy per capita than the United States, does not have the same capability for reducing energy demand growth as the United States. It was for this reason that the 1974 Trilateral Commission Task Force on Energy called for an annual energy demand growth rate in Japan (4 percent) that was twice as large as the target for the United States (2 percent).

12. This point was clearly made in an address by Toshiwo Doko, president of Japan Federation of Economic Organizations, at a Japan Society dinner in New York on June 13, 1977.

13. Statement, Joseph S. Nye, deputy to the undersecretary of state for Security Assistance, Science and Technology, at the International Conference on Nuclear Power and Its Fuel Cycle, Salzburg, Austria, May 2, 1977.

14. Forecast, Japanese Institute of Energy Economics.

15. The conference ended in June 1977.

13
Administration of the World Economy and Japan

Takashi Hosomi

World Economic Issues

The Unfolding Drama

In the thirty-odd years since World War II, there have been three acts in the drama of world economic development. Act I was the recovery from wartime destruction. The United States emerged virtually unscathed from the fires of war as the dominant producer and supplier of the world. The trade surpluses accumulated by the United States were channeled back to deficit countries in the form of transfer payments, aid, and investment. The most serious problem in managing the world economy was the shortage of dollars. The U.S. dollar as an international currency was backed completely by gold. Since the dollar was "as good as gold," all national currencies were pegged to it, and all national economic policies were formulated in the context of compulsory adjustment to the dollar-gold standard. The unipolar mechanism in the world economy centering on the U.S. dollar lasted throughout the 1950s, providing a stable basis for recovery and growth. To countries with strong growth potential like Japan, the "Pax Americana" was an enormous boon for it contributed to holding down inflation, encouraging savings, expanding imports, and raising domestic investment.

The curtain rose on Act II before the world was quite aware of what was happening. The overwhelming U.S. dominance in production and supply had slowly declined, but no corresponding adjustments had been made in the role assigned the United States and the dollar in administering the world economy. This inconsistency was exacerbated in the 1960s by the increasing seriousness of the North-South problem and the Vietnam War.

When the link between the dollar and gold was officially severed in 1971 and the system of fixed exchange rates officially was brought to an end in early 1973, people finally began to realize that what they were watching was no longer Act I but Act II. The awakening actually came a good ten years after the fact. The period from the 1960s through the early 1970s was spent, so to speak, trying to understand the plot of Act II. Unfortunately, it was never revealed. Everyone recognized that some sort of multipolar structure would have to follow the collapse of the unipolar system centering on the dollar. With the benefit of hindsight, however, we can see now that in searching for a new multipolar structure we were too taken with an inflationary approach that placed altogether too much emphasis on the advanced industrial nations. The first conference on the Group of Ten finance ministers was held in 1962, when the excessive burden placed on the United States and the dollar was noticed. That conference was the natural first step toward a multipolar mechanism, and the Group of Ten was to play the stellar role in Act II.

The group's weakness, however, was its inability to move beyond the outmoded plot of Act I, according to which equilibrium among the advanced industrial nations was the necessary and sufficient condition for equilibrium in the world economy. In 1972, when the Bretton Woods system collapsed in fact as well as in name, the search for a new international monetary system led to the formation of the Committee of Twenty, which included the less industrialized nations as well. The committee published its conclusions in 1974 as an "Outline of International Monetary Reform," but here again, the basic tendency was to emphasize equilibrium only among the advanced industrial nations. Most people overlooked the fact that the international economic order within which a monetary system must function had changed fundamentally in the preceding twenty years.

The blow dealt advanced industrial nations by OPEC's sharp unilateral increase of oil prices at the end of 1973 was a severe retaliation for past negligence. Absolutely no efforts had been made in the course of the international monetary adjustment process that followed the summer 1971 Nixon shocks to consider seriously the interests of the developing nations, including those of the oil producers. Moreover, in fear of deflationary impact of monetary adjustment, the advanced industrialized nations gave first priority to domestic employment and exported their inflation. Factors such as these triggered the oil crisis.

Wounds Inflicted by the Oil Crisis

These events led into Act III, and the oil shock provided a curtain-raiser much more dramatic and disorderly than the one that had ushered in Act II. The oil crisis brought a sudden shift in the international capital flow, with the oil-producing nations registering enormous surpluses and importing nations experiencing equally dramatic deficits. That turn was so extraordinary that the 1972 OPEC current-account surplus of $700 million jumped to $3.5 billion in 1973 then soared to $59.5 billion in 1974. The initial shock was so great that the price forecasts and estimates of OPEC surpluses were extremely erratic, ranging from highly optimistic to very pessimistic. The majority, though, foretold doomsday, when the oil-importing nations would be hounded by deflationary pressure beyond all possibility of adjustment, the OPEC countries would continue to amass enormous surpluses, and these surpluses would be unable to be recycled smoothly.

By 1975, however, predictions turned more optimistic. Now the oil-importing countries were thought to be gradually adjusting to the new price system and the OPEC nations to be increasing their import demand. Accordingly, the OPEC current-account surplus was not anticipated to be as great as once was thought. Concerning the reflux of oil money, it was believed that the stable flow was broadening and that the attitude of the OPEC nations was showing definite signs of maturity.

Yet, I cannot but believe that such optimism is premature.

When the outlook for development of alternative energy
sources by the oil-importing nations and the forecasts concerning the probable increases to be expected in the oil
producers' absorptive capacity are taken into consideration,
one can only conclude that a large OPEC current-account
surplus will last for a long time. As a result, the OPEC nations
will amass enormous financial assets. It is possible that those
assets will be held in a stable manner, but it is conceivable
that under some unforeseeable circumstances they could
become a source of disorder. Therefore, gradually increasing
pressure toward instability in the international monetary
situation is probably unavoidable. Moreover, the continuation
of large-scale deficits on the part of the oil-importing nations
is enough to cause continuous leaks in effective demand with
the deflationary gap constricting economic growth.

Under such circumstances, large differences in economic
performance open up among oil-importing nations, including
both advanced industrial countries and developing nations
that are not oil producers, leading to a pronounced polariza-
tion between strong countries and weak ones. The latter will
be forced to adopt retrenchment policies to improve their
balance-of-payments position, but limits will be imposed by
domestic issues such as unemployment. In addition, weak and
strong will find themselves in conflict over how to distribute
the financial burdens, and the danger of protectionism will
grow large. Probably the most serious scars left by the oil crisis
are the perpetual nightmares that experience will inflict on
the economies of oil-importing nations.

Two lessons from the oil crisis were that import prices for
oil are very inelastic and that the initiative in price and supply
determination lies almost entirely with the OPEC nations.
Just how far the OPEC countries will be able to go on arbi-
trarily manipulating price and supply in the future is an open
question. Even if OPEC were to continue efforts to maintain a
reasonable stance, no one can say with confidence that no
further dramatic changes will occur in oil price and supply,
especially when domestic political conditions, tensions between Arabs and Israelis, and the Middle East confrontation
between the United States and the Soviet Union are considered.

It is no doubt true that only our own naivete can explain why such concerns were not voiced before 1973. At any rate, fear of a renewed outbreak of panic and, more fundamentally, apprehension that resources are inadequate to provide the energy necessary for world economic development, act as a fatal depressant on business psychology in the oil-importing nations, particularly those like Japan with a high degree of dependence on imported oil. One of the main reasons why Japan has not yet recovered completely from the recession of two years ago is that managers have insufficient confidence in the future to make the required capital outlays. Business psychology itself has undergone profound structural change.

Overcoming the Malaise

The major problem now facing the world economy is still the scars of disequilibrium left by the oil crisis. Realistically, they cannot be cleared up entirely in the near future. That being the case, we have no alternative but to continue trying to steer the world economy safely while remaining mindful of the dangers.

First, we must strengthen our efforts to reduce the deficits of the oil-importing nations by improving OPEC's absorptive capacity while at the same time expanding the export capability of oil-importing nations vis-à-vis OPEC. Second, on the assumption that it is unrealistic to expect that efforts to develop alternative sources of energy will bear fruit in the near future, constraints on oil consumption must be made as tight as possible, particularly in countries that are large importers. The degree of success of the United States in such efforts will have an important influence on the situation in the rest of the world.

Since the oil importers will still have deficits, realistic measures are essential to make the financial burden bearable. First of all, imbalances among the oil-importing nations must be reduced to the lowest possible level. For that purpose, international consultations for the harmonization of economic policies will be necessary. Second, financial facilities will have to be made available for nations facing balance-of-payments difficulties, and efforts will have to be continued to facilitate the recycling of oil money. Third, and most important, is the difficult task of restoring confidence in the future among management and workers in the oil-importing nations. For this, no instant remedy is available, but the need for a firm policy stance by the governments is readily apparent. The posture of the U.S. government in this regard is extremely influential. To bring the world through this period of instability, the United States will have to display a firm and credible position not only in its economic and energy policies, but in diplomatic and military affairs as well.

Japan's Resource Strategy and Trade Relations with Industrial Countries

The Resource Problem

Little need be said about Japan's lack of resources. In 1976 Japan imported 100 percent of its crude oil, iron ore, cotton, wool, bauxite, and gum rubber, 77 percent of its coal, and 97 percent of its copper ore. If trade were completely cut off, the 110 million people on this group of small Pacific islands would perish in a very short time. Japan is probably the only major nation in the world for which this tragic prospect is a reality. As a result of this acute vulnerability in the realms of raw materials, energy, and food resources, Japan has the least economic security of any major nation.

According to forecasts of long-term technological progress, we should not completely reject the possibility of some epoch-making alternatives appearing in such fields as nuclear power and the use of seawater. For the foreseeable future, however, we will have to continue relying on traditional sources of raw materials and energy. Moreover, we have become increasingly aware that the supplies of these traditional resources are limited. We must conclude that Japan's economic vulnerability may increase for some time to come and certainly will not decline. That being the case, Japan must devote the highest priority to whatever degree of alleviation of that vulnerability is possible by securing a stable supply of raw materials and energy through economic and peaceful means. What Japan should do is:

1. Cooperate in maintaining a stable, peaceful international economic order. It is primarily through the continuity of more than thirty years of stable and peaceful international economic order that Japan, despite its vulnerability, has risen to a position of economic strength second only to the United States in the Free World. A peaceful framework has been particularly essential to Japan because of its relative lack of the diplomatic and military power that other states are able to bring to bear in achieving their objectives.

2. Work hard for the maintenance and enhancement of the principle of free trade. Japan's sources of raw materials and energy resources span the world and must be diversified even further. The areas where close relations are particularly essential are the Pacific-rim nations such as the United States, Canada, Australia, New Zealand, and Indonesia, the Middle East, and certain Latin American nations. It is necessary for Japan to avoid provoking the hostility of any nation and to expand a variegated web of interdependent relationships throughout the world.

3. Promote financial and technical cooperation with nations able to supply resources. Developing nations in possession of resources, particularly oil, are not satisfied with just selling their raw materials as primary products. They demand greater value added and seek to industrialize. In the future, great care will be necessary to avoid giving the impression that the advanced industrialized nations are exploiting primary-product-supplier countries. Japan must provide them with direct aid in terms of both technology and capital, thereby raising their productivity and earning ratios. Moreover, by promoting processing facilities in producer countries, Japan can help them retain value-added earnings and in that manner provide them with direct and indirect aid toward the goal of industrialization. Such a process will burden Japan with higher manufacturing costs, but it is a price we must pay as a vulnerable industrial economy. On the other hand, such a policy will increase mutual dependence and thereby help in securing

a stable supply of resources.
4. Increase long-term contracts for a stable supply of resources. In concluding long-term contracts with the resource-producing nations, Japan will have to consider responding favorably to their demands for export compensation. We must not forget that stability does not come cheaply.
5. Increase reserves of major raw material and energy supplies to the maximum possible extent. Such stockpiles mean added costs, but just as in the case of oil reserves, they improve our bargaining power and must be regarded as a necessary expense for resource-poor economies.

Even these efforts will not in themselves assure our access to all the resources that we need. As already noted, we always will live with a certain degree of economic vulnerability, and as our economy—and that of the world—expands, that vulnerability will increase. It is also true, however, that as our dependence on imports of energy, raw materials, and food expand in volume, our position as a major buyer contributing to the expansion of the world economy will be strengthened.

In 1975 Japanese imports accounted for 45 percent of total world trade in iron ore, 12 percent in grain, 48 percent in lumber, and 18 percent in crude oil. When imports assume these proportions, their weight vis-à-vis the income and employment of supplier nations is so enormous that it cannot be ignored. Rather than begging, Japan is actually guaranteeing a large portion of the exporting countries' income and employment.

Japan's resource position requires delicate handling. It has strengths as well as weaknesses, and it inevitably involves noneconomic factors. Above all, what is necessary is a relationship of true interdependence with resource-producing nations and the rationality on both sides to recognize it.

Trade Relations with Advanced Countries

In the absence of raw materials, Japan is destined to be a processing and trading nation. As an island country that industrialized in relative isolation from the major industrial centers of the world, in the attempt to catch up with them, Japan has always had a strong instinct of self-preservation. That instinct has been manifested in a desire to be self-sufficient in all manufactured products, making Japan fundamentally different from the nations that developed in the Western industrial centers. Horizontal international specialization, therefore, comes less naturally to Japan than to other industrialized nations.

Japan's industrial and trade structure, with its emphasis on processing, makes unavoidable an unfavorable trade balance with the raw-material and energy-resource nations and a favorable balance with all the others, including, of course, the advanced industrialized nations. Moreover, since Japan's economic structure dictates large deficits in trade-related service transactions, it must have a correspondingly high surplus in trade transactions. The Japanese economy has, therefore, an inherent propensity toward friction with advanced industrialized nations. A country that rejects horizontal international specialization and amasses large trade surpluses can hardly be considered a desirable trading partner for industrialized countries.

When Japan's share of the world export market was minimal, this situation was tolerable. But in 1976 Japan accounted for 13 percent of total world exports of manufactured products. Obviously, we can no longer ask for indulgence on the basis of geographical or historical circumstances. That fact is illustrated by the recent trade friction with the United States and the European Community.

Japan wants to maintain a certain level of surplus in its trade with the advanced industrial nations. As long as Japanese exports are high in quality and are competitively priced, they will contribute to holding down inflation in the importing nations and will benefit consumers. Nevertheless, we always must bear in mind the possibility of Japanese exports falling victim to a witch hunt at a time of bankruptcies and unemployment. If Japan intends to continue a trade surplus with the industrialized nations while creating minimum friction, there are several needs that have to be met simultaneously.

In the realm of imports, we must embark on programs to promote horizontal international specialization in manufactured goods and liberalization of agricultural product imports, with full realization that such a course of action will cause long and agonizing changes in our economic and social structures. If Japan is to claim the rights of free trade, it naturally must open its own doors to trade, not just to the advanced industrialized nations, but also to the semi-industrialized areas such as South Korea and Hong Kong. Here, too, adjustment assistance is indispensable. We must pursue a domestic economic policy aimed at stable expansion of import demand. Also, in order to facilitate penetration of Japanese markets by foreign goods, efforts to remove nontariff barriers to trade must continue.

Turning to exports, in order to avoid the monopolization by Japanese goods of too large a market share in any given nation as a result of precipitous increases in exports, there will have to be an effective program of monitoring and control. We should also expand the level of direct investment in the industrialized nations by constructing more plants and facilities there. This will be welcomed as a contribution to employment as well as a stimulus to the local economy.

Direct investment in manufacturing requires large capital outlays, in many instances production in a foreign nation means higher costs and lower quality. Therefore, as long as export is possible, there are few incentives for export industries to produce abroad. Nevertheless, exporters will have to understand that from a long-range perspective direct investment is inevitable.

There are two realities about trade relations with the advanced industrial nations that, if properly recognized, will serve the interests of all. The first is that free trade is a matter of life and death for Japan. Japan must take the lead in championing that principle. Fortunately for Japan, the United States and West Germany still remain strong advocates of free trade, and other nations have not yet reached the point of totally deserting the principle. The second is that Japan must develop an open economic system in which the entire world can enter as both stockholder and customer. These realities will take time to make themselves understood. Haste produces only friction.

A Stable Monetary System

The Need for a Flexible Structure

Two things are demanded of any monetary system: that it work, and that it be stable. Few, therefore, would contest the desirability of a fixed exchange rate system, as long as it is viable. Japan's postwar economic development for twenty-two years depended heavily on the maintenance of the fixed exchange rate of ¥360 to the dollar.

The problem is that we now lack the objective conditions that would allow a fixed exchange rate system to be viable. After the collapse of the unipolar international mechanism centering on the United States and the dollar, no assets existed that would work as a stable standard of value. In addition, there was no easy way to rectify the fundamental worldwide disequilibrium created by the oil crisis.

This situation makes a system of fixed exchange rates unviable in any form. With the world economy in a state of flux, the monetary system must be flexible as well. The new International Monetary Fund Agreement, which is now in the process of ratification by member nations, will leave the choice of an exchange-rate system up to each nation. This amounts to little more than a confirmation of existing conditions, but under the circumstances it is the most realistic approach.

When we cast our eyes back over the tumultuous change that has beset international finance after the oil crisis, it is plain that the system of floating rates was the only practical alternative. As long as large-scale disequilibrium remains, this is the only international monetary system that can function without collapsing. Further, as long as there is no prospect of fundamental change in the present situation of instability, the float will have to continue.

The Float and Issues for the Future

On the other hand, the float has not functioned in a totally satisfactory manner. Even if we look only at the OECD nations, it is evident that rate fluctuations under the float have not functioned to adjust imbalances in international accounts. Nevertheless, because of the floating rate, a significant number of nations are now determined to rectify their balance-of-payments problems through domestic economic policy.

Thus, even though continuing the float is the most realistic alternative, we cannot expect the float alone to redress balance-of-payments problems. It is necessary, above all, for the major nations, particularly the key currency countries, to conduct economic policy in a disciplined and prudent manner. This makes policy coordination among the major nations more important than ever. The new IMF agreement provides for IMF surveillance of exchange-rate policy, and this process, too, functions as an important link in international policy coordination. One practical problem is that under present conditions, policymakers cannot choose between adjustment and finance. Adequate financing facilities must be provided. Nevertheless, it should be made clear that they are always subject to an element of conditionality, in which financing functions only as a support mechanism for the ultimate purpose of promoting adjustment.

When OPEC amasses a large volume of financial assets, stability in key currencies is crucially important. Present circumstances demand on the one hand a system that is not fixed, but elastic. Those circumstances also require, however, that the elasticity not be without guiding principles. If wild fluctuations in key currencies were to cause a general loss of confidence in financial assets held in those currencies, it is not difficult to imagine the disruption that would result. Therefore, the stability of the dollar, yen, and mark, and the stable interrelationship among them, are the ingredients of the best monetary system that we can expect under the circumstances. They are also absolutely essential.

Japanese Conceptions of and Role in Economic Assistance

Japan's foreign aid began in the form of reparations to those Asian nations that suffered at Japanese hands during

World War II. It was treated primarily as a vital link in export-promotion policy. Reparations would help increase the purchasing power of the recipient nations, which would, in turn, enable them to import Japanese products. Thus, aid was perceived as a means of expanding Japan's overseas markets. Such a conception of foreign aid was perhaps natural from the point of view of Japan, which had just lost all of its reliable markets abroad and for which exporting was the only way for survival. In consequence, however, the deferred payment loan became the dominant form of Japanese aid, and official development assistance (ODA) aid was often tied to the export of Japanese products.

It must be admitted that in carrying out its aid programs, Japan gave little heed to the needs of the recipients. No one would expect a car buyer purchasing on installment to express his thanks to the dealer, and likewise, the recipient nations have been little appreciative of this type of aid. The opposite has been the general rule: Japanese aid has usually caused smoldering resentment.

Not until Japanese products gained a high degree of competitive strength and began to create their own demand did our concept of aid move to a higher plane. It was no longer crucial to regard foreign aid as a support for the export drive. Japanese became aware of the global implications of their industrial development and began to see economic assistance in this broader context.

Aid now means for Japan a method of contributing to a stronger, more stable framework for world economics and politics. In concrete terms, it is hoped that aid will help Japan obtain energy and raw materials and heighten the level of its economic security. An aid program with these goals will no longer be geared toward promoting Japanese exports, but toward helping the recipient nation develop itself.

Although such a forward-looking stance is fast becoming part of the attitude toward aid, the programs themselves still retain many drawbacks. First is the lack of efficiency due largely to the complexity of administrative mechanisms for handling aid. The Economic Planning Agency, the Ministry of Foreign Affairs, the Ministry of Finance, and the Ministry of International Trade and Industry jointly administer aid programs, which often gives rise to competition over authority, great amounts of red tape, and a slow process of decision making. The ministers involved also tend to intervene excessively in the affairs of the institutions responsible for executing aid programs, such as the Economic Cooperation Fund, the Import-Export Bank, and the Japan International Cooperation Agency. This interferes with appropriate timing and judgments in the process of identifying, screening, and making decisions on aid projects. In order to overcome this deficiency, authority for planning and disbursement should be integrated under the aegis of a Ministry of Economic Assistance.

The second problem is the lack of revenue sources because of fiscal stringency. Although Japan's defense expenditure is small, government spending plays a major role in the national economy. With the rapid increases in recent years of expenses for what has by now become a sacred cow—welfare— it will be very difficult for the Japanese government to find financial sources for economic assistance.

As a result of Prime Minister Fukuda's recent trip to the ASEAN nations, Japan will have to adopt a much more forward-looking stance in its aid to Southeast Asia. Because of the failure of Japanese colonialism and of other bitter war-related experiences in Southeast Asia, Japan seems reluctant to adopt any clearly defined principle in dealing with the region. When Japanese rid themselves of the thinking that an aid-recipient nation is merely a market for goods, and when they become aware that the objective of aid has to be the building of a stable economic and political system in the recipient nation, then Japanese assistance will enter on a new period of real progress. Such a development would be the realization of what Prime Minister Fukuda has called "heart-to-heart communication" with Southeast Asia. It has taken a long time for Japan to arrive at this stage. Other nations get infuriated over the sluggishness of Japanese decision making, but the correct course finally has been set.

Appendixes

APPENDIX A:
Participants in the Fourth Shimoda Conference

Japanese Participants

Nobuhiko Ushiba: Co-Chairman of the Shimoda Conference, Advisor to the Minister for Foreign Affairs, and Former Japanese Ambassador to the United States.

Tadashi Yamamoto: Co-Director of the Shimoda Conference, and Director of Japan Center for International Exchange.

Naohiro Amaya: Director-General, Basic Industries Bureau, Ministry of International Trade and Industry.

Tasuku Asano: Professor of Political Science, International College of Commerce and Economics.

Hideo Den: Member, House of Councillors (Japan Socialist Party).

Jun Eto: Professor of Comparative Literature and Culture, Tokyo Institute of Technology.

Sanshichi Hanyu: Former Member, House of Councillors (Member, Japan Socialist Party).

Takashi Hosomi: Advisor, Industrial Bank of Japan, Former Vice-Minister of Finance for International Affairs.

The affiliations of the participants are as of September, 1977

Akira Iriye: Professor of History, University of Chicago.

Asahi Kameyama: Foreign Editor, Kyodo News Agency.

Koichi Kato: Member of House of Representatives (Liberal Democratic Party).

Seishi Kato: President, Toyota Motor Sales Company.

Tamio Kawakami: Member, House of Representatives (Japan Socialist Party).

Hiroshi Kitamura: Deputy Director-General, American Affairs Bureau, Ministry of Foreign Affairs.

Yotaro Kobayashi: Executive Vice-President, Fuji Xerox Co., Ltd.

Yohei Kohno: Member, House of Representatives (President, New Liberal Club).

Akinobu Kojima: Director and Managing Editor, *The Nihon Keizai Shimbun (The Japan Economic Journal)*.

Tokusaburo Kosaka: Member, House of Representatives (Liberal Democratic Party).

Masao Kunihiro: Professor of Cultural Anthropology, International College of Commerce and Economics.

Yukio Matsuyama: Senior Staff and Editorial Writer, *The Asahi Shimbun*.

Isamu Miyazaki: Director-General, Coordination Bureau, Economic Planning Agency.

Kiichi Miyazawa: Member, House of Representatives (Liberal Democratic Party).

Akio Morita: Chairman and Chief Executive Officer, Sony Corporation.

Kinhide Mushakoji: Vice-Rector, United Nations University.

Kazuji Nagasu: Governor of Kanagawa Prefecture.

Yoshimi Nakagawa: Member, House of Representatives (Komeito).

Nobuyuki Nakahara: Managing Director, Toa Nenryo Kogyo, K.K.

Kazuo Nukazawa: Senior Assistant Director, International Economic Affairs, Federation of Economic Organizations.

Akira Ogata: Chief News Commentator, Japan Broadcasting Corporation (NHK).

Takashi Oyamada: Managing Director, Japan Foundation.

Hisashi Owada: Secretary to the Prime Minister.

Kiichi Saeki: President, Nomura Research Institute.

Takeo Sasagawa: Director, International Projects, *The Sankei Shimbun.*

Hideo Sato: Assistant Professor of Political Science, Yale University.

Masahide Shibusawa: Director, East-West Seminar.

Ichiro Shioji: President, Confederation of the Japan Automobile Workers' Unions.

Kenichi Ueda: Editorial Staff Writer, *The Mainichi Shimbun.*

Jiro Ushio: President, Ushio Electric Inc.

Koji Watanabe: Director, First North American Division, American Affairs Bureau, Ministry of Foreign Affairs.

Ro Watanabe: Member, House of Representatives (Democratic Socialist Party).

Toshio Yamazaki: Director-General, American Affairs Bureau, Ministry of Foreign Affairs.

Toru Yano: Associate Professor of Political Science, Kyoto University.

Shiro Yasuda: Foreign News Editor, *The Yomiuri Shimbun.*

Takeshi Yasukawa: Counselor, Mitsui and Co., Former Japanese Ambassador to the United States.

American Participants

Robert Ingersoll: Co-Chairman of the Shimoda Conference, Deputy Chairman of the Board, University of Chicago, Former Deputy Secretary of State, and Former U.S. Ambassador to Japan.

David W. MacEachron: Co-Director of the Shimoda Conference, Executive Director, Japan Society, Inc.

Morton I. Abramowitz: Deputy Assistant Secretary for East Asian and Pacific Affairs/Inter-American Affairs, Office of the Assistant Secretary for International Security Affairs, Department of Defense.

Michael H. Armacost: Senior Staff Member for East Asia, National Security Council, The White House.

Les Aspin: U.S. House of Representatives (Democrat, Armed Services Committee).

George Chaplin: Editor-in-Chief, *The Honolulu Advertiser,* Former President, American Society of Newspaper Editors.

Barber B. Conable, Jr.: U.S. House of Representatives (Republican, Ways and Means Committee).

William Diebold, Jr.: Senior Research Fellow, Council on Foreign Relations.

William D. Eberle: President, U.S. Council of the International Chamber of Commerce, Former President's Special Representative for Trade Negotiations.

John H. Glenn, Jr.: U.S. Senate (Democrat, Foreign Relations Committee), Chairman, Senate Subcommittee on East Asian and Pacific Affairs.

Carl J. Green: Representative in Japan, The Ford Foundation.

Charles B. Heck: North American Secretary, The Trilateral Commission.

Walter E. Hoadley: Executive Vice-President and Chief Economist, Bank of America NT & SA.

James D. Hodgson: Former U.S. Ambassador to Japan, Former Secretary of Labor.

Mike Mansfield: U.S. Ambassador to Japan, Former U.S. Senator.

Jiro Murase: Senior Partner, Wender, Murase, and White.

Herbert Passin: Chairman, Department of Sociology, Columbia University.

Michael W. D. McMullen: Executive Assistant to the Chairman of the Board, The Coca-Cola Company.

Herbert Passin: Professor of Sociology, Columbia University.

Hugh T. Patrick: Professor of Far Eastern Economics, Yale University, Director, Yale Economic Growth Center.

William R. Pearce: Vice-President, Cargill, Inc., Former President's Deputy Special Representative for Trade Negotiations.

Russell A. Phillips, Jr.: Secretary, Rockefeller Brothers Fund.

Nicholas Platt: Director for Japan, Office of Assistant Secretary for East Asia and Pacific Affairs, Department of State.

Robert E. Pursley: Partner, J. H. Whitney & Co., Former Commander, U.S. Forces Japan and 5th Air Forces.

Gustav Ranis: Professor of Economics, Yale University.

John E. Rielly: President, Chicago Council on Foreign Relations.

Thomas P. Rohlen: Associate Professor of Anthropology, University of California at Santa Cruz.

Donald H. Rumsfeld: President, G. D. Searle & Co., Former Secretary of Defense, Former Chief Assistant to President Ford.

John C. Sawhill: President, New York University, Former Administrator, Federal Energy Administration.

J. Robert Schaetzel: Former U.S. Ambassador to the European Community.

Isaac Shapiro: Partner, Milbank, Tweed, Hadley & McCloy, Former President, Japan Society, Inc.

Howard Simons: Managing Editor, *The Washington Post.*

Stephen J. Solarz: U.S. House of Representatives (Democrat, International Relations Committee).

Samuel S. Stratton: U.S. House of Representatives (Democrat, Armed Services Committee), Chairman, House Subcommittee on Investigations.

John J. Stremlau: Assistant Director, International Relations Program, Rockefeller Foundation.

Peter C. White: President, The Southern Center for International Studies.

APPENDIX B:
The Agenda of the Fourth Shimoda Conference

General Theme: U.S.–Japan Relations in a New World Order

I. *First Plenary Meeting:* The United States and Japan in a Changing International Environment

(The major goal of the first plenary meeting will be to develop a broad understanding among all the participants of the nature and scope of the changes that have taken place in Japanese–U.S. relations in recent years. We hope, further, to generate a general exchange of views among the participants concerning the major factors that can lead to tension or conflict between Japan and the United States, now and in the future, as well as the roles each country expects the other to play and the perspectives each has of its own role. Discussion to be initiated by remarks from Ambassadors Ingersoll and Ushiba.)

A. What is the nature of changes in the international community, particularly as they pertain to Japanese–U.S. relations?

B. How are the United States and Japan responding to these changes? Are there significant domestic constraints upon such response?

C. What are the Japanese and American perceptions concerning each other's role in an era of transition?

D. What are the long-range and short-range sources of possible conflicts and cooperation?

E. Are the points for discussion listed below for subsequent sessions relevant? Any omissions? Any reorganization?

II.   *First Concurrent Session:* Security in Northeast Asia

(Of major concern here are the changing conditions for a stable and peaceful regional system for Asia as both the United States and Japan are engaged in essential redefinition of their respective world roles).

    A.   How should Japan and the United States be seeking to relate to the two mainland powers?

    B.   What arrangements on the Korean peninsula hold the best promise for peaceful evolution? How can Japan and/or the United States best influence events there?

    C.   What are the proper roles for Japan and the United States in East Asia generally and how should they conduct themselves?

III. *Second Concurrent Session:* Political and Economic Development in Southeast Asia

(In the post-Vietnam environment, Southeast Asia is now a backwater of great-power diplomacy. Problems in the region will be more economic and political than strategic and military. Or will they?)

    A.   What are the essential conditions for regional stability in Southeast Asia?

    B.   What part are the ASEAN nations and Indochina likely to play and how are they likely to interact with each other?

    C.   What roles are the four great powers (Japan, the United States, People's Republic of China, and Soviet Union) likely to play in the region?

    D.   How do the United States and Japan perceive each other in the political and economic development process in the region. Is there a cooperative role they can play?

IV.   *Third Concurrent Session:* Japan, the United States, and the World Economy

(Where do Japanese and American interests and policies diverge and converge in the management of an increasingly interdependent international economic system?)

    A.   What are the most important international economic problems facing the two nations?

    B.   Is the present policy of free international trade still valid? If not, what new policies are needed?

    C.   How can the two nations singly or in cooperation best assure themselves of adequate supplies of energy and other raw materials at reasonable cost?

    D.   What roles should Japan and the United States be expected to play generally in relation to the world development process, individually or in tandem?

V. *Second Plenary Meeting:* U.S.–Japan Relations in a New World Order

(The second plenary meeting will be devoted to summing up the discussions held during the first plenary meeting and concurrent sessions which followed. Special attention will be given to articulating a common understanding of the future course of Japanese–American relations and areas of potential conflict. The session will conclude with an exchange of opinions regarding what forms of dialogue are best suited to finding solutions to those potential issues. Discussion to be initiated by the two moderators).

    A.   What are the implications of the preceding discussions for the relationship between Japan and the United States?

    B.   What are the areas for constructive dialogue between Japan and the United States?

    C.   What are the effective instruments for such dialogue?

VI. *Concluding Plenary Meeting:* Review of "Summary Report"